BUILDING FINANCIAL MODELS

A Guide to Creating and Interpreting Financial Statements

JOHN S. TJIA

McGraw-Hill

New York   Chicago   San Francisco   Lisbon
London   Madrid   Mexico City   Milan
New Delhi   San Juan   Seoul
Singapore   Sydney   Toronto

To my wife, Charlotte, with love and kisses

Library of Congress Cataloging-in-Publication Data

Tjia, John S.
  Building financial models : a guide to creating and interpreting financial statements/by John S. Tjia.—1st ed.
    p. cm.
  ISBN 0-07-140210-1 (hardcover : alk. paper)
  1. Financial statements. I. Title.
  HF5681.B2T57 2004
  657'.3–dc21   2003006579

1 2 3 4 5 6 7 8 9 0 DOC/DOC 0 9 8 7 6 5 4 3

ISBN 0-07-140210-1

This publication is designed to provide accurate and authoritative information in regard to the subject matter covered. It is sold with the understanding that neither the author nor the publisher is engaged in rendering legal, accounting, or other professional service. If legal advice or other expert assistance is required, the services of a competent professional person should be sought.
                              —From a declaration of principles jointly adopted by a committee of the
                                        American Bar Association and a committee of publishers.

McGraw-Hill books are available at special quantity discounts to use as premiums and sales promotions, or for use in corporate training programs. For more information, please write to the Director of Special Sales, Professional Publishing, McGraw-Hill, Two Penn Plaza, New York, NY 10121-2298. Or contact your local bookstore.

C O N T E N T S

INTRODUCTION

This book will teach you how to bring together what you know of finance, accounting, and the spreadsheet to give you a new skill—building financial models. The ability to create and understand models is one of the most valued skills in business and finance today. It's an expertise that will stand you in good stead in any arena—Wall Street or Main Street—where numbers are important. Whether you are a veteran, just starting out on your career, or still in school, having this expertise can give you a competitive advantage in what you want to do.

By the time you have completed the steps laid out in this book, you will have created a working, dynamic spreadsheet financial model with Generally Accepted Accounting Principles (GAAP) that you can use to make projections for industrial/manufacturing companies. (Banks and insurance companies have different flows in their businesses and are not covered in this book.)

Along the way, I will take you through a tour of the essentials in Excel and modeling (Chapters 1 to 5), then "guerilla accounting" to give you some familiarity with this subject (Chapter 6) before plunging into actual model building (Chapters 7 to 11). I cover the performance indicators that a model should have (Chapter 12) and guidelines for making useful forecasts (Chapter 13). In the rest of the book (Chapters 14 to 19), I take you back to building additional "bells and whistles" to add to the basic model that you have built.

FIRST, SOME DEFINITIONS

A spreadsheet can be used to tabulate and organize numbers, but it does not become a *model* until it contains data, equations, and specific relationships among the numbers that organize them into informational output.

The model becomes a *financial model* when it uses relationships of operating, investing, and/or financing variables based on GAAP principles.

And it can be called a *financial projection model* when it uses assumptions about future performance in order to give a view of what a company's future financial condition might be like. By changing the input variables, such a projection model can be very useful for showing the impact of different assumptions and/or strategies for the future.

TWO REQUIREMENTS FOR MAGIC

The task of developing a good spreadsheet model is a combination of many things, but, primarily, it is about good thinking and a sound knowledge of the tools at hand. These two attributes will put you on the right track for producing a model structure and layout that are robust, yet easy and, yes, delightful to use. Arthur C. Clarke, the renowned science writer, once said: "Any sufficiently advanced technology is indistinguishable from magic." I hope that after using the approaches and techniques for building models in this book, you too can look at your work and feel the magic you have created. And I certainly hope that your colleagues, managers, and clients will have the same reaction.

THIS IS A HANDS-ON BOOK

This book will lead you through the development process for a projection model. It is laid out in a step-by-step format in which each chapter describes a step. Each chapter covers a specific phase of building a model. This is a hands-on book. You will get the most out of this book if you perform the steps outlined in each chapter on your computer screen. By the end of the book, you will have the satisfaction of having built your own model, to which you can then add you own changes and modifications.

BUILD MODELS WITH YOUR OWN STYLE

There are as many ways to build a model as, say, to write a book. Most of them will result in working models, but not necessarily very good ones. There are, after all, bad books. But there are also excellent books with very different styles. The intent of this book is to show you the tools—the vocabulary and the syntax of model building, if you will—for developing a model that works properly, and so provide you with the foundation for developing other models. Just as you develop your own style of writing once you have learned the basics of language, you will then be able to develop your own style of model building.

THE MODEL WE WILL BE BUILDING

The projection model we will be developing is one that you might find as the starting point in many forms of analysis. The model will have these key features:

- It will have historical and forecast numbers for modeling an industrial type of company or business. Forecast numbers can be entered as "hard-coded" numbers (e.g., sales will be 1053 this year and 1106 next year, etc.) or as assumptions (e.g., sales growth next year will be 5 percent, etc.).
- The income statement, balance sheet, and a cash flow statement follow GAAP.
- The balance sheet balances: the total assets must equal the total liabilities and net worth. This balancing is done through the use of "plug" numbers (see Chapter 7). With the accounting interrelationships correctly in place, the cash flow numbers will also "foot" (see Chapter 11), i.e., the changes in cash flow must equal the change in the cash on the balance sheet.

THE SPREADSHEET

Microsoft Excel

Although this is not a "how-to" book on Microsoft Excel, the spreadsheet functions and controls discussed in this book are those of Excel as this is now the software of choice for spreadsheets. However, the approaches outlined here for building a model will work on any spreadsheet program, although you will have to make adjustments for any differences between Excel and that program.

The screen captures are from Excel XP, which, aside from the look, show little change from earlier versions of Excel. Other illustrations show the general look of Excel.

Commands

Commands in Excel are described in this book using the ">" notation. Thus, the sequence for saving a file would be shown as File > Save, for example.

ACKNOWLEDGMENTS

This book is just a part of what I have learned in my career as a financial modeler in investment banking, so in thanking those who have helped me in the writing of this book, I must give thanks to all with whom I have worked, including the many hundreds of colleagues in J.P.Morgan (past) and JPMorgan Chase (present), who gave me encouragement and constructive feedback through all of the many generations of financial models I have developed for that firm.

In looking back at my career and how I started to build financial models, I must return to the first time I saw a new-fangled white box sitting on somebody's desk sometime in the early 1980s. I remember asking, "What do you do with this?" And my colleague Lillian Waterbury said: "Type 'Lotus' at the C prompt sign." I did, and at this first PC I caught my earliest glimpse of the spreadsheet (it was Lotus 1-2-3 Release 1A). This would be a new direction for me. Thanks, Lillian.

Thanks to my friends and colleagues from the Financial Advisory Group. Sue McCain and Carol Brunner gave me my first chance to work as a modeler and it made all the difference. Juan Mesa taught me what clear thinking was about when we built a Latin American model with financial accounting. Christopher Wasden was my guide in the arcane accounting for banks when we built a model for banks.

I worked together with Jim Morris and Humphrey Wu in New York and Mike Koster in London and consider them as cohorts and comrades-in-arms in the arcane alchemy of finance, accounting, Excel, and Visual Basic for Applications that is the art of financial modeling. We all gave our best to produce modeling packages that were often more than the sum of their parts. Thanks, Jim, Humphrey, and Mike.

In the new JPMorgan Chase, Pat Sparacio, Marguerita Courtney, and Leng Lao were enthusiastic supporters of my work, and I thank them. Jay Chapin, independent training consultant, read the manuscripts and cheered me on from his homebase in Houston. Thanks, Jay. Fern Jones, a colleague and friend from my earliest days in finance so many years ago, also read the manuscript and encouraged me through the dark hours that probably every author experiences. Thanks also to Sumner Gerard, who took the time late into the night to look over the manuscript.

Finally, thanks to Susan Cabral, now of Cabral Associates, who in 1967 built in the mainframe computer the first financial projection model for J.P. Morgan, and quite possibly for Wall Street. Susan's model design was still in use 15 years later and it was the starting point for me when I began modeling for the PC. Her design is present in almost all the models I have developed in my career. Thank you, Susan, for being the pioneer and for showing me the way.

CHAPTER 1

A Financial Projection Model

This chapter will explain what projection models do and how they differ between industries. There is an overview of how projection models are used and what bits of information are important. The three roles you perform when you do financial modeling are covered. Finally, a suggestion about where to put the computer mouse may help in relieving arm tension.

THE CASE FOR STANDARDIZED PROJECTION MODELS

Although this book will tell you how to create your own financial model, its underlying message is that a model that can be used across a group becomes that much more effective. It is natural to think that a financial model is primarily a tool for quantitative analysis. But, to the extent that a model is the standard for a group, or even for a firm, it becomes much more than that: it becomes a communications platform. A standardized model achieves this in several ways:

1. It conveys to its users the analytical methodologies that others in the group are using, because those are embedded in its structure.

2. It becomes in its own right a teaching tool, letting new users understand how the standard analysis should be conducted.

3. As colleagues agree to use the same model, it becomes the common yardstick of analysis, a way to foster cooperation and partnership across groups. Credit or investment review committee members who are familiar with how the numbers have been produced and how the ratios have been calculated can proceed to the qualitative analysis that much more quickly and reach their decisions with greater confidence. The economic impact is usually significant: good (or better) decisions are made; and bad choices are avoided altogether.

4. When one standard model is used across different projects in different industries, it facilitates management review and oversight. To the extent that the model includes the preferred standard analytical methodologies, it is also a form of insurance against nonstandard approaches to analysis.

AN ESTIMATOR, NOT A PREDICTOR

A projection model is not a crystal ball, and its output does not dictate what the future will be. It is merely a tool to estimate what a company's future financial condition might be, given certain assumptions about its performance. Conversely, it is a tool to test what needs to happen in order for a particular performance goal to be reached.

It is easy, for example, for a chief financial officer to say, "We will have enough cash flow in the next five years to retire $100 million of our debt." This may well be true, but the validity in such a statement lies in what needs to happen. If the statement is based on conservative forecasts consistent with the company's recent performance and its current position and reputation in its industry, then this is good and fine. If, on the other hand, the $100 million is attainable only through rapid, unrealistic, and unprecedented increases in revenues, then it is very likely that the CFO's statement is just so much hot air.

This role as a testing tool means that a projection model is best when it can allow you to change the inputs quickly for a series of sensitivity tests. For example, what would be the operating cash flow if revenues increased by 3, 5, or 10 percent while margins improved, held steady, or worsened? We can add other variations in other accounts. Given all the accounts in a company's financial statement, the permutations of the sensitivities can be nearly limitless. In fact, we can run the danger of having a tool that can produce so much "information" that it becomes useless. So part of the exercise in building and using such a model is knowing how to make the best use of it. Chapter 13 gives a review of the main points to keep in mind in developing projections.

PROJECTION MODELS FOR DIFFERENT INDUSTRIES

Industry/Manufacturing Industries

The type of model that we will be building is most appropriate for manufacturing- or industrial-type companies. In this type, sales are the main revenue generator, and the net income line in the income statement shows the result of revenue less expenses.

The balance sheet is a listing of the assets and liabilities related to the production facilities required to produce the product for sale and the financing to support these activities. Shareholders' equity shows the amount of equity capital in the business.

Service companies, where the revenues are derived from the selling of a service, can also fit this framework.

Banks

Banks produce their revenues not be selling a product or service, but by the interest yield on their main assets: the loans they have in their loan portfolio on the balance sheet. Because banks generally have to borrow the money that they lend, they also incur interest expense. Thus, the equivalent "sales revenue" line for banks is something called "net interest earnings": this is the interest income they receive on their loans, less the interest expense on their funding liabilities.

Developing a projection model for a bank is more difficult, primarily because of the need to include regulatory capital requirements in the model. In the United States, banks have to have two types of capital, called Tier I and Tier II, and a bank must meet minimum requirements for its capitalization. What this means is that as the model makes its projections, it also has to keep these accounts in line with the requirements. Bank modeling is not covered in this book.

Insurance Companies

Insurance companies can be described as a combination of a service company earning premiums and an investment company making interest income earnings from its investments (from all the cash received in premiums, less what has to be paid out in insurance claims).

Insurance companies come in two types: life insurance companies and non-life insurance companies.

Forecasts for life insurance companies need good, extensive, and expensive actuarial data, and even then, assumptions of how many insurees the company will have over time and the long time horizon for its insurees can make the exercise difficult.

Non-life (property and casualty) insurance companies are easier to model, since the claims can be more easily estimated via probability theories and the known finite useful lives for property.

Insurance companies are again a different animal from the basic industrial/manufacturing companies that we want to model, so they will not be covered in the book.

WHERE PROJECTION MODELS ARE USEFUL

Credit Analysis

To lend or not to lend? Or, to put it more bluntly, will we get our money back if we lend it to this particular company? Thus, modeling for credit analysis necessarily requires a focus on cash flows and ratios. If we can show that the company will be producing enough cash in excess of its operational and investment needs over the term of the loan to repay the loan, then it would be a "go" decision to lend, at least insofar as the numbers are concerned. (Good lending decisions must consider other, qualitative factors.) The challenge for the credit decisionmakers occurs when the company is considered a "good" company, but the cash flow is less robust. This is why skilled and experienced credit officers are always in demand by lending institutions.

Equity Investments

Equity investors need projections to estimate their equity returns through the internal rate of return (IRR) calculations. In these calculations, it is important to be as precise as possible in modeling the timing of the investments, so that they are not all the "year end" according to the model. In this case, one often sees quarterly or even monthly models. This is one reason why many equity investment models, such as those used in project finance and leveraged buyout situations, use periodicities shorter than a year.

Leveraged Buyout

In a leveraged buyout (or LBO), a company is bought out by a group of investors, which usually includes the current management, using debt to finance the purchase. Modeling such a transaction requires a focus on both the debt and equity changes at the deal date, the effects on the *stub year* (the portion of the year subsequent to the transaction), and the remaining forecast years. On a purchase LBO, goodwill will have to be calculated; on a recapitalization LBO, it will not.

Mergers and Acquisitions

Where an LBO involves one company, a merger or acquisition would involve two companies. (Of course, a company could buy another company and the new company can then buy a third, and so forth, but we can think of this as a succession of mergers, each involving only two companies.)

Merger modeling really involves modeling three companies: the first company, which is the acquirer; the second company, which is the target; and the third, which is the combined new company. The acquirer and the target should be modeled separately through the forecast period, especially if the two companies operate in different industries or different sectors of an industry.

With the exception of the numbers for the period from the last available data date to the deal date, for which some estimates would be needed, all of the information for the pre-deal period can be taken straight from the historical data.

Merger accounting is complex because of the need to keep track of the flows of the two companies and layering in the effects of the transaction in the capitalization and the cash flows. Asset revaluations and goodwill calculations add to the complexity.

WHAT TO FOCUS ON

Critical Numbers in Any Projection Model

A useful projection model focuses on only five main points:

- The earnings before interest and taxes (EBIT) in the income statement
- The earnings before interest, taxes, depreciation, and amortization (EBITDA) in the income statement
- The net income number
- The operating working capital (OWC) and capital expenditures levels, as measures of the use of cash on the balance sheet
- The level of debt on the balance sheet

EBIT

EBIT is an important number because it shows the earnings related to the main operations of a company. EBIT is revenues less the expenses that are directly related to the revenue-generating operations. These operating earnings give you a clue as to how robust the company's business is, outside of other nonoperating flows such as interest or investment. The trend over the most recent years can show you how well the company is positioned for future growth.

EBITDA

EBITDA is EBIT, but with depreciation and amortization of intangibles added back. Depreciation and amortization are noncash expenses; there is no actual cash that the company has to pay out. So EBITDA is a good way to arrive at the idea of "cash earnings," the amount of cash generated by the operations. This can give you a good indication of a company's absolute ability to pay interest. A zero EBIT can mean that there is still some cash, from the add back of depreciation and amortization; a zero EBITDA, on the other hand, means that there is absolutely no cash coming from the revenue-generating activities.

Net Income

Below EBIT and EBITDA, the net income number is produced by the inclusion of other nonoperational revenues and expenses. Usually there are more expenses than revenues, and the biggest expenses are interest expenses and taxes.

Net income is a useful number because this is the usual measure of whether a company is "profitable" or not and is the basis of calculations such as earnings per share (EPS). However, a company can be profitable but still run out of cash because of large demands for working capital and/or capital expenditures, so net income (and all other measures of a company) is best viewed in the context of other factors and ratios.

Operating Working Capital

Working capital by definition is current assets less current liabilities. However, a more useful measure for working capital is what might be termed *operating working capital* (OWC). This is current assets *without* cash or short-term investments, less current liabilities *without* short-term debt (including the current portion of long-term debt). Thus, OWC is primarily:

Accounts receivable
+ Inventory

+ Other current assets
− Accounts payable
− Other current liabilities

OWC is a measure of how much cash a company must invest in its operations. Cash and debt are the result of separate financing decisions. This is why they are excluded from OWC. A high level of OWC (because of accounts receivables not being collected quickly and/or poor inventory management, for example) means that a company has a large amount of its cash tied up as receivables and inventory, which limits its ability to use its cash for other purposes.

Capital Expenditures

Capital expenditures, or *capex* for short, is the other major use of cash in the balance sheet. Capex is generally an ongoing expense because a company must continue to invest in its production equipment, which over time needs to be maintained or replaced.

Debt

Most companies have debt on their balance sheet. Whether a company has "too much" or "too little" debt is not a function of the dollar value of the debt, but rather its cash flow to "service" the debt (i.e., can it pay the ongoing interest expense and make timely repayments of the debt itself).

In modeling forecast debt levels, you would need to enter known amortization schedules so that you would have a base line of the outstanding (and decreasing) debt. A good model with realistic assumptions will then show what the additional borrowing, if any, would be required in the forecast years.

YOU AS THE MODEL DEVELOPER

Three Hats

You will be wearing many hats when you are a model developer:

- You are the finance expert, working with the elements of the income statement, balance sheet, and cash flow statement, using your knowledge of GAAP conventions to produce the correct presentation of the results.

* You are the spreadsheet wizard, pushing your knowledge of Excel to the limit to squeeze the last ounce of performance out of your model.

* You are the visual designer and virtual architect, manipulating the screen and the structure of your worksheet to make your model as easy and fun to use as possible. You give meaning to the term *user friendly*.

Balancing the Three

How much you focus on each of the three parts will determine the look and feel of your model. Obviously, a model that looks spectacularly attractive and is user friendly but produces inaccurate outputs is not what we want. On the other hand, a model that is powerful and provides useful analytical information but has an interface so forbidding that no one understands how to use it is also not our goal. So a balance among the three approaches is important to get to a final, optimal product.

Give Yourself Time

I hope that the model that you will create if you follow all the steps in the book will be the first of many that you will build. As you develop and create more models, it will seem that there is always a "next" model to do. A good model takes time and passes through many versions. How many versions exactly? My experience is that you would need at least three:

1. The first version is the attempt to gather together the right set of calculations in the right way to get the answer you want, but typically this results in a model that is not very user friendly and has lots of errors.

2. The second version is the version for correcting the calculation errors as well as the gross shortcomings in terms of its usability. This version is a little easier to use and has better accuracy in its calculations. It is also often at this point that there is a sudden understanding into what the model should have been all along, which leads to...

3. The third version is much easier to use and more elegant in structure. Often, this is a radical departure from the first two versions and comes after a smack-your-hand-in-the-middle-of-your-forehead moment of insight. And strangely, this is the one that comes much closer to what the original concept of the model was.

MOUSE OR KEYBOARD?

The byword is "whatever works for you." As you become more and more expert at developing and working with models, you will begin to find yourself spending more time with your PC. This brings us to the question of whether it is better to use the mouse or the keyboard to operate the menus and work with the worksheets.

Using the mouse has the advantage of getting to some of the commands more quickly and "intuitively," but it has the disadvantage of taking more time and hand motion: your hand has to leave the keyboard, find the mouse, position the cursor, click, and then return to the keyboard. In addition, the mouse can lead to wrist and elbow strain when you need to extend your arm to handle the mouse, especially when there is little or no support to the forearm. Using the keyboard has the advantage of being quicker, and learning this method gives you the advantage of being able to continue your work if for some reason you cannot use the mouse. The disadvantage is that it can be quite tedious to step through the menu system, especially when you are confronted with a menu box with drop-down lists, tabs, checkboxes, etc. However, some practice can make the hand movements automatic, so that your hands will seem to have a "keyboard memory."

I do not recommend one over the other and can only say *use whatever works for you*. Indeed, it might be that the best method is a combination of the mouse and the keyboard.

A Suggestion for Mouse Placement

If you place your mouse to the side of the keyboard, an arrangement that most people use, you can have overworked shoulder and elbow joints because your shoulder has to support your arm as you work with the mouse. Additionally, this position forces your hand to point outward as you work, creating an angle at the outer edge of where the hand meets the wrist. It is possible to get tendonitis at the point where the tendon kinks through the angle. To minimize strain, place the mouse in front of you, between you and the keyboard, rather than to the side. So, a view from the top of the desk would be as follows:

Monitor screen
Keyboard
Mouse
Edge of desk
You

There are several advantages to this:

- The arm can be supported by the elbow on your desk.
- The position of the hand directly in front of you is also more natural and closer to the center of your body. You are more "centered," to use a martial arts term.
- It is just as easy, if not more so, to move your hand from the keyboard toward your solar plexus than to move it out to the right and putting your elbow and your shoulder in a twist.
- In this position, the hand holding the mouse will tend to point toward the left side of your body (if you are right handed), extending the outer edge of the hand and wrist and reducing the possibility of tendonitis at this point.
- In this location, given the curve of your arm, the most natural position for the mouse is "sideways", with the cable leading off to the left (again, if you are right-handed). You will move the mouse to the left in order to get the cursor to move "up" on the screen. This adjustment, however, will be an almost instantaneous one.

CHAPTER 2

Design Principles for Good Model Building

This chapter covers the principles you should keep in mind. These are meant to minimize confusion in building the model and in using it. Remember, the confusion you avoid may be your own.

KEY PRINCIPLES

When we design something that exists in a physical form in the world, we have the benefit of having something to pickup, turn over, peer into, kick, or thump when something is not working. Additionally, if we are designing something like a car and find that the dashboard lights are not working, it is a safe bet that the problem lies with the electrical wiring or switches in the vicinity.

Not so with spreadsheet modeling. Despite the fact that we can see a model, it's not actually "there," and when problems arise, we have only our mental map of it to use in figuring out what is wrong. And, unlike a physical counterpart, a problem in one area of the model can be caused by something else not seemingly related to the problem at hand.

So the design principles we apply as we build our model are critical. The more we can do things correctly the first time around, the less trouble and confusion will result.

Some principles to consider:

+ KISS—Keep it simple, stupid.
+ Have a clear idea of what the model needs to do.
+ Be clear about what the users want and expect.
+ Maintain a logical arrangement of the parts.
+ Make all calculations in the model visible.
+ Be consistent in everything you do.
+ Use one input for one data point.
+ Think modular.
+ Make full use of Excel's power.
+ Provide ways to prevent or back out of errors.
+ Save in-progress versions under different names, and save them often.
+ Test, test, and test.

KISS

The overriding principle in model building is the "Keep it simple, stupid" principle. The KISS principle does not mean that a model should be simplistic and do nothing but the most rudimentary of calculations. Rather, it means that whatever you need your model to do, keep it simple. A variation of this is the principle of *Occam's razor*: the best solution is the simplest one.

+ Keep the formulas simple, even if it means using one or more lines to break up the calculations. If you write a formula and then look at it again 10 minutes later and have a hard time understanding it, that is a sign that you may want to break up the formula into two or more cells.
+ Keep the structure of the model simple, with a flow of calculations that, as much as possible, go in one consistent direction in the model, from the "beginning" to the "end." Generally, you can consider the "top" sheet in Excel—whose screen tab is at the leftmost at the bottom of the screen—to be the beginning. The "bottom" sheet is at the end. This will give the user a sense of the start and the end of the model. A "simple" structure will mean different

things to different people. On the one hand, it may mean that there should be only one sheet, with the beginning of the model at the top and the results at the bottom. On the other, it may mean that there should be several sheets, with each sheet containing particular blocks of inputs or calculations.

- Keep your formatting simple, with just enough to make visual distinctions on the screen to help your users, without going into a psychedelic mix of florid colors and heavy lines. **Bold** type is helpful for highlighting items on the screen, but use it sparingly. If the screen holds a profusion of bold type, then the highlighting effect is gone, and the screen now looks visually "heavy."

KISS is a very beneficial principle to follow. Determine what "simple" means to you and those who will be using your model. If there is a difference, go with the "simpler" of the two. The more you can follow that standard, the more your work will be used.

A good model should be powerful and fulfill its analytical goals, allow its settings to be changed quickly and with reliable results, and be fun to use. A truly great model "disappears": the users use the model to get the results they want without the model's functions or interface design intruding into their consciousness.

Have a Clear Idea of What the Model Needs to Do

Having a clear idea at the outset of what your model needs to do is an absolute requirement. If you do not have a clear idea, the best thing to do is to step away from the computer and continue to think out what the model should be. A good way is to build a small pilot model that can give you a proof of concept, or simply to take pen and paper and start sketching out the flows.

The clearer the modeling goal, the less messy the model. Being clear goes a long way in helping you follow the KISS principle.

Sometimes, you have a clear idea but the idea is that the model should have more than one primary function. This is to be expected if you are building a standard model that will get used in many different situations. For example, your model may be used for credit analysis *and* for an equity valuation. The credit model may need a "cash sweep" module, whereby excess cash produced as a result of your assumptions can be used to automatically repay outstanding debt (see Chapter 14). The valuation model would have to pay attention to the development of "free cash flows." In this case, a good approach to take is to develop one solid "calculation engine" at the core of the model, the output of which can be used in different ways.

An important distinction here if you are building a model for others is that their sense of what the model needs to be may be different than yours. Always build your models to match, or exceed, your users' expectations.

Be Clear About What the Users Want and Expect

If you are creating a model for others to use, be absolutely clear about what your audience wants and expects. Do not assume that you know what they want—often they themselves only have a vague idea of what they are looking for, making it likely that what you produce for them will meet with a thumbs-down reception. If they have a model they like that they are already using, it is a good idea to make your (new and improved) model follow some of the layout and analytical steps used in the old model. Users generally like to stick to the steps that they are comfortable with.

You will also have to gauge the skill levels of the users and develop your interface appropriately. Another important tip: check the version of Excel that they have and make sure that there are no compatibility problems with the version in which you are developing your model.

Maintain a Logical Arrangement of the Parts

With the goal clear in your mind, the natural way to set out a good layout is to follow the flow of calculations. The bigger the model, the more important it is that this principle is followed. What do you need to calculate first in order to get to the next round of calculations? After that, what else in order to get to the final result? In this way, it will be easy to follow and check the model's workings.

Many models are unnecessarily difficult to follow because the calculations are done by formulas that are spread out willy-nilly across the model. Granted, there will be times when the calculation blocks cannot follow each other in one smooth flow, but the more they can be ordered in a logical and visually accessible way, the easier it will be for you and your users to work with the model.

In terms of the final output, this can be a separate sheet that organizes and presents the various parts of the model in one summary form.

Make All Calculations in the Model Visible

A corollary of the logical arrangement is that all calculations must be visible. A "black box" model is the most intimidating kind of model. This is the kind of model where the calculations are not visible and the model produces its results with no indication of how it does so.

By the same token, nothing is more reassuring to users than to see how the model is working and to be able to check for themselves the calculations—all the better if the formulas are arranged in a logical fashion. And not only formulas, but also the "toggles" or settings that allow you to set how the formulas work.

Be Consistent in Everything You Do

As much as possible, make the parts of the model be consistent with one another. Use the same label for the same item if it is shown at different places in the model. Calling the same row of information "cash flow from operations" in one place but "operating cash flow" in another is a prescription for confusion and error.

The same columns in the sheets should contain the same year. When you know that every sheet's column H contains the data for year 2003, formula references across sheets become less prone to error.

The same font and font size should designate the same type of item. If you are using colors in your fonts and cells, be sure to follow this consistency rule, too.

Use One Input for One Data Point

There should be only one place in the model to enter one data point. For example, if you need to work with the current stock price of a company, enter it in one place only and have the model always read that input, either directly or indirectly, when it needs to calculate anything that would use the current stock price. Having multiple inputs for the same data item will exasperate your users, and only leaves room for conflicting inputs for the same data point.

Think Modular

Build the model so that it has blocks or modules of formulas that perform discrete operations within them. As a block completes its tasks, it passes the results to the next block. This approach makes the work of building the model, and later of checking and auditing it, that much easier. It also makes changes easier to implement, as you can work with the modules and not have to roam over the whole model to change formulas.

In military parlance, the expression "fire and forget" refers to missiles that unerringly hit their target, no matter what the battle conditions are after the launch. The parallel for developing models the right way is "develop and forget": develop and construct your model robustly, and let it be capable of future changes easily. The "think modular" approach is by far the most effective way to get to this level of model-building expertise.

Make Full Use of Excel's Power

A valid way to describe Excel, or any spreadsheet program, is that it is a big calculator. Just as you would not take a pencil and do a sum on paper before entering that number into a calculator, you also should not have any intermediate tools between you and the spreadsheet. Do everything in it.

Excel has a whole repertory of over 250 functions (pre-formatted formulas) that make it a hugely powerful calculator. These functions are divided into the following types:

- Financial
- Date and time
- Statistical
- Lookup & reference
- Database
- Text
- Logical
- Information

You won't need to know all the functions. In fact, for the financial modeling that is used in investment banking and finance, you will only need to know as a start about 35 or so functions, and these are listed in Chapter 5, "Your Model-Building Toolbox: Functions." Because Excel's functions work with one another, putting combinations of functions together will often give you exponential leaps in your modeling expertise. Excel also lists its functions when you click on the Function icon on the menu bar. Help screens can be called up to help you understand what each function does.

Excel has its own programming language, called Visual Basic for Applications (VBA). This is a powerful language for writing macros to create various user forms to help with the user interface or to automate tasks. Later chapters will provide an introduction to VBA, but VBA is a full-length subject in its own right.

Provide Ways to Prevent or Back Out of Errors

There are two types of errors to worry about:

- *Formula errors.* Formulas can work well when all the data are entered but will show an error if a data point is missing. An example is the #DIV/0! ("divided by zero") error in formulas where a number is being divided by another. In this case, the simple remedy is to write the formula with a way to prevent the error, by checking whether the denominator is zero or not. If it is, the statement just returns a zero.

- *User errors.* A good developer can usually guess what the "typical" user will do, given a particular point in working with a model, but there is no way to guess what the "untypical" will do! There are countless unexpected ways that users interact with a model. Where the number is expected, they may put text and vice versa; formulas that they have been told not to touch get altered, and altered radically; messages displayed in the middle of the screen describing the next step go unread, and the wrong button is clicked; and so on.

  To prevent user errors, we can employ a variety of approaches such as designing the screen to guide the user to do the right thing as much as possible; using Excel's data validation features that prevent the wrong type of inputs (e.g., a number when a text string is expected) from being entered; writing very clear and explicit messages on the screen about what to do. However, there is every likelihood that users will still make mistakes.

Save In-Progress Versions Under Different Names, and Save Them Often

This is not so much a design principle as an operating principle to use when you are designing. Anytime you work with any electronic documents, you should remember to save frequently. And don't just save under the same name. This is because you want to have a record of your work over time, in case the latest version gets corrupted. For example, if you had saved a work-in-progress 30 minutes ago as Newmodel08.xls and the current Newmodel09.xls has up and died, then you can go back to version 08 and pick up the work again. You will have lost only 30 minutes of work. The shorter the interval between saves under different names, the less you lose if you have a system crash. It would be disastrous if you used the same name again and again over days of development work! It is also a good idea to save and rename whenever you have completed a particular feature and you want to start adding something new to the model.

CHAPTER 3

Starting Out

Chapter 2 reviewed the design principles for model building. In Chapter 3, we examine some of the controls in Excel that will help us to put those principles into practice.

THE EMPTY SCREEN, FRAUGHT WITH POSSIBILITIES

The computer is on and Excel is up and running, inviting us to get to work immediately. But at this point, let's pause for a moment and stop ourselves from just rushing in. Artists facing a blank canvas need to lay out their paints and brushes around them so that things will be at hand when they are needed. In the same way, we should prepare our Excel "canvas" and lay out the tools so they will be conveniently at the ready. In this chapter, we will be looking at customizing the following settings in Excel:

- Toolbars to have and how to customize the list of icons
- Gridlines
- Styles
- Column width
- Colors

- ◆ Editing settings
- ◆ Calculation settings
- ◆ Iteration

CUSTOMIZING YOUR TOOLBAR

At the top of your screen, you should see a row of icons. These are little pictures which, when clicked on, will launch particular sequences. For quick print, for example, you can just click on the Print icon. Likewise, if you want to change the color of the font in a cell to a different color, you can click on the Font Color icon.

Standard and Formatting Toolbars on Two Rows

Each icon takes up only a little bit of real estate space. It is helpful to fit as many icons as you can into this toolbar space. I would recommend that you choose to have the "Standard" and "Formatting" toolbars in place and have them shown as two rows. You can do it through this setting:

1. View > Toolbars and then select Standard and Formatting. This will make these two appear in the toolbar space.
2. View > Toolbars > Customize > Options to show the dialog box shown in Figure 3-1. This is for setting how the two toolbars appear and several other options.

   Check the check box for "Show Standard and Formatting toolbars on two rows." Additionally, if you do not want to work with abbreviated menus, check the check box for "Always show full menus." Abbreviated menus can be exasperating because Excel will hide less frequently used menu items. In theory, this is great, unless you need to do something for the first time and cannot find the menu command because it is hidden.

   In the lower section, you can choose other settings, including the animation for menus.

Adding a Third Standard Toolbar: Auditing

A third toolbar that should be part of the default set of toolbars is the Audit toolbar. This will give you a set of icons that will allow

F I G U R E 3–1

you to audit your model (for example, by showing the references used by particular cells or where in the model particular cells are being used).

Click on View > Toolbars > Auditing Toolbar to make the toolbar appear. You can also go through Tools > Formula Auditing > Show Formula Auditing Toolbar for the same effect. In Excel XP, this will cause the toolbar to be inserted automatically into one of the toolbar rows.

(For earlier versions of Excel, the command is Tools > Auditing > Show Auditing Toolbar. The toolbar will then appear floating in the main part of the screen. You can leave it there or drag and drop it into one of the two rows occupied by the other two toolbars; it is short enough to fit without taking up a third row.)

At the left edge of each toolbar group, you will notice a thin highlighted vertical strip. Think of this as a handle. With your mouse, you can click on this handle to drag and drop the toolbar into any position you want, including creating another row of icons. As you add more toolbars, you can add a third or fourth row, although by this time, you may be starting to limit severely the amount of usable screen space. (See Figure 3-2.)

F I G U R E   3–2

Customizing the Toolbars Further

Once you have these toolbars installed, you can further customize them by adding or deleting other icons, which are listed by the type of function that they represent. You can see the full list of functions by going through the following steps: View > Toolbars > Customize > Commands. (See Figure 3-3.)

How to Add or Delete Icons from the Toolbars

You can add or delete more icons, in effect changing the set of icons that come preset with the toolbars. The steps for adding

F I G U R E   3–3

icons is the same for all. Let's take the step of adding the "Save As..." command to the toolbar. "Save As..." is a command that does not have an icon, so when we add this to the toolbar, we will just see a button that spells out "Save As..." The steps are as follows:

1. Click on the category "File."
2. Click on the "Save As..." command and drag it to the top of the screen.
3. In order for it be parked correctly, you must drag and drop this **onto an existing toolbar location**. In this case, you can park it right next to the Save icon (the icon showing a diskette). If you drag and drop it into an empty space outside of an existing toolbar, it will not "take."
4. You can drag and drop it to another location, but again, it must be a location on an existing toolbar.

To delete an icon, just drag and drop it onto a location outside the toolbars. This only works when you are in the "customize" mode. After some use, you will find which of the icons you do not need or use, and can remove them accordingly. This will free up more space for any new icons that you do want to add.

Recommendations for Additional Icons to Have

1. From the File category
   a. Set Print Area: To define your print area quickly.
   b. Print Preview: To preview the page being printed before it comes out of the printer.
2. From the Edit category
   a. Delete Rows: To delete the whole row that your cursor is in, without your having to highlight the whole row.
   b. Delete Columns: The same, except that it works for the column that your cursor is in.
3. From the View category
   a. Zoom: To show you the zoom percentages of the screen so that you can make your change. If you did not have

this icon, you would have to through two steps (click on View, and then Zoom) to get to the same place. This may be minor, but if you are giving a presentation to your project leader or client, an extra step under pressure can make the stress level that much higher.

4. From the Insert category

   a. Rows: To insert a whole row that your cursor is in, without your having to highlight the whole row by clicking on the row number bar at the left of the screen.

   b. Columns: The same effect, except that it inserts a column.

5. From the Format category

   a. Font: This and the following icon will show you the current settings.

   b. Font Size.

   c. Style: If you are using styles (and you should), to tell you at a glance whether you have the right format or not.

   d. Borders: A multipurpose icon that, when clicked on, will show a small window of 12 other border settings that can apply to the cell or range of cells that you have highlighted. However, if you want to make special border attributes (e.g., dashed or double lines in different colors), you will still have to click on Format > Cells > Border.

   e. Bottom Border: Although the Border icon can help you to apply any of 12 border setting quickly, it does not give the bottom border (a line at the bottom of your cell). Adding the Bottom Border icon completes the list of border choices.

THE LOOK OF THE SCREEN

There is quite a bit you can do with the look of the screen that can make your model look spiffy. But be careful: if you are over-enthusiastic about changing the look of the screen, you can get one that looks cluttered and visually unattractive. You can, however, leave well enough alone. If you don't feel like making any changes to Excel's look, you can skip the following few subsections and pick up again on the calculation settings.

Gridlines

The starting screen in Excel has faint lines marking the rows and columns. These gridlines make it easy to locate items on the screen, but you might want to make them disappear for a cleaner and "cooler" look. It is still quite easy to find the row and column address on the screen because Excel turns the row and column coordinates of the current active cell (at the left and the top of the screen) into **bold** type. And, of course, the cursor still goes from cell to cell, whether the gridlines are there or not.

To make the gridlines disappear, do the following:

1. Click on Tools.
2. Click on Options.
3. Select the View tab.
4. Uncheck the Gridlines check box.

Styles

A style is a named format that you can apply to the spreadsheet cells. Through styles, you can change the look of your spreadsheet quickly. A change in a style will change all the cells formatted in that style.

In a new worksheet, the standard style is called "Normal." This is the default style that all cells have. You can change the Normal style to carry any attributes that you want, or you can create new styles of your own that have those attributes. You can delete the new styles that you have created, but you cannot delete the Normal style.

To look at the settings for the Styles, follow these steps:

1. Click on Format in the menu bar.
2. Click on Style.... You will see the user form shown in Figure 3-4 for the Normal style.

F I G U R E   3–4

The checked boxes show the attributes that will be applied with this style. The default setting applies all these attributes.

Number
The General setting is an automatic formatting feature for determining how numbers are displayed. For example, the number of decimal places shown in General follows the number of places that you enter from your keyboard. If you enter a number with a % sign at the end, the cell then holds a percent column.

This is a convenient feature for working up a small table in Excel. However, for larger models where you want a greater control of how the contents are displayed, the Number attribute to use might be as shown in Figure 3-5.

The settings are for:

* One decimal place.
* Use the separator for thousands (e.g., 1234.0 appears as 1,234.0).
* Parentheses for negative numbers. Choose whether you want the negative numbers to be shown in black or in red.

Alignment
You can leave the Alignment settings as they are. The General setting for Horizontal means that text will be formatted as flush left and numbers will be formatted flush right. The

F I G U R E   3–5

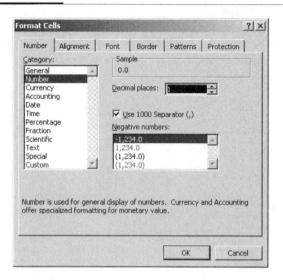

Bottom setting for Vertical means that all your text or numbers will appear at the bottom. This does not matter when the rows are set for only one line. When you make the row height higher so that a row can contain more than one line, the Bottom setting will be obvious. (See Figure 3-6.)

Font

Excel's default font is Arial, a modern-looking sans serif typeface. (*Sans serif* means "without serif"; a serif is the extra stroke marking the end of a stroke in a letter.) Another choice would be Times Roman, a serif typeface which will give your printouts a more classic look. Excel has other typefaces to choose from, but be careful that you don't go overboard and choose an overly ornate typeface. When in doubt, keep it simple and stick to the starting default typeface. (See Figure 3-7.)

One consideration, aside from your own visual preferences, is how well the type prints out in your printer. Arial is a "True Type" font, and as this user form notes, the same font will be used on both your printer and your screen. In other words, what you see is what you get. Other typefaces that are not True Type may appear different when printed.

FIGURE 3–6

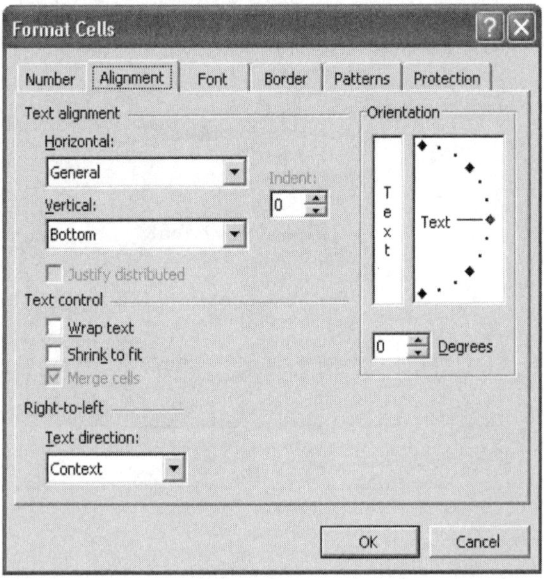

FIGURE 3–7

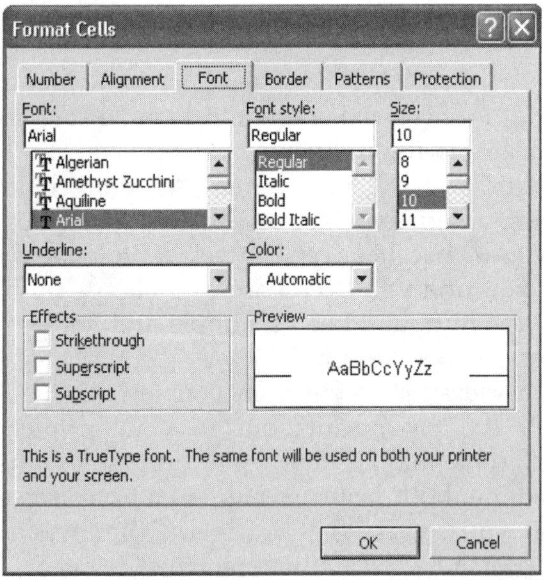

Font Size   Excel's default font size is 10 points. This font is large enough for fairly easy reading on the screen, but often Excel screens are set to a zoom of 75 percent so that the screen can hold more columns.

I would recommend setting the starting font size to 8 points. This will give you a font size that is readable but will still make room for many columns on the screen—and without your having to make zoom adjustments on every one of your sheets.

Border

Border allows you to draw lines on the sides of each cell, or even diagonally across them, and you can specify the weight and type of line and the color. It's easier to control these borders by actually changing the cell, rather than applying a style, so you don't have to touch anything on the Border user form for styles. (See Figure 3-8.)

F I G U R E 3–8

Patterns

Patterns allow you to change the background pattern of a cell.
A pattern can be plain shading. Making a cell look gray is changing its pattern. Like borders, it is easier to control a cell's shading
by changing the cell, so we don't need to touch anything on the
Pattern user form. (See Figure 3-9.)

Protection

Locking a cell means that its contents cannot be changed, so this
is one way to protect a model's formulas from being tampered
with. *Hiding a cell* means that while it shows the results of
the formula it contains, the formula itself cannot be seen in the
formula bar.

   As the note says, if you choose to protect or hide your cells,
then you have to turn on the protection by going to Tools,
Protection, and Protect Sheet. A password is optional. One warning: turning on protection for the sheet means that you cannot
change the contents or the formats of the cell unless you turn the

F I G U R E 3–9

F I G U R E 3–10

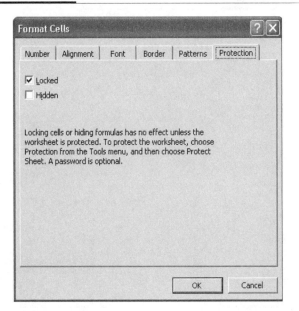

protection off. This is a little inconvenient, and it also means that if you start to put macros into your model to make it go through automatic changes, a protected sheet will cause the macro to stop. (See Figure 3-10.)

Styles are global settings and, as with anything global, you can also set local styles that override the global settings. Thus you can have a "Normal" style set to the Arial font, but you can change a cell or cells by specifying a, say, Times Roman font for that cell. (Potentially, you can select all the cells on a sheet and apply a local setting like this, thus fully overwriting the global setting.)

Local Settings

To change the local setting to override the style, do this:

1. Select the cell.
2. Select Format from the menu.
3. Select Cells and you will see the screen shown as Figure 3-11.

F I G U R E   3–11

This is the first of six tabbed forms. They show formats identical to the ones we saw for the Style settings and work the same way. The Number form shown here is the most different from the one seen for setting styles. Both the global and local settings give you total control of how your model will look.

Column Width

The default column-width setting in Excel is 8.5. You can change the global setting for each sheet by doing the following:

1. Click Format on the menu bar.
2. Click on Column.
3. Click on Standard Width and change the width setting.

A width of 10 gives enough room for more numbers or decimal places, without making the columns look too wide.

For the title column, a width of 30 or so will give you plenty of room for entering the titles for each row.

Colors

In the figures in the following chapters, you will see shaded areas in the spreadsheet illustrations. This is a way of showing where the *input* cells are located. It is a good idea to highlight the background of the cell, using a pale yellow, for example. Additionally, you may want to set the fonts to bright blue. If you use only a blue font on a white background, when the model is empty of inputs, you (and especially other users of your model) will have a hard time knowing which are the input areas and which are not.

You set the shading (called "pattern") for the cell by the command Format > Cells, which will get you to the user form shown in Figure 3-12. The pattern that is most pleasing to the eye is the lightest yellow on the upper part of the grid, above the line. The lower part is used for chart coloring, but because it is not seen when you call up this palette using the Color Fill icon, you should not use it if you want to take advantage of the quick change using the icon.

F I G U R E   3–12

F I G U R E   3–13

It may be that the lightest yellow in the upper section (or any of the colors you wish to choose) is not quite the right shade. My own preference is that the yellow should be the shade of the lower section. In this case, we can modify the color in the given palette through the Tools > Options > Color command. You will see a similar user form. (See Figure 3-13.)

By selecting a square of color in the palette and then clicking on the Modify button, you can change the color for that square. The change can be as dramatic as changing one color to another, or as subtle as just changing the shading or hue.

When you click on Modify, you can change the colors in either of two ways. The "Standard" tab gives you a large color palette from which you can select the color just by clicking on that color. A box at the bottom right shows the new color you have selected against the current setting. (See Figure 3-14.) The second way is to click on the "Custom" tab. You can make literally millions of colors by manipulating the red/green/blue settings or by moving the cross hairs on the spectrum and the arrowhead on the scale at the right. If you are trying to

F I G U R E   3–14

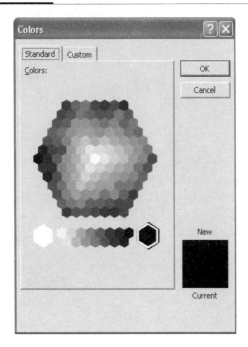

determine a color, it helps to first set the arrowhead lower on the scale to deepen the color. This makes it easier to determine the color you want by just shifting the cross hairs (the deeper color makes it easier to distinguish between hues) before setting the arrowhead up again to get the shading you want. (See Figure 3-15.)

Once you have changed the colors in the basic palette, that setting is saved in the file.

Editing Settings

There are two settings on the Tools > Options > Edit tab that you might want to consider changing. (See Figure 3-16.)

The first setting option is "Edit directly in cell." With this checked, when you double-click on a cell with a formula in it, the formula will appear overlaying that cell. It will also appear in the formula bar at the top of the screen. Although it may be

F I G U R E   3–15

a personal preference to see the formula this way, you lose one benefit: if this is not checked, then double-clicking will make Excel highlight the cells that are the precedent cells to the active cell (i.e., the cells that feed into the current cell). In other words, with this unchecked, you can have a quick audit function of the elements of the current cell.

The second setting option is "Move selection after Enter." With this on, after you press Enter, the cursor will automatically move to the next cell in the direction specified here. For certain tasks when you are going to be entering a list of entries, this may be helpful. But for general work, when you only want to stay at the entry you have just made or move to a different direction, you should uncheck the preset automatic move.

Calculation Settings

As default, Excel will calculate with the settings shown in Figure 3-17. Let's look at the settings in the top two sections.

F I G U R E 3–16

F I G U R E 3–17

Calculation is the mode for refreshing the file. The three choices in this mode are as follows:

- *Automatic.* There is a calculation refresh every time you make a change to your file. For a small model and/or a fast computer processor speed, you can leave this on. But if you have a larger model and/or an old computer, this refresh can take a discernable—and annoying—pause *every time* you make a change, however small. When that happens, you might want to select another mode.
- *Automatic except tables.* This is also an automatic refresh, with the exception of the calculation of data tables. Data tables are tables that you can set up in Excel in order to make sensitivity tables. Excel creates the internal calculations for a table that can test, for example, the IRRs (internal rate of return) for a set of cash flows based on different exit years (for the x axis) at different exit multiples (for the y axis). However, data tables are hugely calculation intensive and can slow down the calculation refresh of the whole model, even if the nondata table calculations are fairly straightforward. When this happens you should select this option. When you do want to calculate the data tables, press F9.
- *Manual.* This setting turns off the automatic calculation refresh and may be the best if you are working with larger models in slower machines. In order to have the number in the file calculate correctly, you must press the F9 key. An important point to remember with this setting is to refresh the numbers before printing.

Under the Manual setting is a check box for automatically calculating the file before you save it. This check box is enabled only when the manual setting is on (since on the other settings, the worksheet is always refreshed). The only reason for having this checked is if you are working with external links and you need to get the data in before you save it. Of course, if you remember to press F9 before saving, you need not have this checked.

Iteration

In the context of Excel, iteration would be required if you have circular references and you want the calculation to be performed over the formulas in the "loop" again and again. Iteration, after all, means "to do something again or repeatedly."

Usually, circular references are to be avoided, but, for our modeling work, circular references can be useful. A short circular reference happens when Formula A reads Formula B, which reads in turn Formula A. (The shortest is when Formula A reads itself.) Longer circular references have more intervening formulas, but the last one reads Formula A.

A circular reference is useful for converging into a solution. Here is an example for the calculation of interest expense based on the amount of debt required in a balance sheet:

1. You are calculating the amount of debt that a company requires based on the "plug" number that fills the financing gap between the assets and the nondebt liabilities and shareholders' equity. Let's say the plug is $100.
2. This new plug carries an interest rate of 10 percent or $10 for the year.
3. The additional interest expense decreases net income (let's assume no tax) and therefore shareholders' equity through retained earnings. This creates another financing gap of $10, so the plug is now $110.
4. The interest expense is now $1 more at $11 ($110 * 10%), not $10.
5. An additional financing gap of $1 is produced. Now the plug is $111.
6. The interest expense is $11.10 ($111 * 10%).
7. The financing gap increases by $0.10.
8. The interest expense is $11.11 ($111.10 * 10%).
9. The financing gap increases by $0.01.
10. The interest expense is $11.111 ($111.11 * 10%).
11. And so on. . . .

In this example, the numbers are converging: they are coming to a relationship with each other in which the changes between each iteration become progressively smaller. It is this kind of calculation that tells us that circular references can be useful. Don't let anyone tell you that circular references must be avoided at all times, or that having circular references in a model is a sign of bad modeling. If anything, having circular references that work is a sign of sophisticated modeling.

By the way, the interest calculations used above have been highly simplified. In actual calculations, we might want to consider that the interest expense is calculated on the average of the beginning and ending plug numbers. We will discuss this more fully in later chapters.

Some Warning Signs You Might See

If you put in a circular reference and the Iteration is not on, you will see the alert shown in Figure 3-18 from Excel. In this case, either turn the Iteration setting on if you want to have the circular reference or just correct your formula if you put in the circular reference by mistake. Notice that the message on this alert box does not consider the possibility that you might actually have wanted to put in the circular reference.

If the Iteration setting is on, but you have somehow entered the wrong relationships in the circular formulas, your numbers go berserk and become astronomically huge. This happens when the numbers diverge, rather than converge. Luckily, Excel has a setting that limits the number of iterations it will perform.

F I G U R E   3–18

Microsoft Excel

Microsoft Excel cannot calculate a formula. Cell references in the formula refer to the formula's result, creating a circular reference. Try one of the following:

• If you accidentally created the circular reference, click OK. This will display the Circular Reference toolbar and help for using it to correct your formula.
• For more information about circular references and how to work with them, click Help.
• To continue leaving the formula as it is, click Cancel.

OK   Cancel   Help

Maximum Iterations

This is the number of iterations that it will perform. The maximum is 200. The kind of model we are building should iterate no more than 25 times or so. Recommendation: set it to 100, which will definitely give you an indication if something is not calculating properly, without having to wait for the second hundred iterations.

Maximum Change

This is the maximum change setting below which the iterations will stop. The change describes the biggest change in each of the numbers in the worksheet between one iteration and the next. The smaller the maximum change setting, the more iterations that Excel will have to make. Recommendation: 0.001 is fine. If the maximum iterations setting is 100, but the maximum change of 0.001 is reached in 5 iterations, then Excel will stop after 5 iterations.

CHAPTER 4

Your Model-Building Toolbox: F Keys and Ranges

In Chapter 3 we went through the Excel controls "outside" the spreadsheet area (i.e., the settings that control how the spreadsheet itself looks and functions). In this chapter we will go over specific keyboard controls and look at how Excel considers blocks of cells in the spreadsheet area, specifically:

- The F keys on your keyboard
- Range names in Excel

F KEYS

Along the top row of your keyboard is a series of keys marked F1 to F12. Each of these "F keys" launches specific commands in Excel, but you will find that the ones you will be using often are really only about half of the F keys. The ones used more often are shown in **bold**:

- F1   Help
- **F2   Edit the active cell**
- F3   Paste a name into a formula
- **F4   Repeat the last keyboard action**
- **F5   Go to**

- F6   Move to the next pane
- F7   Check spelling
- **F8   Anchors the start of a range**
- **F9   Calculate all sheets in all open workbooks**
- F10   Make the menu bar active
- F11   Create a chart
- F12   Save As... command

Additionally, there are four other frequently used sequences that use the F keys in combination. These are:

- F2 + F4   Cycle through absolute references
- F2 + F5   Trace back to formula sources
- F2 + F9   Recalculate portions of formulas
- Ctrl + Alt + F9   Forced calculation

In addition to these, Excel gives you even more commands if these F keys are used with Shift, Ctrl, Alt, Ctrl + Shift, or Alt + Shift. Most of these are not often used in day-to-day modeling, but you should explore the full list of functions by going to F1 Help. Type any of the F keys (e.g., F1) in the input box at the top of the Find tab. Then select the "Function keys in Microsoft Excel" in the list of items shown in the list box at the bottom of the form for a full list of the function keys in Excel.

F1: Help

This is the key you use to get help from Excel.

F2: Edit

Pressing this key will bring you to the "edit mode." It will allow you to edit the cell that your cursor is on. Pressing this key and other F keys will have other results (see below).

In the F2 Edit mode, you can choose to edit the formula directly in the cell that the cursor is on, or in the formula bar near the top of the screen. In both cases, the cells of the precedent cells (the cells that feed the current cell, i.e., the ones carrying data that "precede" the current cell) will be highlighted by different-colored borders. The setting to determine this is in the Tools > Options > Edit tab, with the check box marked "Edit directly in cell."

This choice is a matter of personal preference, but there is also one important difference. If the "Edit directly in cell" is checked, double-clicking a cell has the same effect as pressing F2; it just gets you into the Edit mode. However, if this is not checked, double-clicking on a cell will "jump" you to the precedent cell (or the first precedent address if there is a long formula in that cell). A *precedent cell* is the cell that contains data that is being used in the cell that you are on; it is the cell whose data "precedes" the current one. The opposite of this, referring to the cell that makes use of the data in the current cell, is the *dependent cell*.

F2 + F4: Cycle Through Absolute References

Cell addresses in Excel change automatically when you copy them from cell to cell. The cell in B2, shown in the box as the formula, will change as it is copied into different cells. Across the same row, the column letter reference will change; down the same column, the row number reference will change.

	A	B	C	D	E	F	G
1							
2		=B4		=D4	=E4	=F4	
3		=B5					
4							

In some instances, it would be preferable not to have this relative referencing work. When we copy the cell to other places, we can make an absolute reference. We do this by putting the dollar sign "$" in front of the column letter or the row number, or both. There are four possibilities for specifying the B4 address, and pressing F4 successively after you are in the F2 Edit mode will cycle you through these settings.

As you copy:

* B4:   Both the column letter and the row number will move.
* B4: Both stay unchanged.
* B$4:   The column letter will change, but the row number will stay unchanged.
* $B4:   The column letter stays unchanged, but the row number will change.

You can also insert the $ symbol manually by typing it into the appropriate place(s) in the cell address.

F2 + F5: Tracing Back to Formula Sources

Once in the edit mode with the F2 key you can highlight a cell address and then press F5. This is a quick "go to." This is most helpful for tracing back to the source(s) when the cell you are editing contains a long formula.

F2 + F9: Recalculating Portions of a Formula

Press F2 while you are in a cell with a long formula, then highlight a portion of the formula with your mouse and press F9. The highlighted portion of the formula will be shown as the result. This is a great way to check if your formulas are calculating correctly, because you can highlight increasingly larger portions to follow the sequence of calculations.

Here's an example:

1. Press F2 to edit the formula in E6. Highlight D2 in the formula.

	▼	=	=D2*E2+D3*E3+D4*E4			
	A	B	C	D	E	F	G
1							
2				60.0%	140.0		
3				80.0%	20.0		
4				4.0%	50.0		
5							
6					102.0		

2. Press F9. D2 now changes to 0.60, the contents of the cell D2.

	=	=0.60*E2+D3*E3+D4*E4				
	A	B	C	D	E	F	G
1							
2				60.0%	140.0		
3				80.0%	20.0		
4				4.0%	50.0		
5							
6					102.0		

3. Now highlight E2 in the formula and press F9. E2 changes to 140, the number it contains.

	=	=0.60*140+D3*E3+D4*E4				
	A	B	C	D	E	F	G
1							
2				60.0%	140.0		
3				80.0%	20.0		
4				4.0%	50.0		
5							
6					102.0		

4. Now highlight the expression 0.60*140 . . .

	=	=0.60*140+D3*E3+D4*E4				
	A	B	C	D	E	F	G
1							
2				60.0%	140.0		
3				80.0%	20.0		
4				4.0%	50.0		
5							
6					102.0		

5. ... and when you press F9, this expression changes to 84.

	A	B	C	D	E	F	G
			▼	=	=84+D3*E3+D4*E4		
1							
2				60.0%	140.0		
3				80.0%	20.0		
4				4.0%	50.0		
5							
6					102.0		

You can continue doing the successive highlighting and pressing F9 through any formula, no matter how long. F2 and F9 will always show you the result.

Be careful. After you have finished your checking, make sure you press the Esc key and not the Enter key. Pressing Esc will undo all the results and revert the formula to its original form. Pressing Enter will convert the portions of the formula you have been editing in this way into the result. If you pressed the Enter key after step 5, the formula will now be permanently changed to $=84+D3*E3+D4*E4$. Fortunately, you can still reverse this action by pressing Ctrl + z, for Undo.

F3: Paste a Name into a Formula

This function pastes a name from the list of range names into a formula (see the section on Ranges later in this chapter). As you write or edit the formula, press F3 and a "Paste Name" dialog box will pop up on your screen. From this, you can select the range name you want to paste into the formula. Once you click on OK, then Excel returns you to the formula and you can continue working with the formula.

F4: Repeat the Last Action

F4, by itself, will repeat the last command. This can be a short-cut sequence, like Ctrl + B for bold, or even the keyboard sequence equivalent, Format > Cells > Font > Bold. This is a time-saving

key when you need to do something that involves hitting multiple keys across many cells in your sheet, and this is worth
remembering.

If you are doing a sequence that requires two operations
(e.g., selecting a row across the worksheet and then performing
an Insert command to add a whole row across), F4 will only
repeat the last command. This means that you will be inserting
a row on only one column (the last command), since F4 does
not also select the whole row (the second-to-last command). In
such a case, exploring the keyboard alternative may prove useful.
The keystroke sequence for inserting a whole row is Alt>
Insert>Rows. Your cursor can be on any column in the row to
do this. Now when you press F4, this sequence is repeated and
you can then quickly insert rows anywhere else on the worksheet.

F5: Go To

Pressing F5 will show you this form. If you have a file that
has no range names, the "Go to:" box will be blank, as shown
in Figure 4-1.

If there are range names, and you want to go to a particular
one, just highlight it and then click on OK. If you want to go to
another address, type it in the "Reference" box. Here is a feature
to remember: once you get to your destination, you can press F5
again and just press OK to return to your starting point.

Click on the "Special" key to see another form that lists
other destinations to go to with the F5 key. (See Figure 4-2.)

The Go To Special form is more of a specialized "find"
function. It is a "go to" function to go to cells that meet the
condition that you have selected from the radio buttons. Most
of the options are self-explanatory.

Of note are the following options:

- *Row differences.* If you have two or more columns of
  numbers and you want to check if any of the cells are
  different across the rows, highlight the columns and then
  choose this option. It will show you all the rows where the
  numbers are not identical.

F I G U R E   4–1

- *Column differences*. This is the same idea as with Row differences, but only for differences across columns.
- *Last cell*. This shows you the cell at the bottom right-hand corner of the area of the screen that you have used. You use a cell by inputting an entry. The more cells you use, the bigger the amount of memory that your file needs (and the bigger the size of the file). For this reason, if you have been working on a sheet and making many changes, it is a good idea to check where the last cell is, so that the sheet is not any bigger than it needs to be. The keyboard alternative to check this is Ctrl + End.

To reduce the used area on your sheet, do the following:

1. Select the row just below the last row with data and highlight all the rows below it to the last row being used. Do this by clicking and dragging on the row numbers on the left of the screen.

F I G U R E   4–2

2. Right-click on your mouse and select Delete.
3. Do the same with columns by selecting the column just to the right of the last column of data and highlighting all the used columns to the right of that. Do this by clicking and dragging on the column letters on the top of the screen.
4. Again, right click on your mouse and select Delete.
5. Save the file and close it. When you reopen it, the used area will have reduced itself.

(Another way to see the used range and one that does not use the F5 key at all is to go to cell A1, which you can do by pressing Ctrl+Home. Then press Shift+End+Home keys together. This will highlight the used range. Pressing End+Home alone will make the cursor go to the last used cell, without highlighting the used range.)

F6: Move to the Next Pane

If you have split the screen (Windows > Split) so that it has up to four areas or panes, then pressing F6 will move you from one pane to another in a clockwise direction.

F7: Spelling Command

This will launch a spell check for the active sheet only. If you want to check the spelling on other sheets, you will have to go to those sheets and press F7 again. F7 is the shortcut for Tools > Spelling.

F8: Anchor the Start of a Range to Extend a Selection

This is not a well-known key but it is useful when you want to highlight a large range. Whereas highlighting a small range can be easily done with the mouse, anything beyond one screen wide and one screen high is a little tricky. What if you wanted to highlight 80 columns across and 2000 rows down? This is where the F8 key becomes handy. Go to the top left corner of the range you want to highlight, then press F8. This anchors the start of the range. If you use the keyboard arrow keys, the highlighted range automatically expands as you move the cursor any way from the starting point. If you are using the mouse, clicking on a cell will define that bottom right corner. You can keep redefining this corner with the mouse. The final range is selected only when you press Enter, and the active cell becomes the top left corner, even as the whole range remains painted on your screen.

If you changed your mind about highlighting a range after you pressed F8, just press Esc.

F9: Recalculate

This key recalculates the whole file, and any other file that is also open in Excel. If you have set your worksheet to have automatic calculation, this key is not critical, as that setting means that

Excel will always be refreshing the worksheet to take into account any changes that have been made.

If you have set the calculation setting to "Automatic except for tables," then you must press this F9 key if you want to update your data tables. Other calculations will be refreshed automatically.

If your setting is for manual calculation, then you must remember to press this key to ensure that the screen shows the latest set of calculated numbers. This is especially important prior to any printing.

Ctrl+Alt+F9 Forced Calculation

As your model becomes more complex and sizable, Excel must keep track of the myriad of calculations in it. Occasionally, though not very often, you may find that the numbers do not seem to be updating properly. One reason is that Excel has an "intelligent recalculation" feature that is supposed to minimize the recalculations it has to do (i.e., it "knows" when cells do not need to be recalculated because the results will not change with further recalculations). This feature can lead to a situation where the recalculation does not happen when it should happen. In this case, use this sequence to override the intelligent recalculation feature and force Excel to go through a refresh.

One hint: as we go deeper into modeling, you will be using circular references. As mentioned in the previous chapter, you will need to set Excel to the calculation setting to allow iterations. If you find that the numbers are not recalculating, no matter how many times you press F9 or Ctrl+Alt+F9, check that the iteration setting has been enabled. If you have circular references and the iteration setting is off, the recalculation cannot proceed.

F10: Make the Menu Bar Active

F10 will allow you to select items on the menu bar by the keyboard. When you press F10, you will see that the File menu item on the menu bar seems to be on a raised level. This indicates that the menu bar can now be selected by pressing the keys on the keyboard that correspond with the underlined letter in the menu item. F10 is equivalent to just pressing the Alt key.

F11: Create a Chart

This is the key that will quickly show a set of numbers that your cursor is on as a chart.

F12: Save As Command

This is the alternative of File > Save As command. F12 allows you to save a file quickly, but potentially under a different name than it has. This is different from Ctrl + S, or File > Save, which saves the file under the name it already has.

RANGES

In Excel, we often work with a block of cells for various operations. Such a block is called a range. The top left corner of a range is defined by one cell, and the bottom right corner is defined by another. In this way, a range is always rectangular and in fact can only be this four-sided shape. One cell can also be thought of as a range, whose top left address is the same as the bottom right. Likewise, the whole sheet from A1 to IV65536 is range.

	A	B	C	D	E	F	G
1			2002	2003	2004	2005	2006
2	Taxable income		100	110	121	132	145
3							
4	Tax rate	35%					
5	Provision for taxes		=C2*B4				
6			=C2*TaxRate				

Once you have a range, you can name it, and this is where it becomes a powerful tool for your model building.

Defining a Range Name Quickly

When defining a range name, use the Name Box at the upper left-hand corner just above the corner where the column letter A and the row number 1 meet.

TaxRate ▼		=					
	A	B	C	D	E	F	G
1							
2							
3		[ ]					
4							
5							
6							

With the cursor already placed in the cell or cells that you want to name, click on the Name Box, type the range name, and press Enter. Here, cell B3 has been named TaxRate. This quick shortcut is good for naming any size range.

Let's build on this with an example of calculating "Provision for taxes" line:

TaxRate ▼		= 0.35					
	A	B	C	D	E	F	G
1							
2		Tax rate					
3		35.00%					
4				2002	2003	2004	
5		Taxable income		100	110	121	
6		Provision for taxes		=D5*TaxRate			
7				=D5*B3			

With the range named as TaxRate (remember, range names do not allow spaces in them) in cell D6, we can type a formula that uses both a cell address and a range name. Range names also have absolute addresses, so that if you copy this across, the range name TaxRate will continue to point to cell B3. This named range becomes convenient to use when you are further down in the spreadsheet and need the input number. You can just type TaxRate instead of having to find the exact cell address. The cell D7 shows the formula that you would have to write if you did not use the TaxRate range name.

The Long Way of Naming Ranges

If we do not use the Name Box for naming ranges, we have to use the sequence Insert > Name > Define to get to the user form that will allow us to define, or name, the range. As you can see, this requires more steps.

Naming Many Single-Cell Ranges at the Same Time

A variation of this longer sequence is actually useful and is a time saver when you want to name many single-cell ranges at the same time. This can occur when you need to set some toggle ranges, for example. Here's how to do it:

1. Type the range names that you want to create in the spreadsheet. For our example, write them down vertically. In this example, we are going to name the cells in column C with the names that we have entered in column B:

	A	B	C	D	E	F	G
1							
2		StartDate					
3		EndDate					
4		NoOfYrs					
5		Rate					
6		TaxDeduct					
7							
8							

2. Highlight the block B2 to C6 and press Insert > Name > Create.

	A	B	C	D	E	F	G
1							
2		StartDate					
3		EndDate					
4		NoOfYrs					
5		Rate					
6		TaxDeduct					
7							
8							

3. A user form like that shown in Figure 4-3 will appear.

F I G U R E   4–3

4. Click on OK.

Done! The user form explains, if rather cryptically, that Excel is creating the named ranges based on the names in the left column of the block you have highlighted. By this approach, you could also have created named ranges based on labels you have into the top, bottom, or right of the highlighted block.

Making Range Names More Informative

Use range names that are clear and spell out the name as much as possible, while keeping it easy to type. In the example, "TaxRate" is more immediately clear than "TxRt." If you are going to be typing this range name many times as you develop your model, strike a good balance between clarity and ease of typing.

You can also use range names to describe switches. For instance, you may have a cell that holds the switch for the use of a U.S. tax rate or a foreign tax rate for a tax calculation, which will be either a 1 or a 0, respectively. If you named the cell "TaxRate," you would have no easy way to remember what 0 or 1 means. You may remember this in the current modeling session, but there is a good chance that when you continue your work the next day you won't remember it as easily. In this case, consider making the range name more self-explanatory. Instead of "TaxRate," call the toggle cell in A3 "TaxUS1Frn0" instead. So it may look like this in a formula:

C7 ▼		=	=C4*IF(TaxUS1Frn=1,C5,C6)				
	A	B	C	D	E	F	G	H
1								
2	TaxUS1Frn0		2002	2003	2004	2005	2006	
3	1							
4	Earnings before tax		100	110	120	130	140	
5	U.S. rate		35%	35%	35%	35%	35%	
6	Foreign rate		21%	21%	21%	21%	21%	
7	Tax		35	38.5	42	45.5	49	
8	Net income		65	71.5	78	84.5	91	
9								
10								

Deleting a Range Name

To delete a range name, do the Insert > Name > Define sequence. At the dialog box that you see, select the range name in the list box and then click on the Delete button.

CHAPTER 5

Your Model-Building Toolbox: Functions

In this chapter, we continue to look at the spreadsheet aspect of Excel and what we can do with it. We have gone over F keys and ranges, but now we come to the true power of Excel: its ability, through preformatted formulas called *functions*, to do a whole host of calculations.

FUNCTIONS

Functions allow you to do arithmetic and other operations very quickly and conveniently. Excel has a list of functions that it offers, and you can see them by clicking on the icon that looks like *fx* on the formula bar (in versions earlier than XP, the *fx* is visible in the toolbar). This will display the full list of functions. In XP you can also see the functions by clicking on the drop down arrow on the icon that looks like the Greek *sigma* (Σ) and selecting More Functions.

There are some 230 functions in all, in 10 major classes, but you do not need to be familiar with all of them. In fact, you can be quite good in Excel and in modeling by just knowing about 50 or so. The list below presents the 36 functions that I would consider important to have in your basic repertoire. The list that follows presents 18 others that would be helpful to know as part of a more advanced skill set.

Basic Functions to Know

* Logical functions: IF, TRUE, FALSE, AND, OR. Theses are functions that allow some measure of decision-making ability in your formulas.
* Math and trigonometry functions: INT, MOD, ROUND, SUM, SUMIF. These are for working with numbers.
* Statistical functions: AVERAGE, COUNT, COUNTA, MIN, MAX. These are for combinations of counting and summing.
* Lookup and reference functions: CHOOSE, HLOOKUP, INDEX, MATCH, OFFSET, VLOOKUP. These are for ways of looking up data.
* Date and time functions: DATA, DAY, MONTH, NOW, YEAR. These are for specifying dates and time intervals.
* Information functions: ISERROR, ISNUMBER, ISTEXT, ISBLANK. These are for finding out different types of information in cells.
* Text functions. LEFT, LEN, MID, RIGHT. These are for working with text.
* Financial functions: IRR, NPV. These are for calculating returns and net present value.

More Advanced Functions to Know

* Math and trigonometry functions: ABS, CEILING, FLOOR, ROUNDUP, ROUNDDOWN, SUMIF, SUMPRODUCT
* Statistical functions: COUNTIF
* Lookup and reference functions: INDIRECT
* Date and time functions: DAYS360
* Text functions. LOWER, PROPER, TEXT, TRIM, UPPER, VALUE
* Financial functions: XIRR, XNPV

ARGUMENTS IN FUNCTIONS

Anytime you use these functions, you will write them starting with an equal (=) sign, followed by the name of the function you want to use, and then a set of parentheses. Within the parentheses, you need to specify the types of information, called *arguments*, that the function needs. Some functions, like =NOW(), which returns the current time setting, do not need any arguments, but you will still need to type in the parentheses. Others may need one, two, or more arguments. Some take optional arguments. You can enter them or leave them out.

Arguments can be:

- A cell or range reference, or multiple references: SUM(A1:A10) or SUM(A1:A10,A20,B30)
- A whole column: COUNT(A:A)
- A whole row: MAX(20:20)
- A range name: AVERAGE(Revenues)
- Another formula or expression: SUM(250/3, 12*34.5)
- Other functions: SUM(AVERAGE(C1:C10), AVERAGE(H1:H10)
- Optional with a marker: OFFSET(B1,0,2) or OFFSET(B1,,2). The space between the double commas is where the argument "0" has been left out.
- Optional without a marker: HLOOKUP(D5,B2:B3,2) or HLOOKUP(D5,B2:B3,2,TRUE)
- Or any combination of the above

A time-saving note: When you enter an argument that is a range reference (e.g., A1:A10), you can use the period (.) as the separator. Excel will automatically convert that to the colon (:). In this way, you only have to press one key, rather than two (the Shift and semicolon keys to get to the colon).

LET'S START

Now that you have some background in how functions work, let's go through the list. Because the purpose of this chapter is to have you become familiar with the functions in the context of their use, the following is organized a little differently from the list of categories that Excel has. We will talk about them in the following way:

1. The starting point: IF
2. Alternatives to IF
3. Functions for adding
4. Functions for counting
5. Functions for dates
6. Functions for looking up data
7. Dealing with errors
8. Other functions to know

THE STARTING POINT: IF

The IF statement is the "granddaddy" function in formulas. It makes the spreadsheet more than just a calculator because IF allows "what-if" scenarios: different results can be shown based on different conditions that have been set.

It has three arguments, and its syntax is as follows:

```
=IF(ThisConditionIsTrue,DoThis,ElseDoThis)
```

As an example, you can have the condition "If A1 contains a number that is not a zero, then show the contents of B1, otherwise show the contents of C1." This would be written as:

```
=IF(A1<>0,B1,C1)
```

Let's look at this formula carefully and note the following:

- Functions are formulas, so you should begin with the equal sign (=). This in effect tells Excel: "Get ready to calculate the following." If you write the formula above into a cell without the equal sign, Excel will show it as text, a string of characters that will not calculate.
- The formula given will show the contents of the cells B1 or C1. We can, however, have the choices occur in the IF

function itself. We could write:

IF(A1<>0,10,22)

* You can put other operators (=, >, <, <=, >=) in the place of the <> sign in the condition. If we want the choices to show text, we have to enclose those messages in double quotes:

IF(A1>10,"Sell","Hold")

* You do not have to write the IF word, or any other function word, in capitals. It will always appear as capitals. Of course, any text you want the formula to show like the "Sell" and "Hold" will show up exactly as you typed them.

It's TRUE or FALSE

Internally, Excel actually keeps track of whether something is true or not. Try this. In an empty spreadsheet, put the number 1 in cell A10. Then, in A11, write just the condition of the IF statement we have been experimenting with.

=A10=1

Remember to put the = sign at the beginning. We want Excel to calculate this. A11 will now show

TRUE

Change A10 so that it contains something else: a number that is not 1, or the text "1" (type an apostrophe and then the number 1), or make A10 a blank. Then the formula will show

FALSE

These words appear even though you did not type them in. The words TRUE and FALSE are keywords in Excel. They are part of Excel's own vocabulary of words with a distinct meaning and function in Excel. All the names of functions (IF, SUM, etc.)

are also keywords. To avoid confusion, do not use these key-words for naming range names.

What this means is that in the IF formula we were using:

```
=IF(A10=1,B10,C10*12)
```

Excel's IF function was testing

```
=IF(TRUE,B10,C10*12)
```

What the formula returns is based on whether the test is TRUE or FALSE.

Booleans: The Value of TRUE or FALSE

More interestingly, TRUE and FALSE have values. TRUE is 1, and FALSE is 0. This is the basis of something called Boolean logic, a system of algebraic logic invented by the English mathematician George Boole (1815–1864). What can we do with this?

We can use this Boolean logic as another way to create an IF condition. Here is an example:

```
=(A10=1)*100
```

You will need the parentheses around the A10 = 1 to make it clear to Excel that this is the Boolean unit. Otherwise, it will simply try to test if A10 is equal to 1*100.

Thus, when A10 is 1, the formula will return 100, the result of 1*100, or 100. When A10 is not 1 (it is another number, a word, or blank), the formula is 0, the result of 0*100, or 0. We're getting the same result as:

```
=IF(A10=1,100,0)
```

Boolean formulas are nice to use when you want to put in a simple switch to turn a cell's numeric contents on and off. If you want to mimic the conditional switch of *DoThis, ElseDoThis* of an IF statement, you have to string two Booleans together. The IF statement:

```
IF(A1<>0,10,22)
```

would look like this in a Boolean:

$$=10*(A1<>0)+22*(A1=0)$$

The only caveat with Booleans is that they are so compact that somebody unfamiliar with them can be totally confused.

In Most Cases, You Can Drop the "<>()"

One of the most common IF statement tests is to check whether the test cell is a zero or not. This formula, for example, tests whether A10 is not a zero. If it is not, then use it as the denominator in the fraction. If it is, then just return a 0. We do not want to calculate the ratio if A10 is 0, because dividing by zero will lead to an error:

$$=IF(A10<>0,A5/A10,0)$$

You can simplify by leaving out the "<>0" portion:

$$=IF(A10,A5/A10,0)$$

This may look strange at first, but you will find that you work faster, not just because you are saving the keystrokes, but also because the internal voice in your brain no longer says "is not zero" as you check your formulas.

A word of caution: Dropping this will have no effect for basic or even nested IF statements (see the section below), but if you are testing multiple conditions through the use of AND or OR, you should continue to include the "<>0".

Nested IF Statements

We have been doing only one thing so far. This is to look at an IF statement that looks at whether *one condition* is true or not, which leads to two choices, *do this* or *do that*.

There will be occasions when you want to look at more than one condition that leads to more than two choices. In other words, if *one condition* is true, *do this*; otherwise, if *a second condition* is true, then *do that*; otherwise, *do a third thing*.

We can build this kind of formula using the basic form as a start. Essentially, the *do this* or *do that* can be other IF statements.

So let's write a formula that says if A10 = 1, then show the number 100; otherwise, if A10 = 2, then show the number 200; otherwise (i.e., if A10 is not 1 or is not 2), show the number 999.

```
=IF(A10=1,100,IF(A10=2,200,999))
```

We can keep slipping IF statements into this kind of formula in a process called "nesting," and the result is called a nested IF statement.

```
=IF(A10=1,IF(D10=20,100,500),IF(B10=5,200,
IF(C10=10,999,300)))
```

Excel has a limit of seven nesting levels, but I think you will find the before you reach that final level, your own brain will have reached its limit of being able to keep track of which IF goes with which *this* or *that*. The limit of seven nesting levels refers to any combination of functions, not just IF.

Be Careful: A Zero May Not Be a Zero

In cases where the condition of an IF formula is whether a cell is 0 or not, be aware that sometimes a cell may look like it contains a 0, but does not. Excel translates numbers from the base 10 numbers to the hexadecimal (base 16) code of the computer for its calculations and then retranslates that back again. A discrepancy may result. This discrepancy is miniscule (you may see a number like 0.00000045, for example) and generally will not have a material effect on calculations. It can, however, have a great effect on an IF condition. If you set a formula such as:

```
=IF(D17=0,A10,B10)
```

that small discrepancy in D7 will make the D17 = 0 condition return a FALSE. If you do need to use this test, do a ROUND function to 1 or 2 decimal places, thus:

$$= IF(ROUND(D17,2)=0,A10,B10)$$

ALTERNATIVES TO IF

The following functions are full-fledged functions in themselves, but they are also useful as alternatives to the IF function. They are the following:

- MIN
- MAX
- CHOOSE
- OFFSET
- AND
- OR

MAX and MIN

MAX is a function that shows the greatest value among its arguments. MIN shows the smallest value.

To show results that are always above zero, you can write it with an IF statement:

$$=IF(A10>0,A10,0)$$

This means that if A10 is over 0, then show it, otherwise (if it is a zero or negative number), just show a zero. You can write it with the formula that is more efficient, like this:

$$= MAX(A10,0)$$

This reads: Show the maximum of or the greater number between A10 or 0. Thus, if A10 is a negative number, 0 is the greater number, and that is the result you will see. If it is positive, then A10 will be the number displayed.

Likewise, the following are equivalents:

$$= IF(A10<0,A10,0)$$
$$= MIN(A10,0)$$

Here is the variation if you want to say: Show A10 only if it is less than zero, but show it as a *positive* number:

`=IF(A10<0,-A10,0)` Note the minus sign in front of A10
`=-MIN(A10,0)` Note the minus sign in front of the MIN

or an alternative using MAX

`=MAX(-A10,0)`   Note the minus sign in front of A10

MIN and MAX become a much better choice over IF when there are more elements:

`= MAX(A10,B10,C10,0)`

or

`= MAX(A10:C10,0)`

An equivalent IF statement would be

`= IF(AND(A10>= B10, A10>= C10, A10>= 0), A10,`

`IF(AND(B10>= A10,B10>= C10, B10>= 0),B10,`

`IF(AND(C10>= A10,C10>= B10,C10>= 0),C10,0)))`

As you can see, this tortuous formula is horrendously diffi-cult to write correctly and check, and this is only to test just three cells against the value 0.

In the case where we want to find the maximum or mini-mum values of a range or a row, there is no other way but to use MAX or MIN:

`= MAX(A1:G16)`
`= MIN(10:10)`

MIN and MAX Together

If you want to show the value only as between 0 and 5, you can use the two together in the same formula:

$$= \text{MIN}(\text{MAX}(\text{A10},0),5)$$

In this way, any number that is in A10 will be shown only as a number between 0 and 5. The MAX function will show only numbers in A10 that are equal to or greater than 0. Potentially, this could be, say, 27. The MIN will show that result only between 0 (the bottom limit of the MAX) and 5 (the limit set by the MIN). So this is a way to limit the number that is being read elsewhere in the model to only the values between 0 and 5.

Another way is to put a limit on the input cell so that only this range of values can be entered. You can do this through the Data Validation feature of Excel. See Chapter 18, "Bells and Whistles."

MIN and MAX with Negative Numbers

MIN will always return the lowest value, in positive or negative numbers; MAX likewise returns the highest value.

If the range named TestRange contains 1,2,3, then

$= \text{MIN}(\text{TestRange})$ will return 1

$= \text{MAX}(\text{TestRange})$ will return 3

Note the results for negative values. If the range named TestRange contains −1,−2,−3, then

$= \text{MIN}(\text{TestRange})$ will return −3

as this is the lowest value

$= \text{MAX}(\text{TestRange})$ will return −1

as this is the highest value

Because of this, be careful with using MIN and MAX with negative numbers if your intent is to find a result that is closest, or farthest, from zero on the numbers scale.

CHOOSE

CHOOSE is a simple function for selecting an item from among a list.

```
=CHOOSE(index_number, choice1, choice2,...choice29)
```

Based on the index number (the first value), CHOOSE selects from the values listed. The index number cannot be a 0. The following example is a CHOOSE function that will return one of the four entries depending on the value entered in cell C10:

```
=CHOOSE(C10,"Apples","Bananas",
  "Cherries","Dates")
```

This example uses text strings, but the choices listed can be any of the acceptable forms for function arguments.

If we had written this with IF, it would have looked like this:

```
IF(C10=1,"Apples",IF(C10=2,"Bananas",
  IF(C10=3,"Cherries","Dates")))
```

As you can see, the benefit of CHOOSE is that it is much more straightforward. The disadvantage is that you have to list the choices individually because CHOOSE does not work with ranges. You cannot write CHOOSE(C10,D10:G10), for example. (You cannot do that with IF either.) Not being able to work with ranges makes writing CHOOSE rather awkward when you have upward of 10 choices. The limit for the values listed is 29; thus, the index number must be between 1 and 29.

To have the option of entering a 0 in order not to select any value, use the following variation. Since the first position is taken up by the "", you can only list 28 other options.

```
=CHOOSE(C10+1,"","Apples","Bananas",
  "Cherries","Dates")
```

OFFSET

OFFSET is a kind of CHOOSE that can work with ranges. In fact, it has to work with ranges so that you cannot pick choices from different parts of a worksheet or from different worksheets. However, it does not have a limit of the number of choices, so you can actually choose from a lot more choices than CHOOSE. The syntax is

= OFFSET (*Reference, RowsOffset, ColumnOffset*)

OFFSET is actually a different "animal" than CHOOSE because at its core it is a function of finding a cell that is so many rows and so many columns away from a starting reference cell. We can use this ability to pick a remote cell as a way to choose, but it is important to remember this is a far more powerful function. Here's how it works.

The formula

= OFFSET (K10, 2, 1)

will return the contents of the cell 2 rows down and 1 column to the right of the reference cell K10, which is to say, the contents of cell L12. The first number after the reference cell is the number of rows away from the reference cell. A positive number means the row is below the reference cell; a negative number means it is above. The second one is the number of columns away; a positive number means to the right of the reference cell; a negative number means to the left.

(In other functions in Excel where you need to define rows and columns, the system is the same. It is always rows first and then columns.)

OFFSET(K10,−2,−1), with the negative rows and columns numbers, will return the contents of the cell 2 rows above and 1 column to the left of the reference cell K10, or cell J8. You can have a negative row count and a positive column count, and vice versa.

If we write

OFFSET (K10, 0, 0)

we get the contents of K10, because the formula is asking for 0 rows and 0 contents away from K10.

Here is a comparison of IF, CHOOSE, and OFFSET. These are set to work an input toggle in cell A1. All these will return "Apples" if A1 is 1, "Bananas" if it is 2, and so on.

	A	B	C	D	E	F	G	H
1	1	Apples	Bananas	Cherries	Dates			
2								
3			=IF(A1=1, B1, IF(A1=2, C1, IF(A1=3, D1, E1)))					
4								
5			=CHOOSE(A1, B1, C1, D1, E1)					
6								
7			=OFFSET(A1,0,A1)					

With OFFSET, the list of items has to be in a contiguous range, because the function is simply counting how many cells away the data cell is from the reference cell. In this example, there is another important point to note. If we move the list of items to a vertical range, the IF and CHOOSE references will automatically change, but we would need to manually adjust the OFFSET formula:

	A	B	C	D	E	F	G	H
1	1							
2	Apples							
3	Bananas		=IF(A1=1, A2, IF(A1=2, A3, IF(A1=3, A4, A5)))					
4	Cherries							
5	Dates		=CHOOSE(A1, A2, A3, A4, A5)					
6								
7			=OFFSET(A1,A1,0)					

AND

As part of writing the IF statement, you can use the AND function, which combines the conditions. It is not an alternative to IF as such, but you could say that it is an alternative to a second IF. Rather than writing a nested second IF, you could combine the conditions with one AND, and write just one IF. The AND syntax is:

AND(*condition1, condition2,...*)

Notice that the AND precedes everything and the conditions are enclosed in parentheses. The function will return a TRUE if all the conditions in the function are true, and it will return a FALSE if even only *one* is not true. AND can contain up to 30 conditions.

AND is very helpful if you need to write a formula for the following, for example: If the employee's age is 50 or over, and his age plus length of employment is 70 or over, then he can retire. In the formula, "Age" and "Employment" are range names for individual cells containing the relevant data.

= IF(AND(Age>=50,Age+Employment>=70),

"See retirement counselor","Keep working")

OR

OR has the same syntax as AND:

OR(*condition1,condition2,...*)

Again, notice that OR precedes everything. Any *one* of the conditions must be true before the OR function returns a TRUE.

FUNCTIONS FOR ADDING

SUM

The SUM function allows you to add across ranges and still have the ability to add and subtract individual cells. You can also nest other SUMs and the results of other functions:

= SUM(A10,A11,254,10)

= SUM(A1:A50)

= SUM(A1:A50,B10,-C10,-SUM(D1:D10),MAX(D11,0))

SUM is also more forgiving and will allow you to add numbers to text (which is regarded as 0). If you have two cells, where C10 has a number and C11 has a text (let's assume this is an "n/a" text that appears because another cell is 0),

= SUM(C10:C11)

will return a 10. On the other hand, if you had written: C10+C11, the result would be #VALUE!

The range in SUM will automatically expand as you insert intervening rows (or columns, if you are SUMming across a table). However, you must be careful to recheck the range if you have been inserting or deleting rows at the top or bottom (or left and right edges) of the table.

SUMIF

This is a combination conditional and summing function. It will add the items in a range of values only if they fulfill a condition. The syntax is:

= SUMIF(*Range,Criteria,SumRange*)

Range is a list of items. *Criteria* is a condition related to *Range*. *SumRange* consists of the items that will be summed depending on the results of *Criteria* and *Range*.

Here's an example: We want to find out the total items related to the listing for Alex, and the formula in F2 is:

= SUMIF(B2:B7,E2,C2:C7)

The first range in B2:B7 is the *Range*. The *Criteria* is the cell E2, in which we have entered the word "Alex." (You could also just enter the test "Alex" directly into the formula.) The formula sums all the items in C2:C7, *SumRange*, that is associated with "Alex." And the answer is 6.

F2	▼	=	=SUMIF(B2:B7,E2,C2:C7)			
A	**B**	**C**	**D**	**E**	**F**	**G**
1						
2	Alex	3		Alex	6	
3	John	2				
4	Alex	1				
5	Lena	4				
6	Hillary	5				
7	Alex	2				
8						

SUMIF does not work with multiple conditions. You cannot write SUMIF(B2:B7,AND("Alex","John"),C2:C7), for example. However, if you wanted this result, the easy solution is to write the formula again, first using "Alex" and then using "John":

SUMIF(B2:B7, "Alex",C2:C7)+SUMIF(B2:B7, "John",C2:C7)

Variation of SUMIF

In the following illustration, SUMIF is being used to sum the cells that meet a quantitative condition, in this case the condition of "over 3." Note the *Range* is now defined as the range of numbers, rather than names. *Range* is the same as *SumRange*.

F2	▼	=	=SUMIF(C2:C7,E2,C2:C7)			
A	B	C	D	E	F	G
1						
2	Alex	3	>3		9	
3	John	2				
4	Alex	1				
5	Lena	4				
6	Hillary	5				
7	Alex	2				
8						

Because *Range* is the same as *SumRange*, we can actually write the formula in an abbreviated form:

= SUMIF(C2:C7, E2)

If you want to write the condition within the formula itself, you have to put it as a text string (i.e., put it in quotes):

= SUMIF(C2:C7,">3")

How You Can Use SUMIF in a Model

You can use SUMIF in a particularly powerful way: as a way to total lines in a model, especially where you expect the model to have rows added or deleted by the user.

Let's say you have a sheet for listing divisional revenues. Rather than summing the revenues at the bottom using SUM, use SUMIF. Here is an abbreviated sheet, listing three divisional revenues in rows 20, 40, and 60. In row 61, we put the SUMIF formula. The highlighted formula in D61 is shown in the edit box. We copy this formula across that line to columns E and F. Note four important points:

1. The formula in cell D64 has absolute references for the columns in *Range* and *Criteria*, since we want these always to read column C.
2. The two ranges must be of the same size. In this case, they are 60 rows each. If they are not of equal size, this formula can give wrong answers.
3. The *Criteria* is a reference, given here as a text "DivRev" within the formula itself. As noted above, we could have used a reference here to another cell which holds this text. If you do put in another cell, make sure that that cell is not part of the two ranges, as this would cause a circular reference.
4. Do not have the two ranges include the rows they are on.

D64		=	=SUMIF($C1:$C62,îDivRevî,D1:D6 2)			
	A	B	C	D	E	F	G
				2002	2003	2004	
20	Divisional revenue 1		DivRev	100	120	140	
21	COGS 1			81	87	98	
22	SG&A			7	9	12	
Ö	Ö						
40	Divisional revenue 2		DivRev	60	70	80	
41	COGS 2			45	48	53	
42	SG&A 2			5	6	7	
Ö	Ö						
60	Divisional revenue 3		DivRev	40	45	50	
61	COGS 3			31	33	36	
62	SG&A 3			3	4	6	
63							
64	Total revenues			200	235	270	
65							

If you add more divisional sales lines between rows 1 and 63, they will automatically be part of the sum of Total Sales. You must be careful to include the new rows as part of the range shown in the SUMIF function.

By the same magic, if you delete any divisional sales segments, the total will continue to work and will not return any error messages.

SUMPRODUCT

This is a quick way to multiply two ranges of numbers together. The syntax consists of two or more ranges, both of which must be the same size, and the function multiplies each element in one range with the corresponding element in the other range.

The illustration shows how the SUMPRODUCT accomplishes the task of deriving the total interest expense from a list of debt items and their individual interest rates.

	E2	▼	=	=SUMPRODUCT(B2:B5,C2:C5)		
	A	B	C	D	E	F	G
1		Debt	Int rate		interest		
2		100	3.0%		42		
3		200	4.0%				
4		300	5.0%				
5		400	4.0%				
6							

In this one cell, we can accomplish what otherwise would take separate multiplications of each debt by each interest rate and then the summing of the products.

FUNCTIONS FOR COUNTING

COUNT

This counts the items in a range. An important point to note is that the COUNT function counts only numbers. It will disregard entries of text.

E2	▼	=	=COUNT(B2:C4)			
A	**B**	**C**	**D**	**E**	**F**	**G**
1						
2	Adam	12		3		
3	Billy	3				
4	Charlie	5				
5						
6						

The formula returns 3, the number of times numbers appear in the range B2:C4.

COUNTA

Unlike COUNT, COUNTA counts both numbers and text. In the illustration above, COUNTA(B2:C4) would return the number 6.

COUNTIF

This is a combination conditional and counting function. It is similar to the SUMIF but returns a count of the items that meet the condition, rather than the sum. It only has two arguments. The syntax is:

$$= COUNTIF(Range, Criteria)$$

Range is a list of items. *Criteria* is a condition related to *Range*. The following shows the number of items related to the category "Alex."

F2		=	=COUNTIF(B2:B7,E2)			
A	**B**	**C**	**D**	**E**	**F**	**G**
1						
2	Alex	32		Alex	2	
3	John	27				
4	Alex	19				
5	Lena	43				
6	Hillary	51				
7	Alex	22				
8						

If you want to count the number of items that are equal (or above or below) a certain value, you can also use COUNTIF. In this case, the *Criteria* must be stated as a test. The following example shows the number of items that are above 25 and looks to the range C2:C7.

F2	▼	=	=COUNTIF(C2:C7,E2)			
	A	B	C	D	E	F	G
1							
2		Alex	32	>25		4	
3		John	27				
4		Alex	19				
5		Lena	43				
6		Hillary	51				
7		Alex	22				
8							

AVERAGE

This is really the SUM and COUNT functions together, or even more basic, the sum of the elements, divided by the number of elements. The syntax is:

$$= \text{AVERAGE}(number1, number2, \ldots number30)$$

The *number* arguments are numbers, arrays, or references that contain numbers. If the argument is a text, AVERAGE will consider it the same as a blank. Some points to note when using AVERAGE:

+ A blank cell is totally disregarded in the averaging calculations. A cell with a 0 is part of the calculations. This is shown in the following illustration:

	A	B	C	D	E	F	G
1					Average		
2	10		2		6	=AVERAGE(A2:C2:)	
3							
4	10	0	2		4	=AVERAGE(A4:C4)	
5							
6							

- If the elements all point to blank cells, you'll have a #DIV/0! error. This is the result of the denominator count's being zero. However, if they point to at least one cell that contains the value 0, then the function will work.

FUNCTIONS FOR DATES

Dates can be simple four-digit numbers that go up by 1 with each column, representing years. Occasionally, you may have to enter quarterly dates or work with days, months, and years. If we want to have a good control of the dates in the column so that we can easily change them, then we will have to understand how dates work in Excel.

How Excel Keeps Track of Dates

Excel keeps track of dates by assigning a number, or a *serial value*, to a date, starting with the number 1 for January 1, 1900. The upper limit is the serial value 2,957,063 for December 31, 9999. Excel's formatting takes this another step. By using different data formats, you can make the serial value appear in the date format you want, including non-U.S. dates ("31/12/2003"), or even as times of the day or the day of the week.

Monthly Dating

Here is a simple dating problem: How do we make a date go up by one month? Or more specifically, how do we get from the end of one month to the end of the next month?

Even with serial values for dates, we cannot just add 30 or 30.42 (that's 365/12) to a starting date if we want to make it go up by one month at a time. Adding 30.42 to December 31, 2003 will give us January 30, 2004, and not January 31. Adding 30.42 to January 31 will give us March 1, not the end of February.

The solution is to work with years, months, and days. If we want to go up one month, we simply add 1 to the month designator, no matter what the length of the month is. Likewise, to go up one year, we add 1 to the year designator, leap year or not. We can do this in Excel, because Excel will show you what year, month, or day it is for any serial value representing any time between January 1, 1900 and December 31, 9999. The functions to use are YEAR, MONTH, and DAY.

Thus, if we picked a serial value like 37986:

$$= YEAR(37986)$$

returns 2003;

$$= MONTH(37986)$$

returns 12; and

$$= DAY(37986)$$

returns 31.

This is to say that December 31, 2003 is 37,986 days away from December 31, 1899 (January 1, 1900, being day 1 in the serial value, is 1 day away). We would get the same results if we actually used the date 12/31/2003:

$$= YEAR("12/31/2003")$$

returns 2003;

$$= MONTH("12/31/2003")$$

returns 6; and

$$= DAY("12/31/2003")$$

returns 16.

Note: I am using here the U.S. convention for dates, which uses the order of month/day/year. Excel can be set to show different dating formats so that the serial value will appear with the correct order of days, months, and years. Go to Format > Cells > Number and select Date in the "Category" list box. Look at the drop-down box for "Locale (location)."

You will have to use the double quotes on the date to mark it as a text string. However, if the date were placed in another cell and the function referenced that cell, you do not have to worry about double quotes.

Going the other way, we can write a date using the component parts of year, month, and day. For this, there is the DATE function.

$$=\text{DATE}(2003,12,31)$$

This returns the serial value 37986, which can be formatted to appear as 12/31/2003.

Because Excel functions can use the results of other functions, we can write the following in cell C1. Let's put 12/31/2003 in a separate cell, say, cell B1:

$$=\text{DATE}(\text{YEAR}(B1),\text{MONTH}(B1),\text{DAY}(B1))$$

This returns the same date: 12/31/2003. Now, let's return to the dating problem we had at the beginning of the chapter: How do you make a date go up by one month?

We start with 12/31/2003 in B1. To make it go up by one month, we add 1 to the MONTH. In C1, we write:

= DATE(YEAR(B1),MONTH(B1)+1,DAY(B1))

This will return 1/31/2004 (January 31, 2004). Success! Building on this, let's try the next column again. In D1 we add another digit to the MONTH(C1):

= DATE(YEAR(C1),MONTH(C1)+1,DAY(C1))

This returns 3/2/2004 (March 2, 2004). This is not quite right. What's happening? The problem arises because January has 31 days and, with this formula, we are asking Excel to give the date for something like February 31, 2004. (We had no trouble with the first formula for January, because that month has the same number of days as December.) Since February in this leap year only has 29 days, Excel keeps counting until the "day 31" of February, and comes up with the equivalent March 2.

How do we find the ending day of each month, given that months' lengths vary? Instead of trying to find the ending day of each month, we could look for the *first day of the next month* and then subtract one day. Since the first day is always day 1, this is quite easy. So January 31 is really February 1 minus 1 day; February 28 is March 1 minus 1 day, and so on. But wait. Since Excel can deal with something like "February 31" to return March 2 (or March 3 in a non-leap year), can Excel consider January 31 as being "February 0," and February 28 as "March 0"?

Yes, in fact, it can. So now we have a solution for our dating problem. We add an extra month to the month interval we want to go up, but specify 0 for the DAY.

Let's have 12/31/2003 in B1 again. In C1, to make the date go up by one month, we write:

= DATE(YEAR(B1), MONTH(B1)+2,0))

to get "February 0, 2004," which is 1/31/2004.

In D1, to continue to the next month, we write:

= DATE(YEAR(C1),MONTH(C1)+2,0)

to get "March 0, 2004," which is 2/29/2004.

Yearly Dating

Increasing dates by 1 year is fairly simple matter now. Just add 1 to the YEAR number. We will use the same table, with 12/31/03, in cell B1. In cell C1, we would use the formula:

= DATE(YEAR(B1)+ 1,MONTH(B1),DAY(B1))

We will not have to worry about the DAY being off, since we are dealing with the same month in the year, just a year apart. However, if we are working with a February year-end, this formula will not return the leap day of February 29 in the leap years, since the DAY will always be based on the count of 28 for 2003 (or 29 if the starting year had been 2004). We could use the approach of using the 0 day of the next month, however:

= DATE(YEAR(B1)+1, MONTH(B1) + 1, 0)

This is the approach to use if you want the leap day to appear on the leap years. Alternatively, instead of adding 1 to the YEAR number, we can add 13 (12 + 1) to the MONTH and still use 0 for the DAY. That will bring us to exactly a year later.

Non-Annual Intervals

Using the MONTH part makes it easy to change the periodicity of your model from annual to quarterlies, or to some other non-annual interval. When you do this, it is a good idea always to use the "plus 1" approach to the MONTH and use 0 for the DAY, because the intervals you have can bring you to months with dissimilar ending days.

Finding the Number of Days Between Dates

Because of the serial value system, it is easy to find the number of days that have elapsed from one date to the next. For example, to find the number of days between August 17, 1953 and October 1, 2003, we do the following:

$$= DATE(2003,10,1)-DATE(1953,8,17)$$

which returns 18,307 days.

Alternatively, we can represent the actual date as a serial value by using the DATEVALUE function, which converts the text of the date to the serial value:

$$= DATEVALUE("10/1/2003")-DATEVALUE("8/17/1953")$$

which returns 18,307 days.

Finding the Number of Months Between Dates Using DAYS360

Finding the number of months between two dates is a little tricky, because of the different lengths of the months in the interval. In the last example we could divide 18,307 by the average number of days in a month (i.e., 365/12, or 30.42), but this is inelegant. A better way is to use the DAYS360 function. With DAYS360, Excel considers each year to be 360 days by assuming that there are 12 months, each composed of 30 days. So Excel has a way of considering the ending days of each month so that everything falls into line properly. The syntax is:

$$= DAYS360(BeginningDate, EndingDate)$$

The beginning date can be one defined by the DATE function, but DAYS360 is also smart enough to take the text of the dates:

$$= DAYS360(DATE(1953,8,17),DATE(2003,10,1))$$

which returns 18,044 days. Or

$$= DAYS360(``8/17/1953", ``10/1/2003")$$

which returns 18,044 days.

Because each year is 5 days shorter than the actual year (6 in a leap year), the number of interval days is fewer than the previous calculation. This is not a problem if we are looking to get a sense of the portion of the month or the year using this method. To find the number of months, we simply take the interval in days in a 360-day year and divide it by 30. Now, to get the number of months or the number of years:

$$18,044/30 = 601.47 \text{ months}$$
$$18,044/360 = 50.12 \text{ years}$$

When to Use DAYS360 in a Model

DAYS360 is useful in calculating a portion of the year. Let's say that a transaction happens on June 14, and we just want to get a value for the *stub portion*, or the portion of the year remaining after the deal. Let's assume a December 31 year-end:

$$= DAYS360(``6/14/2003", ``12/31/2003")/360$$

which returns 197/360, or 0.55.

Solving a Problem with DAYS360

In some situations, DAYS360 does not give you a 30-day month. Take the case where cell A1 has the date of 12/31/02 (the end of December) and cell A2 has the date 2/28/03 (the end of February in a non-leap year):

$$= DAYS360(A1,A2)$$

which returns 58 days.

Under the logic that each month is 30 days, the function should return 60 days for the two full months' interval. It does not in this case because Excel looks at the end of the month and tries to fit the 28-, 29-, 30-, 31-day endings into some order, and somehow the 28-day ending is confusing it. We can help Excel get unconfused by bringing the dates into the beginning of the month, where the interval algorithm is more straightforward. We do this by adding the number 1 to the cell references. In this way, we also do not need to change the dates themselves:

DAYS360(A1+1,A2+1)= 60 days

Assuming that you are always using period-end dates, adding 1 to the components of DAYS360 is a good way to make sure that the function works properly.

FUNCTIONS FOR LOOKING UP DATA

Two of the functions for looking up data have been introduced as variations of the IF functions: CHOOSE and OFFSET. Looking up data is really pinpointing the location of the data point that you want, whether it is from a collection of alternatives or from its location as defined by rows and columns.

MATCH

Use MATCH if you are looking for the location of a specific number or text in a range. Depending on how you write the formula, this function will return either the row or column number (but not both) within the range that you specified. The syntax is:

= MATCH(*LookUpValue*, *LookupArray*, *MatchType*)

LookUpValue is the item that you want to look up. This can be a number, a text, or a reference to another cell that holds the *LookUpValue*.

LookUpArray is a contiguous range of cells, or a range name.

MatchType can be either 1, 0, or −1. If it is 1, the MATCH will find the largest value that is less than or equal to the *LookUpValue*. In this case, the items in the *LookUpRange* must be arranged in ascending order.

If it is −1, it will find the smallest value that is greater than or equal to the *LookUpValue*. The data must be in descending order.

If it is 0, then it will find the exact match for *LookUpValue*. The data can be in any order. MATCH is very useful in this mode, and this is what we will illustrate below.

In this simple example, let's find the location of the word "Bob" from the list of names:

	A	B	C	D	E	F	G
1							
2							
3		Alice	2	=MATCH("Bob",B3:B6,0)			
4		Bob					
5		George					
6		Bob					
7							

The argument "Bob" is written directly into the function formula, but it could well have been a reference to another cell that actually holds that word. The range in the middle specifies the one-column block. The "0" at the end indicates we are looking for the exact match for "Bob."

In this instance, the formula will return the value of 2, meaning that it has found Bob in the second row of the target range, which in this case is row 4 on the sheet. Note also that the function disregards the second "Bob" altogether, because it has already found the exact match in the first, and the function essentially stops there.

If we made a slight change to the formula and made the target range start at row 1: then the function will return 4, since "Bob" is now in the fourth row of this range. There is an interesting point here. We have just identified the actual row number in the sheet of where "Bob" is located (or at least the first instance of "Bob"). Being able to identify a row number of a data point can be useful in other instances, especially if we already know which column it is in.

	A	B	C	D	E	F	G
1							
2							
3		Alice	4	=MATCH("Bob",B1:B6,0)			
4		Bob					
5		George					
6		Bob					
7							

To make this function useful to return a row number, the range used in *LookupArray* should start with row 1 in the column. In fact, the range can be the whole column, which can be easily defined by leaving out the row numbers, thus:

$$= \mathtt{MATCH(\text{"Bob"}, B:B, 0)}$$

This will identify where the first occurrence of "Bob" would be in all 65,536 rows of column B.

INDEX

INDEX returns the value of a cell within a range, by locating its row position and its column position. The syntax is:

$$= \mathtt{INDEX}(\mathit{Array}, \mathit{RowNumber}, \mathit{ColumnNumber})$$

The *Array* is any range storing the data.

The *RowNumber* is an integer greater than 0 that specifies which row within the *Array* the data point is in. *RowNumber* 1 means that the data point is on the first row of the *Array*. This can be omitted if the *Array* is a one-row range.

The *ColumnNumber* likewise is an integer greater than 0. It specifies which column the data point is in. *ColumnNumber* 1 means that the data point is on the first column of the *Array*. You can omit this if the *Array* is a one-column range.

	A	B	C	D	E	F
1						
2						
3		Alice	12	13		
4		Bob	22	23		
5		George	32	33		
6		Bob	42	43		
7						

If we define the *Array* as B3:D6, then INDEX(B3:D6,1,1) will return the value in the top left corner of the range (i.e., "Alice"). Using this table, we will get the following results from these other variations:

= INDEX(B3:D6,3,1)   George

= INDEX(B3:D6,4,3)   43

When you use INDEX, the row and column specifiers must specify positions within the *Array*. If they point to a location outside the range, you will get a #REF error message.

Using MATCH and INDEX together

The power of Excel functions can be magnified by using them together. Because MATCH can locate a row number based on matching it with a specific label or value, you can use the result of MATCH as a row parameter in INDEX. In the following illustration, we specify the company "Charlie" in cell E7. The following in cell E8 returns the stock price for the company:

= INDEX(D2:D5 , MATCH(E7,B2:B5,0))

The INDEX *Array* range is a one-column range, so we do not have to specify the *Column number* argument.

	A	B	C	D	E	F	G
1		Company		Price			
2		Alpha		$12.25			
3		Baker		$8.50			
4		Charlie		$22.00			
5		Delta		$17.35			
6							
7		Enter company name ===>			Charlie		
8		Stock price:			$22.00		
9		Formula in E8:			=INDEX(D2:D5,MATCH(E7,B2:B5,0))		

HLOOKUP/VLOOKUP

HLOOKUP and VLOOKUP are functions that work together in the same way as MATCH and INDEX in searching for a data point in data range. HLOOKUP is for searching the data range horizontally, by columns; VLOOKUP is for searching vertically, by rows.

HLOOKUP and VLOOKUP are powerful functions and are often used when simpler functions like OFFSET or INDEX will do just fine. These functions are most useful when the answer does not depend on an exact match with your search parameters. The syntax for HLOOKUP is as follows:

> = HLOOKUP(*LookUpValue*, *TableArray*, *RowNumber*, *LookUpType*)

The *LookUpValue* is the value to be looked up in the first row of the *TableArray*.

The *TableArray* contains the data for the lookup.

The *RowNumber* is the row that contains the data to be returned by the function.

The *LookUpType* is optional. If omitted or TRUE, this means than an approximate match can be returned if there is no exact match. The approximate match will be based on the value that is less than the *LookUpValue*.

	A	B	C	D	E	F	G
1				Price			
2	Income	$0	$2,500	$25,000	$50,000		
3	Tax rate:	15%	28%	31%	36%		
4							
5							
6							
7		Enter income:		$23,000			
8		Applicable tax rate:		28%	=HLOOKUP(D5,B2:E3,2,TRUE)		
9							

The applicable tax rate returned is 28 percent because the income entered is over $2500 but below $25,000, and the *LookUpType* entered is TRUE. If the *LookUpType* were set to FALSE, the result would be an #N/A error because there is no exact match to the entry of $23,000.

VLOOKUP uses the same syntax, but the table would have to be arranged vertically:

	A	B	C	D	E	F	G
1		Income:	Tax rate:				
2		$0	15%				
3		$2,500	28%				
4		$25,000	31%				
5		$50,000	36%				
6							
7		Enter income:		$23,000			
8		Applicable tax rate:		28%	=VLOOKUP(D7,B2:C5,2,TRUE)		

DEALING WITH ERRORS

As we develop the formulas in our model, Excel has a way of telling us when we are going about it the wrong way. The four most common error messages that Excel will show are the following:

- ◆ #DIV/0!
- ◆ #VALUE!
- ◆ #NAME?
- ◆ #REF!

#DIV/0! Errors

Excel will display this error when you attempt to divide a number by 0. It is easy to write a formula that inadvertently divides by zero because as you develop the formula, you may be using some test numbers. However, once you clean up the model, these test numbers go away and you will have formulas that then show the #DIV/0 errors. It may be that as the model starts to be used, there will be values coming in that will make these formulas calculate properly again. However, it is sometimes quite disconcerting for a new user unfamiliar with your model to see these error messages. For this reason, for any formula you write that involves a division, you should take steps to do an error trap by using an IF statement.

Thus, instead of the formula

$$= D10/D12$$

we should write it as:

$$= IF(D12,D10/D12,0)$$

Remember that D12 is the short way of writing D12<>0. Another variation is this formula:

$$= IF(D12,D10/D12,"na")$$

This formula will return the text "na" if D12 is zero. This is fine, unless there is the chance that this formula will be read by another cell as part of the calculation in that cell. If the first cell shows "na," then the calculation in the second cell will run into trouble because it will not be able to use this text in its calculations. That second cell will show the #VALUE! error (see below).

One trick you can use if you do want the "na" to show but avoid having other cells running into calculation problems is to use the first formula that returns a 0. To do this, we use Excel's formatting capabilities to show "na" when it is the value for 0. Please turn to Chapter 18, "Bells and Whistles" to see how this is done.

The #VALUE! Error

The usual occurrence of this error message is when you have written a formula whose components include a text. Essentially, this is Excel saying: "I don't want text. I want values only, please."

The #NAME? Error

You will get this error if your formula uses a range name that does not exist. This can be because of a misspelled range name, or a range name that you have created and used before but which has now been deleted. A misspelled function name will also give you this error.

The #REF! Error

This happens when the formula uses an invalid cell reference. For example, start with a formula in cell A10 like this:

$$= A1+10$$

If you copy this up one row, the formula will return a #REF!. In copying, Excel will try to keep the relative referencing, so as you go up one row, it changes the reference to A0. Since A0 does not exist, the error message shows up.

You will also get this error if you are in a situation where a formula, looks like this:

$$= B10+C10$$

and you cut and paste something into B10 and/or C10. Copying and pasting will not cause a #REF! error, however.

The ISERROR Function for Trapping Errors

Errors in a spreadsheet are generally easy to find and correct. Understanding what the error messages mean allows us to get an idea of what kind of error to look for and make the necessary corrections.

When we build a model, however, errors can be a little more troublesome. As you will see when we start developing the formulas in the model, we will be using circular references.

A circular reference occurs when a formula refers to itself, whether directly or indirectly. For example, if you enter =SUM(A1:A10) in cell A10, you would get a circular reference because every time A10 is calculated, it must include itself in the SUM calculation, in a never-ending cycle.

When you create such a circular reference, Excel will give you a warning message:

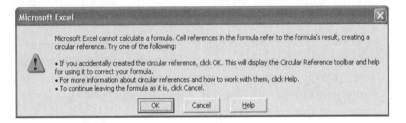

There are two ways of dealing with circular references and Excel's attempts to warn you about them:

1. One way is to correct the inadvertent circular references. Clicking on the OK on this message form will get Excel's circular reference toolbar to show, which will help you to start to zero in on where the troublesome reference is.

2. The second way, and this is only if you actually want to have circular references, is to set Excel's calculation to the iteration mode by the following sequence: Tools > Options > Calculation > Iteration. This will set Excel to allow circular references. An *iteration* is simply a cycle of calculation in which you can imagine a "wave" of calculation sweeping through the whole model, sheet by sheet.

Why do we want iterative circular references? Simply put, it is a simple way to get the model to converge on its calculations of interest expense. As you will see in the next chapters, in the forecast years the model will be creating "plug" numbers to balance the balance sheet. A plug number that is assumed to be debt will create an additional interest expense, which will affect the plug number itself. The model then has to recalculate (or iterate) to adjust for this increase, which in turn will create another, but incrementally smaller, increase. The iteration will go through several more cycles before there is convergence within the limits set in the model.

So, circular references can be used to good advantage. The dangerous thing is that as there is now a calculation loop in the model, if there is an error that gets inadvertently introduced into the calculations, this error message will continue to cycle around in the loop. Even after the source of the error has been removed, the error message continues to be caught in the loop! In this case, there are two ways to correct the situation:

1. Manually change one of the formulas so that the calculation loop is "broken." Make sure that the source of the original error is corrected, and recalculate the model again to clear out the error message. Once this is done, restore the formula again.

2. A more elegant way is to use the ISERROR function to trap the error. Simply put, at a location in the calculation loop, we write a formula that returns a 0 when it encounters an error condition. Let's say we put this in cell C51:

   = IF(ISERROR(C50),0,C50)

C50 is a cell that is part of the loop, as is C51. If there is an error in the loop, this formula in C50 will revert to a 0, which is then read by C51 and the rest of the calculations. The 0 breaks the circular loop and gives the error message a chance to be cleared out, so that when C50 calculates again, it does not see the error sign and automatically reconnects to C50. The loop is restored.

OTHER FUNCTIONS TO KNOW

Working with Parts of Numbers:
ROUND, INT, MOD

- ROUND(*number, number of digits*) will round the number to the specified number of digits. =ROUND(1.564,1) will return 1.6, for example. Likewise, =ROUND(1.564,0) will return 2.

Neat trick 1: You can put a negative number for the number of digits: −1 will round the number to the nearest ten, −2 to the nearest hundred, −3 to the nearest thousand, etc. Thus, =ROUND(1,234.2,−2) will return 1,200.

Neat trick 2: To round to the nearest 5 cents in a price, double the number first before doing a ROUND to 1 digit, and then divide by 2. The nearest 5 cents for $1.96 is $1.95. We get there by =ROUND(1.96*2,1)/2.

- INT(*number*) will get you the integer part of the number, the part to the left of the decimal point.
- MOD(*number, divisor*) will return the remainder of the number after it has been divided by the divisor. To get to the part of a number to the right of the decimal point you must use 1 as the divisor, thus, =MOD(1.564,1) will return 0.564. You can use other divisors for other results. For example, =MOD(1.564,0.5) returns 0.064. The divisor can be any other number except 0.

Working with Numbers in a Direction: ABS, CEILING, FLOOR, ROUNDUP, ROUNDDOWN

We can imagine that numbers lie on a line, with the 0 point separating the negative and the positive numbers. The following functions work in identifying or shifting numbers on the numbers line.

- ABS(*number*) returns the value of a number without the sign. Thus =ABS(−5) and ABS(5) will both yield 5, or the measure of the distance of 5 from the 0 point on the numbers line.
- CEILING(*number,significance*) returns the number rounded away from zero. For a positive number, this means it is rounded up. =CEILING(2.01,1) returns 3. For a negative number, it is rounded down, so it becomes more negative. CEILING(−2.01,−1) returns −3. Both the *number* and *significance* must have the same sign. If they do not, a #NUM! error results.

- FlOOR(*number, significance*) is similar to CEILING, but rounds the number toward zero. FLOOR(1.99,1) returns 1. FLOOR(−1.99,−1) returns −1. Similar to CEILING, both the *number* and *significance* must have the same sign. If they do not, a #NUM! error results.
- ROUNDUP(*number, number of digits*) behaves like ROUND, but rounds a number away from zero (in this sense it also works like CEILING). The *number of digits* can be a positive or negative number, and works exactly the same way as in ROUND.
- ROUNDDOWN(*number, number of digits*) is similar to ROUNDUP, but rounds the number toward zero.

Other Information Functions: ISNUMBER, ISTEXT, ISBLANK

These functions are useful for determining the kind of information that you are dealing with.

- ISNUMBER(*Value*) will return a TRUE if *value* is a number and a FALSE if it is a text or is blank. One example where this is useful is when you are writing an IF statement where you want the formula to read the entry in a cell, *even if it is a zero*. (The usual IF statement testing for the value "if it is not a 0" will return a FALSE when it encounters the number 0.)
- ISTEXT(*Value*) will return a TRUE if the value is a text string.
- ISBLANK(*Value*) will return a TRUE if the *value* refers to an empty cell.

Working with Text: LEFT, RIGHT, MID, LEN, LOWER, UPPER, PROPER, TEXT, VALUE

These functions are useful when you work with text strings. In these functions, the space between words counts as one character.

- LEFT(*Text, number of characters*) will return the leftmost portion of the *text* consisting of the *number of characters* defined. =LEFT("Good Morning",7) will return "Good Mo."

- RIGHT(*Text, number of characters*) will return the rightmost portion of the text, consisting of the *number of characters*. =RIGHT("Good Morning",7) will return "Morning."
- MID(*text, start number, number of characters*) will return a portion of the *text* from the letter of the *start* number. The portion will have the length of the *number of characters*. =MID("Good Morning",2,5) will return "ood M."
- LEN(*text*) returns the number of characters in the *text*. LEN is short for "length." =LEN("Good Morning") will return 12.
- LOWER(*text*) will return the *text* all in lowercase. =LOWER("Good Morning") will return "good morning."
- UPPER(*text*) returns everything in uppercase. =UPPER("Good Morning") will result in "GOOD MORNING."
- PROPER(*text*) will return *text* with the first letter of each word in uppercase and the remaining letters in lowercase. =PROPER("goOd moRNing") will return "Good Morning."
- TEXT(*value, format*) is a useful function for creating dynamic labels that include values. Excel is able to handle text strings and values together, but if you want the values to carry a particular format when you want to show the two together, you must use TEXT and define the *format* of how that value will appear.

  =TEXT(1.386, "$0.00") will return "$1.39." Note that the conversion also includes a rounding effect. The "$1.39" is now a text string, so that you can link it to other text strings by using the ampersand (&) symbol. Amazingly, you can still apply an operation to this text string so that it still performs as a value, but the format does not work on the result. TEXT(1.386, "$0.00")*2 will return "2.78," not "$2.78." The rounding effect in TEXT also causes 1.386 to become 1.39.
- VALUE(*text*) converts the *text* of a number into the value of that number. However, you do not really need this function as Excel can convert text to values as necessary.

Financial Functions: NPV, XNPV, IRR, XIRR

NPV (net present value) and IRR (internal rate of return) are the necessary functions to know when you start working with cash flows and estimating the returns of various projects. Both these functions deal with the *time value of money*. Time value of money is a way of saying that a dollar today is not worth the same value as a dollar will be in the future, or as it was in the past. No, we are not talking about inflation here. We are talking about the fact that money can earn interest.

Let's take a brief detour: Let's say that we can earn 5 percent interest every year on our dollar. Thus, our $1.00 today will be worth $1.05 next year (the arithmetic is simple: $1 \times 1.05 =$ $1.05), and $1.1025 ($1.05 \times 1.05) a year after that. By the same token, to have our $1.00 today, we actually needed to have only $0.9524 last year ($1.00 divided by 1.05. The proof that we have the right answer is 0.9524×1.05 =$1.00) and $0.9070 two years ago. The important point to remember is that the following values:

2 Years Ago	Last Year	Now	Next Year	2 Years Later
$0.9070	$0.9524	$1.0000	$1.0500	$1.1025

represent the *same time value of $1.00*. So to rephrase what we said in the previous paragraph, a dollar today is the same as something more than a dollar in the future, and something less than a dollar in the past. The term for adjusting the $1.00 across time to become a higher future number is called *future valuing*; reducing it by going backward in time is *present valuing*. Present valuing is also called *discounting*, although you can use it to describe future valuing by saying "discounting forward." We used the idea of an interest rate above, but the rate for looking at time value of money is usually called the *discount rate*.

Back to our functions. You should keep in mind the following points.

If you are dealing with annual periods, the NPV and IRR functions will work perfectly for your calculations. These functions use the spacing of the columns, with data in each column regarded as one year's data, as the annual timing for the calculations. If you have a year where there are no flows and you want these functions to include that year, you must have a 0 there. NPV and IRR disregards blanks. However, if you are dealing with uneven flows—they do not happen every year, or they happen at irregular intervals across the years, or both—then you should use the XNPV and XIRR functions. These more powerful functions look not just to the flows in each column, but also to the date labels in each column, and calculate the results based on the time intervals.

NPV and IRR are in the standard set of functions in Excel. However, XNPV and XIRR are part of the extended set of functions that are available only when the Analysis ToolPak Add-In is enabled. You can check whether it is enabled or not by the sequence Tools > Add-Ins.

- NPV(*rate,value1,value2,...*) returns the net present value of the annual flows represented by the *values*. These *values* can be positive or negative numbers, representing, by the usual convention, inflows and outflows of cash, respectively. Instead of individual *values*, you can use a range of *values*. *Rate* is the annual discount rate.

  Be very clear about the timing of the discounting when you use the NPV function, because the *values* are assumed to occur at the end of each year. So you have to be careful about whether you want to discount the first *value* in the function. In the following illustration, cell B6's NPV of 151.34 shows the result of the first *value* of (100)—representing an investment outflow of 100 at the end of 2004—being part of the NPV function. This means that it is also being discounted at 10.00 percent (entered in cell B1). Thus, this shows the NPV as of the beginning of 2004 for the cash flows that occur at the end of the year for the period 2004–2008.

  In contrast, the formula for cell B9 shows that the first *value* in cell B4 is simply added to the columns C to F that is part of the NPV function. Thus, the (100) is not being discounted at all, and cell B9's value of 166.48

represents the NPV of the flows at the end of 2004, at the time the investment is being made.

	A	B	C	D	E	F	G
1	Discount rate	10.00%					
2							
3		Dec-31-2004	Dec-31-2005	Dec-31-2006	Dec-31-2007	Dec-31-2008	
4	Cash Flows	(100)	50	60	110	130	
5							
6	NPV	151.34	=NPV(B1,B4:F4)			NPV at beginning of 2004	
7			Outflow at end of 2004; Other flows recognized at year-end				
8							
9	NPV	166.48	=B4+NPV(B1,C4:F4)			NPV at end of 2004	
10			Outflow at end of 2004; Other flows recognized at year-end				

A necessary simplification with the use of the NPV function is the fact the cash flows are assumed to occur at the end of the year. Let's consider what this means. In the example we have been looking at, each of the inflows from year 2005 onward are recognized as if they suddenly appeared on December 31 of each year. Realistically, this is not so as a project produces cash flows throughout the whole year. Thus, a more accurate conceptual representation would be to recognize them at the average of their individual timings, i.e., at the middle of the year. If we want to find out the NPV of the cash flows as of December 31, 2004, the 50 flow we see for 2005 should really be discounted only 0.5 years, rather than 1 year. Likewise, all the other flows should be discounted at 1.5, 2.5, and 3.5 years. The undiscounted starting investment value of (100) aside, the NPV function as it is being used means that we have an NPV of the 2005–2008 flows as of June 30, 2003.

In this case, if we agree that:

- The initial investment outflow is December 31, 2004, and
- Project inflows should be recognized at the middle of the year, then we can make an adjustment to our NPV calculation by future valuing the NPV part half a year. The formula multiples the NPV(B1,C4:F4) part by $(1+B1)^{0.5}$. B1 contains the discount rate,

and the ^0.5 is an exponent for the half year. The final NPV value of 179.48 is larger than the 166.48, reflecting the fact that there has been less discounting done on the flows for this third NPV value.

	A	B	C	D	E	F	G
1	Discount rate	10.00%					
2							
3		Dec-31-2004	Dec-31-2005	Dec-31-2006	Dec-31-2007	Dec-31-2008	
4	Cash Flows	(100)	50	60	110	130	
5							
6	NPV	151.34	=NPV(B1,B4:F4)			NPV at beginning of 2004	
7			Outflow at end of 2004; Other flows recognized at year-end				
8							
9	NPV	166.48	=B4+NPV(B1,C4:F4)			NPV at end of 2004	
10			Outflow at end of 2004; Other flows recognized at year-end				
11							
12	NPV	179.48	=B4+NPV(B1,C4:F4)*(1+B1)^0.5			NPV at end of 2004	
13			Outflow at end of 2004; Other flows recognized at mid-year				
14							

- XNPV(*rate,values,dates*) returns the net present value occurring at the *dates* specified.

	A	B	C	D	E	F	G
1	Discount rate	10.00%					
2							
3		Dec-31-2004	Dec-31-2005	Dec-31-2006	Dec-31-2007	Dec-31-2008	
4	Cash Flows	(100)	50	60	110	130	
5							
6	NPV	151.34	=NPV(B1,B4:F4)			NPV at beginning of 2004	
7			Outflow at end of 2004; Other flows recognized at year-end				
8							
9	NPV	166.48	=B4+NPV(B1,C4:F4)			NPV at end of 2004	
10			Outflow at end of 2004; Other flows recognized at year-end				
11							
12	NPV	179.48	=B4+NPV(B1,C4:F4)*(1+B1)^0.5			NPV at end of 2004	
13			Outflow at end of 2004; Other flows recognized at mid-year				
14							
15	XNPV functions						
16							
17	XNPV	166.45	=XNPV(B1,B4:F4,B3:F3)			NPV at end of 2004	
18							
19		Dec-31-2004	Jun-30-2005	Jun-30-2006	Jun-30-2007	Jun-30-2008	
20							
21	XNPV	179.57	=XNPV(B1,B4:F4,B19:F19)			NPV at end of 2004	
22							

The illustration shows a comparison between XNPV and NPV. In the first XNPV on row 17, the result 166.45 represents the net present value of the flows based on an investment outflow of (100) at the end of 2004, and the subsequent year-end inflows. This is very close to the second NPV we did; the discrepancy comes from the more exact count of days that the XNPV has. Note also that we do not have to exclude (100) from the function because XNPV associates the flows with dates. It regards the first flow as occurring at the time of the XNPV, so there is no discounting of that.

The second XNPV example, on row 21, uses the same cash flow but a different dating for the post-December 2004 columns. So with this function, you can change the discounting intervals to use the midyear recognition by changing the dates that the function is reading. The result of 179.57 is virtually identical to the NPV calculation on row 12; the slight difference is due to the different count of days that XNPV is using.

The dates in XNPV can have irregular intervals of months or years.

- IRR(*values,guess*) returns the internal rate of return on the range of *values*. An IRR is the rate that would bring the NPV on a set if it flows to 0. The *values* must contain at least one number that is positive and one that is negative. The *guess* rate is a rate you can enter, such as 0.10 (10 percent), to help the function to begin its calculations correctly. You can omit this guess, in which case Excel will begin its calculations with the guess rate of 10 percent.

- XIRR(*values,dates,guess*) will return the IRR on a range of *values* associated with the *dates*. These two ranges must span the same columns so that Excel will know which year's data are associated with which year. The dates in XIRR can have irregular intervals of months or years.

CHAPTER 6

Guerilla Accounting for Modeling

We can do "modeling" for historical numbers without knowing any accounting. Showing past data is not modeling, really, because it is only an exercise in setting down perfectly reconciled and matching numbers on the worksheet. When we want to do financial projection modeling, however, we will be creating numbers based on new and changeable assumptions. We will need to know how to make these numbers mesh with one another so that they become useful information. We do this through accounting.

A BEAUTIFUL SYSTEM

Accounting may not seem to be the easiest—or most interesting—subject to learn at first glance. But this system of keeping track of the numbers in a business, first found in the records of the trading centers of Venice and Genoa in the thirteenth century, is really an elegant and beautiful system. Its core essence is a simple system of logical and clear thinking. For this reason, if we can have a good grasp of accounting flows, then the models we create will likewise be logical and clear.

This chapter will attempt to explain just the basic principles in accounting—the principles we need to understand in order to create a working financial model, especially a working financial *projection* model.

Accounting is a big subject since it needs to cover all aspects of business operations, whether it is accounting for billions of dollars of sales or keeping track of small internal flows like expenses for office supplies. However, to do modeling, we need to know only its main principles. Thus, this chapter is a small "guerilla attack" on the subject: it will get us the best return on investment in terms of comprehension for the time and effort required.

The process of creating a model in itself is a terrific way to get more comfortable with accounting. With a model that immediately tells you how the numbers are flowing through the financial statements, you will get a sense of accounting as a dynamic system that keeps track of all the flows. You will never be fazed again when you need to look at financial statements.

THE FINANCIAL STATEMENTS

There are three types of financial statements:

1. The income statement
2. The balance sheet
3. The cash flow statement

Whenever stakeholders—whether they are a business's management, employees, investors, customers, supplies, or what have you—look at a business, they want to ask questions such as these:

1. How much revenue does the business have, and how well does it control its expenses so that there is positive net income?
2. What does the business have as its assets (what it has under its control), as its liabilities (what it owes), and as its equity (what it owns outright)?
3. How is the money being used? For buying production equipment? Paying down debt? For stocking up on inventory? How much cash does the operation have at the end of its accounting period?

Answering each of these three—and other—questions is the main function, respectively, of each of the three financial statements.

The Income Statement

The *income statement* is an ongoing record of the revenues and expenses through the accounting period. The typical accounting period is one year, and this fiscal year usually ends on December 31, to coincide with the calendar year. However, some companies end the fiscal year in other months to be at the most favorable position within the business season. Large retailers, like department stores, like to have the fiscal year end in January or February, when the year-end holiday shopping season leaves them with their inventories low and cash in the bank high.

The Balance Sheet

The *balance sheet* is the snapshot of the company's assets, liabilities, and equity at the end of the accounting period. Note that whereas the income statement is a record covering 12 months, the balance sheet is a one-point-in-time record.

The Cash Flow Statement

The *cash flow statement* shows the flows of cash in the company: how much is coming in and how it is being used. The cash flow statement looks at the income statement for the year and the balance sheet at two points in time: the end of the current year and the end of the prior year. (The end of the prior year can be thought of as the beginning of the current year.) It is the most difficult to build, or, to put it another way, the easiest to build incorrectly.

We Need Just Two of the Three Types of Statements

To make our model useful, we will be including the three statements in it. Although all three are interrelated, it is useful to understand that we need only the information from the income statement and the balance sheet. We always need the income statement, as it gives the lists of revenues and expenses. We will also need the balance sheet information, as it lists the assets, liabilities, and equity. The cash flow statement information, however, can be derived from what we know of the income statement and the balance sheet. In fact, we should understand that *the cash flow statement is nothing more than a reconciliation of the flows in the income statement and the changes in the balance sheet.* You will see later on that the balancing mechanism for the projected balance sheet does not require the cash flow statement either.

THE ACCOUNTING EQUATION

Let's look at the balance sheet first. This is where the trickiest question arises when you do modeling. The accounting equation is this:

$$\text{Asset} = \text{Liabilities} + \text{shareholders' equity}$$

Or to use the language of guerilla accounting:

$$\text{What you have} = \text{What you owe} + \text{what you own}$$

This is most easily illustrated when we buy something by paying with some of our own cash and some with a loan, such as a house. We can say that we "have" a house. But really, what we "owe" the mortgage bank is an amount that represents a big portion of the house, and so the part we truly "own" is just a small part of the house. In this case, the balance sheet for owning a house would look like this:

Assets	Liabilities
We have a house: $100,000	We owe on the mortgage: $80,000
	Shareholder's (SH) Equity
	The portion of the house we truly own because we put in our own cash: $20,000
Total assets: $100,000	Total liabilities and SH equity: $100,000

In our real life, our personal balance sheet will have a lot more items. Literally, it should have a listing of all that we have, all that we owe, and all that we own. But that full balance sheet will have the same idea as this simplified balance sheet: what we have as assets must equal the resources for purchasing them— our debts and our equity. Put another way, *the two sides of the balance sheet must have the same total; they must always equal, or balance, each other.* In a more graphically oriented way, these are the two stacks of numbers that must be the same "height":

DOUBLE-ENTRY BOOKKEEPING

Now we come to what makes accounting a beautiful system: double-entry bookkeeping.

"Double entry" refers to the fact that any change in any of the three—what we "own" (shareholders' equity), what we "have" (assets), and what we "owe" (liabilities)—will cause a change somewhere else, in one of the other two or in itself.

So let's again imagine the house/mortgage/equity balance sheet we saw above:

BALANCE SHEET NO. 1

House:	$100,000	Mortgage:	$80,000
		Equity:	$20,000
TOTAL:	$100,000	TOTAL:	$100,000

If we suddenly won $10,000 in a small lottery, we can add an item called "cash" in our assets side. This is a new thing that we "have." Do we also "own" this? Yes, we do, because the cash is ours. So we can also add this amount to our "equity":

BALANCE SHEET NO. 2

Cash:	$10,000	Mortgage:	$80,000
House:	$100,000	**Equity:**	**$30,000**
TOTAL:	**$110,000**	**TOTAL:**	**$110,000**

Note: **Bold face type** indicates the changes in the balance sheet caused by the transaction.

The two steps that we have just taken to add the cash amount on the left- and right-hand sides of this simple balance sheet demonstrate *double-entry bookkeeping*. Note that the totals have also increased.

Let's continue. Now that we are flush with cash, we can splurge on some furniture. Let's say we spend $5000 of our cash. Cash decreases by this amount (step one of double-entry bookkeeping) and a new item called "Furniture" worth $5000 appears (step two). In effect, the $10,000 in starting Cash has been redistributed, so that half remains as Cash and the other half is now classified under Furniture. There is no change in the totals for either side of the balance sheet.

BALANCE SHEET NO. 3

Cash:	$5,000	Mortgage:	$80,000
House:	$100,000	Equity:	$30,000
Furniture:	**$5,000**		
TOTAL:	$110,000	TOTAL:	$110,000

We still have extra cash and decide to use that to reduce the mortgage. The cash amount goes down by $5000 to $0 and, to complete the double entry, the mortgage amount also goes down by $5000. The totals also change.

BALANCE SHEET NO. 4

Cash:	$0	**Mortgage:**	**$75,000**
House:	$100,000	Equity:	$30,000
Furniture:	$5,000		
TOTAL:	**$105,000**	**TOTAL:**	**$105,000**

Even in this simple balance sheet, you can see how the double-entry steps have helped us keep track of the transactions.

The final balance sheet is quite different from the first one. We own more than before—our equity is up by $10,000. This increase is fully accounted for by having $5000 more in total assets and owing $5000 less on the mortgage.

So, we can derive the following rules of thumb from this.

* If the change is on both sides of the balance sheet (balance sheets 2 and 4), the change is in the same direction: if the left side goes up, the right side goes up too, and vice versa. Consequently, the totals also change accordingly.

* If the change is on one side only (balance sheet 3), then the change is in the opposite direction: if one account goes up, the corresponding double-entry account must go down, and vice versa. The totals do not change in this case.

In either case, the lesson to remember is this: the two sides of the balance sheet must always balance. This is the beauty of double-entry bookkeeping: you cannot get lost in the balance sheet. Keep in your head the image of two blocks on the balance sheet and their having to be the same height as we go deeper into modeling. This mental concept will carry you quite far in helping you to figure out accounting flows.

DEBITS AND CREDITS

The material in this section is not really needed to create a financial model, but later on as you grapple with new accounts and need to understand what the flows look like, understanding these concepts will be very helpful.

We have been talking about accounts going "up" and "down," and that is a serviceable way of describing the changes in the balance sheet. However, for your background knowledge, let's go over the more precise terms used in accounting to describe the two entries of double-entry bookkeeping:

* *Debit*, sometimes written as Dr
* *Credit*, sometimes written as Cr

T-Accounts

A debit must always have a credit (and vice versa, of course). Debits and credits are the entries for something called a *T-account*. This is just a little diagram to show the two sides of a bookkeeping entry. The left side is called "debit" and the right side is called "credit," and you must always use this order. The diagram itself looks like the letter "T," hence the name:

Debit	Credit

Despite how we use the word in everyday language, a *debit* does not always mean a decrease. Likewise, a *credit* does not always mean an increase! Confused? Here is the real deal:

- A *debit* describes an increase of an asset, but a decrease of a liability or equity account.
- A *credit* describes a decrease of an asset, but an increase of a liability or equity account.

Let's use the steps in the previous balance sheet illustrations and show them as T-accounts:

BALANCE SHEET NO. 2: WINNING THE $10,000 LOTTERY

Debit	Credit
Cash: $10,000 (Asset increases)	
	Equity: $10,000 (Equity account increases)

BALANCE SHEET NO. 3: BUYING $5000 WORTH OF FURNITURE WITH CASH

Debit	Credit
Furniture: $5000 (Asset increases)	
	Cash: $5000 (Asset decreases)

BALANCE SHEET NO. 4: PREPAYING $5000 OF MORTGAGE WITH CASH

Debit	Credit
Mortgage: $5000 (Liability decreases)	
	Cash: $5000 (Asset decreases)

We have established the facts that a debit must go hand-in-hand with a credit and that changes "across" the balance sheet move in the same direction, whereas changes in the same side go in opposite directions. The T-account works beautifully to show the one-two sequence of double-entry bookkeeping, but if you are like me when I first learned this, the direction of changes is still hard to remember. What goes up and down with a credit? What goes up and down with a debit?

How to Remember Debits and Credits

Here is one way of remembering what debits and credits do that I have found works for me. Perhaps it will work for you, too. Think of the schematic cross-section of a river, split into two halves. Like a balance sheet, the left half is assets, the right half is liabilities and equity.

On the left half, the left bank is the debit and because it is high, this represents an increase; the river bottom is the credit and because it is low, this represents a decrease.

On the right half, the low river bottom is the debit, and this represents a decrease. The high right bank is the credit, and this represents an increase.

HOW THE INCOME STATEMENT CONNECTS WITH THE BALANCE SHEET

We have been discussing how the balance sheet changes as various accounts change. One way that a balance sheet changes is through the infusion of earnings from the income statement, which comes in as additions to the retained earnings. (Pop quiz: is that a debit or credit to retained earnings?) This is the connection between the income statement and the balance sheet. The balance sheet "collects" the flow that comes from the incoming statement it is in, whether it is positive (a profit) or negative (a loss). Either way the flow is a credit to retained earnings.

The following is the continuation from the last balance sheet. Now, let's assume that in the next year, we receive a paycheck of $5000. There's income tax of 30 percent, so our take-home net income is $5000 \times (1 - 0.30) = \$3500$. In terms of a T-account, it would look like this: The retained earnings account increases and, on the other side, the corresponding entry to the credit is a debit to cash:

Debit	Credit
Cash: $3500 (Asset increases)	
	Retained earning: $3500 (Equity increases)

Here's what the balance sheet changes would look like:

INCOME STATEMENT

Revenues	$5000
Tax (at 30%)	$1500
Net income	$3500

BALANCE SHEET NO. 5

Cash:	$3,500	Mortgage:	$75,000
House:	$100,000	Equity:	$30,000
Furniture:	$5,000	New equity:	$3,500
TOTAL:	$108,500	TOTAL:	$108,500

These are the basic flows that we will work with as we continue with our modeling.

CHAPTER 7

Balancing the Balance Sheet

Now that we know a bit about accounting, we know that a balance sheet must balance. In creating forecast numbers for that financial statement, we have to make sure that our projected balance sheet will also balance. We will go over how to build the mechanism in our model to do this.

THE USE OF "PLUGS"

It is easy to set up a model for historical data because, by definition, the balance sheet has numbers that balance. However, forecast balance sheets will always need to be balanced, because we forecast the individual items without regard to how the overall totals will add up. Accounts receivable, inventory, and accounts payable are likely to be projected at percentages of revenues; capital expenditures may be defined by another measure. In the meantime, debt levels will be based on a known amortization schedule, while equity will increase from the net income after dividends. The net income itself will be defined by various margin assumptions. Other asset and liability accounts will grow at the revenue growth rate, or other rates. They may hold constant or drop to zero altogether at some point in the future.

These varying effects serve to make the balance sheet go out of balance from the first forecast period on. Either the assets side will be greater than the liabilities and equity side, or vice versa. Either way, we will have to consider the use of a "plug" number to even out the sides:

Historical balance sheets are balanced by definition

Imbalance in forecast years, which needs to be corrected by a liability "plug" (shown in gray)...

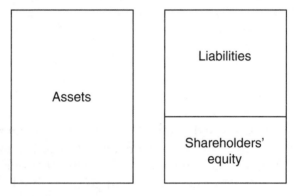

or an asset "plug" (shown in gray)

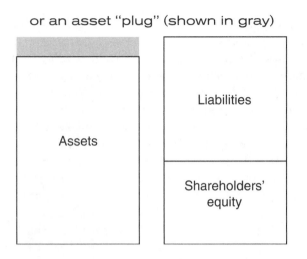

SURPLUS FUNDS (SF) AND NECESSARY TO FINANCE (NTF)

The plug is a number that appears on either side of the balance sheet and serves to make both sides equal. From our discussion in the last chapter, we can think of the balance sheet in visual terms, and the purpose of the plug is to make both sides of the balance sheet equal in height. If it is on the left hand side of the balance sheet, let's call the plug *Surplus funds*. If it is on the other side, then we call the plug a *Necessary to finance*.

There are other terms we can use for these two plugs. For *Surplus funds*, or *SF* for short, we can well call it *Excess cash*. This is to make a distinction from the account called *cash*, which is not a plug number but a specified entry. However, as the two terms *Excess cash* and *Cash* appear similar, I like to call the plug item *Surplus funds* to make the distinction more clear.

For *Necessary to finance*, another term can be *Revolver* (a revolver is a debt facility that keeps being renewed, or revolved). However, this glosses over the fact that this new funding required on the right-hand side is not always necessarily debt. The funding need can well be for new equity. For this reason, the term *Necessary to finance*, or *NTF* for short, is closer to the concept that this is really only a funding requirement.

We will regard it as debt, but we should not be constrained to think of it only as debt.

If you specify known projected debt levels (from the company's current borrowings and known amortization schedules), the company's total outstanding debt will decrease. It is likely that in normal operations the company's assets will increase at a pace that cannot be funded by the increase in shareholders' equity alone. To keep the balance sheet balanced, we need to assume that it will need additional new debt, and this is where the NTF comes in. It can work as an automatic indicator of the company's funding deficit—the additional debt that the company needs to maintain its balance sheet growth.

If you then forecast a level of earnings that allows the company to grow its shareholders' equity, the company's cash position will improve. *This is seen first as a reduction in the NTF number*—this is so because with more cash, the company has less of a funding deficit and the NTF amount decreases.

An Important Use of the NTF Number

You can also use the NTF number as a way to show a company reducing its *total* debt outstanding as fast as its earnings and other growth elements allow it. Do this by deliberately entering zeroes for the company's debt at the start of the projection year, thus forcing an NTF number to appear to fill in the gap. Any earnings in future years, to the extent that they exceed the company's balance sheet needs, will work down the NTF number automatically.

TWO WAYS TO BALANCE
THE BALANCE SHEET

We now proceed to the task of balancing the balance sheet. There are two ways to balance the balance sheet:

1. Through the cash flow statement
2. Through the balance sheet

I recommend the balance sheet method, simply because it is simpler and less prone to errors. However, let's go over the cash flow statement method first.

Cash Flow Method

The first approach uses the cash flow statement to bring together (1) the net income number from the income statement, which is really the change in the retained earnings, and (2) the changes between the current year and the prior year in every account of the balance sheet, except the retained earnings account. As we add together all these changes, we get a net number. If this net number is a positive number, then this is the Surplus funds plug on the current balance sheet; if it is a negative number, then it is the NTF plug.

SCHEMATIC OF THE CASH FLOW BALANCING METHOD

Net income from the income statement

+

Changes in every asset account
(increases in assets are negative flows;
decreases are positive flows)

+

Changes in every liability and equity account, except the
retained earnings account
(increases are positive flows;
decreases are negative flows)

=

Net cash available in the year
Positive number is the Surplus funds plug
Negative number is the NTF plug

The cash flow method is the more difficult of the two because:

1. We have to make a lot of calculations to get to the final net number. We have to look at the flows from the income statement and also the changes in each account on the balance sheet from one year to the next.

2. We have to know how to create a cash flow statement, which is the trickiest statement to build of the three financial statements.

3. This approach does not give an indication of what the final number of the plug should be. Essentially, we would be making all the calculations in the cash flow statement

blindly, with no real indication of what the final target net number should be.

4. The ending net cash available from the cash flow calculations represents the *change* in the plug for the current year, because it is derived from the net changes for the current year. In order to use the net cash available as a plug, we have to add it to the prior year's plug numbers on the balance sheet.

If we arrive at the correct solution at the first try, well and good. However, if the net number is not the correct one for balancing the balance sheet, there is no one definitive clue about what the number should be, or where we should look for it.

With this approach, we would also not be able to balance the first year of the model. Since the cash flow method requires two balance sheets, the current one and the one from the prior year, there is no "prior" when the current one is the first year. Of course, the first year in the model is typically a historical year and there would be no need to balance those numbers, so this may be an unimportant point.

Either method will give the same set of numbers for the model. But in addition to being the more difficult of the two, it is also possible that the cash flow approach makes it more difficult to see and understand how a model and its accounting are working. This is because the direct relationship of one side of the balance sheet to the other, very clearly seen in the visual representation of two columns next to each other, gets blurred when you have to run the numbers through a third format, the cash flow statement. Now let's look at the balance sheet method.

Balance Sheet Method

To use the balance sheet method, look at the numbers on the left-hand and right-hand sides of the balance sheet. Find the difference. It is better to subtract the left-hand side (assets) from the right-hand side (liabilities and shareholders' equity) simply because the sign of the result gives a good reminder of what kind of a plug it is: A positive difference means it is a plug on the assets side, the Surplus funds. A negative difference means it is an NTF amount. There is no need to use the cash flow statement at all for this approach. As mentioned before, the cash flow becomes nothing more than a reconciliation of the flows from the income statement and the changes in the balance sheet.

SCHEMATIC OF THE BALANCE SHEET METHOD

Total liabilities and Equity – Total assets
Positive number is the Surplus funds plug
Negative number is the NTF plug

There are two variations in this method, and we will show both. The first uses a total assets number that excludes the Surplus funds number, and a total liabilities and equity number that excludes the NTF number. The second includes them.

Once you have this total and the balance sheet is balanced (with the interest income and interest expense from the plugs properly accounted for in the income statement), then the cash flow statement can be created. This task is made easier by the fact that all the relevant numbers have been laid out in the other two statements, and you know what the plug number is for each year because of the calculations you have made comparing the two sides of the balance sheet. This is a big help, especially if you are still grappling with the intricacies of the cash flow statement.

USING THE BALANCE SHEET METHOD—VARIATION 1

We are going to use the balance sheet method in our starting model. At the end of this chapter, you will also see the cash flow way, but only as a quick comparison to the balance sheet approach.

SCHEMATIC OF THE BALANCE SHEET METHOD—VARIATION 1

Total liabilities and Equity (excluding the NTF line) –
    Total assets (excluding the Surplus funds line)
Positive number is the Surplus funds plug
Negative number is the NTF plug

To get the most out of the following discussion, I recommend that you switch on your computer and open up Excel and create the numbers for a test balance sheet as shown below.

For the next set of illustrations, although we will be looking at the differences between the totals of the left- and right-hand sides of the balance sheet, the illustrations will put the two sides in a vertical format, with the assets on top and the liabilities and shareholders' equity numbers below.

The only formulas you need to put in are for the rows shown. Note that the ranges in the SUM functions for the total assets and total liabilities include a blank row each. This is so that we can include the rows for the plug numbers (which we have yet to enter). The two sides of the balance sheet are unbalanced at the start. For the rows without formulas, enter the numbers shown as "hard-coded" numbers.

I have put the second year's numbers in column D so that column C can be used to show the formulas for the first year. As you build your own balance sheet, feel free to put the columns for the two years next to each other.

	A	B	C	D	E
1					
2	BALANCE SHEET	Year 1		Year 2	
3					
4	Current assets 1	100		200	
5	Current assets 2	100		100	
6	Long-term assets	300		400	
7	Total assets (TA)	500	=SUM(B3:B7)	700	=SUM(D3:D7)
8					
9					
10	Current liabilities 1	80		100	
11	Current liabilities 2	80		80	
12	Debt 1	320		320	
13	Total liabilities (TL)	480	=SUM(B9:B12)	500	=SUM(D9:D12)
14					
15	Common stock	80		80	
16	Retained earnings	40		70	
17	Shareholders' equity (SHE)	120	=SUM(B15:B16)	150	=SUM(D15:D16)
18	Total liabs & SH equity	600	=B13+B17	650	=D13+D17
19					
20					

Now enter the formulas shown in row 20.

	A	B	C	D	E
1					
2	**BALANCE SHEET**	**Year 1**		**Year 2**	
3					
4	Current assets 1	100		200	
5	Current assets 2	100		100	
6	Long-term assets	300		400	
7	**Total assets (TA)**	**500**		**700**	
8					
9					
10	Current liabilities 1	80		100	
11	Current liabilities 2	80		80	
12	Debt 1	320		320	
13	**Total liabilities (TL)**	**480**		**500**	
14					
15	Common stock	80		80	
16	Retained earnings	40		70	
17	**Shareholders' equity (SHE)**	**120**		**150**	
18	**Total liabs & SH equity**	**600**		**650**	
19					
20	Difference (TL+SHE-TA)	100=B18-B7		-50=D18-D7	

Note the imbalances in row 20: in the first year, the imbalance is a positive number when we use the formula total liabilities (TL) + shareholders' equity (SHE) – total assets (TA); in the second year, it is a negative number with the same formula. We could have written the formula as TA – (TL + SHE) and gotten to the same magnitude of difference. However, by doing it the way we did, we can follow the helpful clue that a positive difference indicates a need for an asset plug (the *Surplus funds* plug). Likewise, a negative number indicates a need for a liability plug (the *Necessary to finance* plug).

Now that we know what the plugs are, as a quick way to illustrate what we want to get to, let's just enter them as hard-coded numbers in the respective cells on row 3:

These two plugs on rows 3 and 9 are what we want to appear in the worksheet. For the next step, since we are in

	A	B	C	D	E
1					
2	BALANCE SHEET	Year 1		Year 2	
3	Surplus funds plug	100	Hard-coded	0	Hard-coded
4	Current assets 1	100		200	
5	Current assets 2	100		100	
6	Long-term assets	300		400	
7	Total assets (TA)	600	=SUM(B3:B6)	700	=SUM(D3:D6)
8					
9	Necessary to finance plug	0	Hard-coded	50	Hard-coded
10	Current liabilities 1	80		100	
11	Current liabilities 2	80		80	
12	Debt 1	320		320	
13	Total liabilities (TL)	480	=SUM(B9:B12)	550	=SUM(D9:D12)
14					
15	Common stock	80		80	
16	Retained earnings	40		70	
17	Shareholders' equity (SHE)	120	=SUM(B15:B16)	150	=SUM(D15:D16)
18	Total liabs & SH equity	600	=B13+B17	700	=D13+D17
19					
20	Difference (TL+SHE-TA)	0	=B18-B7	0	=D18-D7

Excel, let's have the spreadsheet do the work of showing these numbers by writing a formula in the plug cells that directly refer to the Difference line.

Important: Before we go any further, make sure that you have turned on the Iteration setting in Excel by this sequence: Tools > Options > Calculation tab, check the Iteration check box, and set the Maximum iteration setting to 100.

Having done that, we can write formulas that refer directly to the Difference row. We'll use the MAX and MIN function to read the numbers. Note the minus sign in front of the MIN function: this formula reads the source only if it is a negative number, but shows that result as a positive number.

But now, something odd happens. The balance sheet "flip-flops": it seems to bring the plug numbers in properly, but then the plugs seem to flip to 0. Next the plugs show up again and then flip back to 0! You can see this more clearly by setting the

	A	B	C	D	E
1					
2	**BALANCE SHEET**	Year 1		Year 2	
3	Surplus funds plug	100	=MAX(B20,0)	0	=MAX(D20,0)
4	Current assets 1	100		200	
5	Current assets 2	100		100	
6	Long-term assets	300		400	
7	**Total assets (TA)**	600		700	
8					
9	Necessary to finance plug	0	=-MIN(B20,0)	50	=-MIN(D20,0)
10	Current liabilities 1	80		100	
11	Current liabilities 2	80		80	
12	Debt 1	320		320	
13	**Total liabilities (TL)**	480		550	
14					
15	Common stock	80		80	
16	Retained earnings	40		70	
17	**Shareholders' equity (SHE)**	120		150	
18	**Total liabs & SH equity**	600		700	
19					
20	Difference (TL+SHE-TA)	0	=B18-B7	0	=D18-D7

"Maximum iteration" setting to 1. In this way, Excel only iterates (calculates) once. Press the F9 key again and again to go through the calculation stages to see the flip-flop in a one-step-at-a-time slow motion.

Here is why this happens. Let's go through the steps just for the first year:

1. Cell B20 calculates the difference before the plugs appear. The difference is 100.
2. This number is carried up into the Surplus funds line. Total assets, because the total includes the Surplus funds line, go up by 100.
3. Cell B20 now shows 0, because the difference has been corrected by the inclusion of the plug number.
4. At the next iteration, the 0 difference number in B20 is carried up to the Surplus funds line. The Surplus funds

line becomes 0. Now Total assets go down, since the 100 of the plug is no longer there.

5. Cell B20 shows 100 again....

If you follow these steps, you will see that there is a circularity here (this is why it was important to make sure that the Iteration setting is on). The Difference line in row 20 is using numbers that include itself through the plug numbers.

The basic idea of getting to a plug number by looking at the difference between the two sides of the balance sheet is still sound. But we need to understand a little more how these numbers work with each other to get to a good, workable, and stable balancing system.

"STATIC" AND "DYNAMIC" NUMBERS

Let's look at the same balance sheet again, but now let's understand that the numbers can fall into two types:

* *Static numbers* are numbers that do not change during any iteration calculations. Of course, you can change them in order to reflect changes in your assumptions. The main distinction is that they remain unchanged during the iteration calculations. All the balance sheet account numbers in the illustration, except for the Surplus funds and the Necessary to finance lines (and the sums which include these plugs), are static numbers.

* *Dynamic numbers* are those that change during the iteration calculations. The Difference numbers and the Surplus funds and Necessary to finance plugs are dynamic numbers in the worksheet we are working with.

The important thing to know at this stage is this: to prevent the "flip-flops," we have to keep the dynamic numbers out of the calculations for the plugs. Here's how to do it.

This illustration shows all formulas for the rows used in the balancing:

	A	B	C	D	E
1					
2	**BALANCE SHEET**	Year 1		Year 2	
3	Surplus funds plug	100	=B23	0	=D23
4	Current assets 1	100		200	
5	Current assets 2	100		100	
6	Long-term assets	300		400	
7	**Total assets (TA)**	**600**	=SUM(B3:B6)	**700**	=SUM(D3:D6)
8					
9	Necessary to finance plug	0	=B24	50	=D24
10	Current liabilities 1	80		100	
11	Current liabilities 2	80		80	
12	Debt 1	320		320	
13	**Total liabilities (TL)**	**480**	=SUM(B9:B12)	**550**	=SUM(D9:D12)
14					
15	Common stock	80		80	
16	Retained earnings	40		70	
17	**Shareholders' equity (SHE)**	**120**	=SUM(B15:B16)	**150**	=SUM(D15:D16)
18	**Total liabs & SH equity**	**600**		**700**	
19					
20	Assets without SF	500	=SUM(B4:B6)	700	=SUM(D4:D6)
21	Liabs & SHE without NTF	600	=SUM(B10:B12)+ B17	650	=SUM(D10:D12) +D17
22	Difference	100	=IF(ISERROR (B21-B20),0, B21-B20)	-50	=IF(ISERROR (D21-D20),0, D21-D20)
23	SF plug calculation	100	=MAX(B22,0)	0	=MAX(D22,0)
24	NTF plug calculation	0	=-MIN(B22,0)	50	=-MIN(D22,0)

At the bottom of the block of numbers, we put two additional lines:

- In row 20, Assets *without* the Surplus funds line. Shown in the C column is the formula, which looks only at the three rows on rows 4 to 6.
- In row 21, Liabilities and Shareholders' equity *without* the Necessary to finance line. The C column shows the formula being used.

These two lines consist of static numbers. From these two, we calculate the Difference (row 22). The next two rows

(rows 23 and 24) are a nice way to organize the Difference into either the Surplus funds plug or the Necessary to finance plug, using the MAX and MIN functions. The balance sheet lines for the plugs read these two rows. (We could have written the MAX and MIN formulas directly in the balance sheet, by the way. However, doing it this way makes things a little bit clearer.)

Now the balance sheet does not flip-flop. (Remember to reset the maximum number of iterations to a number such as 100, if you had changed it to 1.)

The Difference row has the ISERROR function as an error trap. When there is an error message, the ISERROR is true, and so the formula returns a 0, effectively breaking the circular reference. This prevents the error from being caught endlessly in the loop. Once the source of the error is removed, the ISERROR test is false, and so the Difference formula is active again.

For showing the full totals on the balance sheet, Total Assets (row 7) and Total Liabilities (row 13) should include the rows for the plugs. We just don't use these for our calculations.

USING THE BALANCE SHEET
METHOD—VARIATION 2

Here is the second variation for the balance sheet balancing. Having made a big fuss about static and dynamic numbers, this second method *makes no distinction between static and dynamic numbers*. It uses the difference between Total assets and Total liabilities + Shareholders' equity, but in a way that does not lead to the "flip-flops."

SCHEMATIC OF THE BALANCE SHEET METHOD—VARIATION 2

Find the *incremental* difference between Total assets (including Surplus funds line) and Total liabilities and Shareholders' equity (including the NTF line) with each iteration
Add *incremental* difference to a "holder cell"
Positive number in the holder cell is read by the Surplus funds plug
Negative number is read by the NTF plug

Recall that the flip-flops occur because the plug depends on the difference between the two sides of the balance sheet. However, once the plugs are included in the two sides, the difference no longer exists, and the plug goes back to 0. As Excel makes another round of iterative calculations, the difference shows up again, creating the plugs. And so on.…

This second method uses two rows of formulas, which together prevent the plugs from disappearing as the difference gets balanced out. Look at the illustration below and note the lines at the bottom of the balance sheet. In addition to the line labeled "Difference," there is a new line in row 21 called "Accumulated difference." The MAX and MIN plug formulas now read this row.

	A	B	C	D	E
1					
2	BALANCE SHEET	Year 1		Year 2	
3	Surplus funds plug	100	=B22	0	=D22
4	Current assets 1	100		200	
5	Current assets 2	100		100	
6	Long-term assets	300		400	
7	Total assets (TA)	600		700	
8					
9	Necessary to finance plug	0	=B23	50	=D23
10	Current liabilities 1	80		100	
11	Current liabilities 2	80		80	
12	Debt 1	320		320	
13	Total liabilities (TL)	480		550	
14					
15	Common stock	80		80	
16	Retained earnings	40		70	
17	Shareholders' equity (SHE)	120		150	
18	Total liabs & SH equity	600		700	
19					
20	Difference (TL+SHE-TA)	0	=B18-B7	0	=D18-D7
21	Accumulated difference	100	=B20+B21	-50	=D20+D21
22	SF plug calculation	100	=MAX(B21,0)	0	=MAX(D21,0)
23	NTF plug calculation	0	=-MIN(B21,0)	50	=-MIN(D21,0)

At first glance, the formula in row 21 looks just plain wrong. Look at B21 closely again. It is the sum of the row above it (B20) and *itself* (B21). How does this work?

Reminder: We should still be using Excel with the Iteration setting turned on, as before.

The Difference row produces the difference between the two sides of the balance sheet. The Accumulated difference row acts as a bucket that holds this difference; it "collects" the Difference number. Let's imagine what happens during successive iterations in Excel. Let's assume the same first year balance sheet as above. At the start, before Excel starts calculating, the two lines read as follows:

Difference   0
Accumulated difference   0

As the sweep of calculation hits the Difference line, it changes to 100

Difference   100
Accumulated difference   0

Now it is the Accumulated difference's turn to be calculated. Remember the formula is Accumulated difference = Difference + Accumulated difference. As it calculates, it becomes 100 (the Difference) + 0 (the Accumulated difference value *before* it is calculated) and so ends up as 100 (the Accumulated difference *after* it is calculated).

Difference   100
Accumulated difference   100

The Accumulated difference number is read by the Surplus funds line. Now the balance sheet is balanced. So, as the iteration occurs again, the Difference number now flips to 0.

Difference   0
Accumulated difference   100

Now as the calculation hits the Accumulated difference row, it stays at 100, because the formula reads: Difference (0) + Accumulated difference (100, from the prior iteration), which equals 100. Remember, the plug is using the Accumulated difference row. This is why there is no flip-flop.

This formula is simplicity itself. It's a little puzzling at first, but it is truly elegant. The only change we need to make beyond the formula you see is the addition of an ISERROR function to trap any errors that might be introduced into this loop. Thus, the formula in cell B21 should read:

$$=\text{IF(ISERROR(B20+B21),0,B20+B21)}$$

Of course, the formula in cell D21 should have the same structure:

$$=\text{IF(ISERROR(D20+D21),0,D20+D21)}$$

So here is the final screen, with the rows holding formulas for the balancing calculations shown:

	A	B	C	D	E
1					
2	BALANCE SHEET	Year 1		Year 2	
3	Surplus funds plug	100	=B22	0	=D22
4	Current assets 1	100		200	
5	Current assets 2	100		100	
6	Long-term assets	300		400	
7	Total assets (TA)	600	=SUM(B3:B6)	700	=SUM(D3:D6)
8					
9	Necessary to finance plug	0	=B23	50	=D23
10	Current liabilities 1	80		100	
11	Current liabilities 2	80		80	
12	Debt 1	320		320	
13	Total liabilities (TL)	480	=SUM(B9:B12)	550	=SUM(D9:D12)
14					
15	Common stock	80		80	
16	Retained earnings	40		70	
17	Shareholders' equity (SHE)	120	=SUM(B15:B16)	150	=SUM(D15:D16)
18	Total liabs & SH equity	600	=B13+B17	700	=D13+D17
19					
20	Difference (TL+SHE-TA)	0	=B18-B7	0	=D18-D7
21	Accumulated difference	100	=IF(ISERROR (B20+B21),0, B20+B21)	-50	=IF(ISERROR (D20+D21),0, D20+D21)
22	SF plug calculation	100	=MAX(B21,0)	0	=MAX(D21,0)
23	NTF plug calculation	0	=-MIN(B21,0)	50	=-MIN(D21,0)

Compared to the first balancing method, this second approach has the following pluses:

- It is simple to set up: you use the totals on the two sides of the balance sheet to get going. Of course, this assumes that the totals correctly include all the accounts.
- It is helpful to use when you are still building your balance sheet and adding new lines here and there. Because the balancing formula uses the totals of each side of the balance sheet, you do not have to tinker with the balancing formula every time you insert new accounts. So long as the new accounts flow properly into the totals, the balancing system will work.

But it has these minuses:

- It takes a little bit of thinking to understand it, and if you use it in a model for distribution to others, expect a few questions from people asking how it works and quite possibly voicing their suspicions about the self-referencing structure.
- You cannot use this approach if you need to create a "cash sweep" feature, which is shown in Chapter 14.

The formulas for both approaches to balance sheet balancing work quickly because we have neither included any effects of the interest income from Surplus funds (remember, it is assumed to be cash), nor have we included the interest expense from Necessary to finance (assumed for the moment to be a form of debt). This is because we have not linked the income statement, where these interest numbers would be calculated, to the balance sheet. When we do, the formulas will still work, but they will have to iterate a few times, with each round of calculations showing incrementally smaller additions to the Accumulated difference line as the model converges.

FOR THE NEXT STEP: EFFECTS OF THE INCOME STATEMENT

Let's connect the income statement to the balance sheet. We do that by having the last line in the income statement flow into the retained earnings account of the model. The last line in our simple model is the Net income after taxes line. However, models often come with other flows after this, such as Extraordinary income or expense and Dividends. In that case, the last line in the income statement would be something called "Net to retained earnings" and is equivalent to Net income after taxes less the additional expenses, and that would be the line we link into the Retained earnings account.

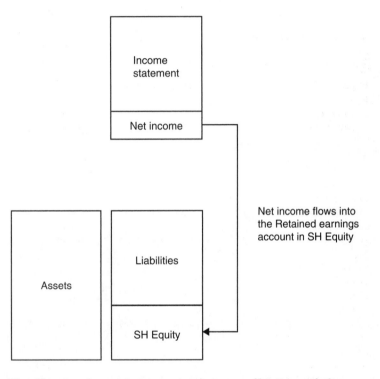

The Retained earnings account is a collection of the current year's earnings from the income statement and all previous year's earnings. So, each formula for this account is the sum of the net income from the previous year and the current year.

Let's insert about 12 rows or so at the top of the balance sheet that you have been working on. For the following illustration, I will be using the balance sheet with the first balancing method, but all the formula changes will also work for the second method.

As we insert the lines, Excel will, of course, automatically adjust all the formula references.

	A	B	C	D	E
1					
2	**INCOME STATEMENT**	**Year 1**		**Year 2**	
3	Sales	200.0		240.0	
4	Expenses	120.0		140.0	
5	**EBIT**	**80.0**=B3-B4		**100.0**=D3-D4	
6					
7	Interest income of SF (5%)	4.6=B17*5%		2.3=AVERAGE(B17, D17)*5%	
8	Interest expense of NTF (10%)	0.0=B23*10%		2.4=AVERAGE(B23, D23)*10%	
9	Interest expense of Debt (10%)	32.0=B26*10%		32.0=AVERAGE(B26, D26)*10%	
10	**EBT**	**52.6**=B5+B7-B8-B9		**67.9**=D5+D7-D8-D9	
11					
12	Taxes (40%)	21.0=B10*40%		27.2=D10*40%	
13	**Net income**	**31.5**=B10-B12		**40.7**=D10-D12	
14					
15					
16	**BALANCE SHEET**	**Year 1**		**Year 2**	
17	Surplus funds plug	91.5=B37		0.0=D37	
18	Current assets 1	100.0		200.0	
19	Current assets 2	100.0		100.0	
20	Long-term assets	300.0		400.0	
21	**Total assets (TA)**	**591.5**=SUM(B17:B20)		**700.0**=SUM(D17:D20)	
22					
23	Necessary to finance plug	0.0=B38		47.7=D38	
24	Current liabilities 1	80.0		100.0	
25	Current liabilities 2	80.0		80.0	
26	Debt 1	320.0		320.0	
27	**Total liabilities (TL)**	**480.0**=SUM(B23:B26)		**547.7**=SUM(D23:D26)	
28					
29	Common stock	80.0		80.0	
30	Retained earnings	31.5=B13		72.3=B30+D13	
31	**Shareholders' equity (SHE)**	**111.5**=SUM(B29:B30)		**152.3**=SUM(D29:D30)	
32	**Total liabs & SH equity**	**591.5**=B27+B31		**700.0**=D27+D31	
33					
34	Assets without SF	500.0=SUM(B18:B20)		700=SUM(D18:D20)	
35	Liabs & SHE without NTF	591.5=SUM(B24:B26)+ B31		652.3=SUM(D24:D26+ D31	
36	Difference	91.5=IF(ISERROR (B35-B34),0, B35-B34)		-47.7=IF(ISERROR (D35-D34),0, D35-D34)	
37	SF plug calculation	91.5=MAX(B36,0)		0=MAX(D36,0)	
38	NTF plug calculation	0=-MIN(B36,0)		47.7=-MIN(D36,0)	

In this layout, we now have the complete and fully functioning system of flows between the income statement and the balance sheet. We have created a model! If you have been following these steps on your own computer, you can experiment by changing any of the static numbers such as the sales line, the current assets and liabilities, and even the interest and tax rates in the model you have created. As you make the changes, the model will recalculate and show a balanced balance sheet.

The model remains a very rudimentary model at this stage, however. So, some points to note:

* The interest rates used for interest income and expense have been written directly into the formulas in order to make the illustration more compact. In practice with a real model, this is not a good idea. Instead, you should have these rates in separate cells, with the formulas referencing them. In this way, the rates are clear and plain to see. Changing them later if you want to test different assumptions also becomes much easier.

* The calculations of interest income and expense are usually done on the average of the beginning and ending cash or debt. For the first year, however, we have just used a full year's calculations for simplicity of illustration.

* In the second year, the formulas use the average of the balance sheet numbers multiplied by the interest rates. For the interest on the NTF plug, this is a calculation of 25 multiplied by 10 percent, to yield 2.5. The number 25 is the average of 0 (the first year's number) and 47.7 (the second year's number). We use the average because the NTF number in the second year did not appear on the first day of that second year. You can imagine that as the plug was 0 at the end of the first year, it was just a little over 0 on the first day of the second year. Only after a full year has passed did the NTF become 47.7. The plug is the result of the flows occurring during the year, and in the absence of any other information,

we make the assumption that the NTF grew in a
linear fashion from 0 to 47.7 over the course of the year.
To get the interest expense for this, we have to take the
average of 0 and 47.7, and multiply the result with the
interest rate.

◆ Usually, because the first year of a model is a historical
period and you will have the hard-coded interest data in
your source document, you do not need to calculate the
interest numbers. So, you could have the formulas for the
first year use the average calculation—they won't be used
anyway, and this makes the formulas more consistent
across the periods.

◆ The Retained earnings account on the balance sheet for
the second year (and for other subsequent years) is a
formula that looks at the prior period's retained
earnings and adds the net income to that. This is because
retained earnings is the cumulative total of a firm's
earnings.

EFFECTS OF THE PLUGS ON THE INCOME STATEMENT

Because the Surplus funds and the Necessary to finance are cash
and debt, respectively, we can assume that they will produce
income interest and income expense. What this means is that
the very act of calculating such a plug number will create a
change in the income statement, which will cause the retained
earnings to vary and the balance sheet to become unbalanced
again.

Effect of Interest Income from Surplus Funds

Here is an illustration of the effects of the interest income from
the Surplus funds plug. We start with step 1, which assumes

that the accounts on the balance sheet on their own have created a Surplus funds (shown as SF) amount:

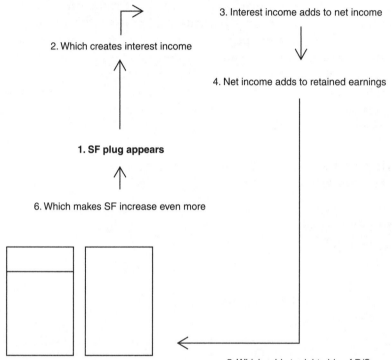

3. Interest income adds to net income

2. Which creates interest income

4. Net income adds to retained earnings

1. SF plug appears

6. Which makes SF increase even more

5. Which adds to right side of B/S

As you can see, there is a circular reference in the model. Step 1, for example, is affected by step 6, which is the result of calculations based on step 1 itself! Not to worry, we still have Excel's iteration setting on (Tools > Options > Calculation, check the Iteration box).

Note also that it is not likely that the numbers will "blow up"—get ever larger with each iteration by diverging from each other. In this system, there is an increase in the numbers with each iteration, but each increment is only a small portion of the previous increase, so the numbers can be said to *converge*. Each increase is progressively smaller than the previous increase, until we arrive at a final iteration with such a small increase that Excel stops the calculations. The convergence happens because each increase in the Surplus funds causes a corollary increase equivalent to the (Surplus funds × Interest income rate). If there is an Income tax rate in the income statement calculations, the increase is further reduced and becomes (Surplus funds × Interest income rate) * (1 − Income tax rate). Of course, the numbers can still not converge if we put in an Interest income rate that, on an after-tax basis, would create an interest income number greater than the starting amount (e.g., a starting Surplus funds number of $100 creates an after-tax interest income of $101, but this is clearly not a situation that we can expect to find in normal economic environments).

Effect of Interest Expense from Necessary to Finance

The same kind of calculation circularity is seen when the plug is on the liabilities side as the Necessary to finance plug. The steps are seen below:

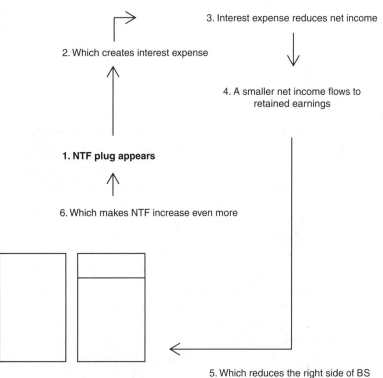

In both illustrations, the same thing is happening: the appearance of a plug sets in motion a chain of calculations that results in the plug converging to a slightly higher ending number. One might say that is due to the phenomenon of the model's calculating "interest on interest."

Reality Check

How does this fit into the real world? Actually, quite well. For our projected numbers, we can imagine a company having to borrow $100 million at the beginning of the year to meet its working capital needs. Over the year, with a 10 percent interest rate, it will have to pay $10 million in interest expense, money it does not have (that's why it has to borrow, after all), so it really should borrow $110 million. But borrowing the additional $10 million means that it will have $1 million interest on that borrowing (this is the "interest on interest" idea), so it really should borrow another $1 million. And that is going to create another $0.1 million in interest, so we should borrow that much more, but then, there will be interest on that borrowing and so on....

DEVELOPING THE MODEL FURTHER

Now that we have an understanding of how to create a working and balancing model, the next steps are to develop it so that it fits real world conditions. We have been using just a limited set of unspecific accounts, after all. Furthermore, the cash flow statement is not developed yet. That is best done when we have a more complete set of accounts, the better to illustrate the components of that statement. Chapter 8 is a return to some accounting points that cover just the types of accounts that you will come across. In Chapter 9, we will return to the task of building the cash flow statement.

Income Statement and Balance Sheet Accounts

In Chapter 7, we used a very simple and simplistic income statement and balance sheet to demonstrate the balancing mechanism. In this chapter, we address what the "real life" counterparts of these financial statements should have.

THE INCOME STATEMENT

The income statement is a listing of revenues and expenses and shows the flows of the company over the reporting period. The typical reporting period is annual. The fiscal year of a company is the span of the year over which it chooses to report its earnings. Although most companies' fiscal year is the same as the calendar year, ending on December 31, a company can choose any date in the calendar year as its fiscal year-end in order to show the best possible seasonal condition. Many department stores, for example, use January 31 as their fiscal year end. This is a point in the year after the year-end holiday sales when their inventories are low and their cash holdings are high.

The basic form of the income statement is this:

Sales
− Cost of goods sold
= Gross profit
− Selling, general, and administration (SGA) expenses
− Depreciation
− Amortization of intangibles
− Operating expenses
= Earnings before interest and taxes (EBIT)
− Other non-operating expense
+ Interest income
− Interest expense
= Earnings before taxes (EBT)
− Taxes
= Net income
− Dividends
= Net to retained earnings

Compare this layout with the simplified layout we used in the previous chapter. The essential lines in that layout are the inclusion of the interest income and interest expense lines, which allow any interest produced by the balance sheet plugs to be included in the modeling flows; these lines are also seen in the layout here. The moral of the story is that the basic structure that we created in the last chapter can be used as the basis for a "real" model. It is a matter of adding more lines to capture the various accounting items. These additional lines are *static* as we defined the term in the last chapter: they do not change with each iteration of the model during the balancing convergence. What this means is that, if you wish, you can expand the number of rows for, say, operating expense from one row to any number of rows, and the model will still work. And the same applies for the balance sheet.

EBIT stands for Earnings before interest and taxes, and one would think that below this line there will only be interest and taxes. But EBIT is a very specific accounting term that defines the earnings that are related to a company's main avenue of business, or what are called the operating earnings or operating profit. So below EBIT, you will often see other expenses that are not directly related to the main avenue of business (that is, other than interest or taxes). This is why you see the line "other non-operating expense" here, in order to be able to capture any such flows.

In some fields of analysis, EBITDA (Earnings before interest, taxes, depreciation, and amortization) is an important number because it shows operating earnings on a cash basis, since depreciation and amortization are noncash expenses. In this case, you may want to shift depreciation and amortization down a few lines and the layout will look like the following sample to the EBIT line. Below EBIT, the format will be the same as shown above. This may not conform to the layout of the source data you are using, but all the numbers remain accurate, and you will have an EBITDA line in the model that you can use for other calculations.

Sales
 − Cost of goods sold
 = Gross profit
 − Selling, general, and administration (SGA) expenses
 − Operating expenses
 = Earnings before interest, taxes, depreciation, and amortization (EBITDA)
 − Depreciation
 − Amortization of intangibles
 = Earnings before interest and taxes (EBIT)
 − Other non-operating expense
 − Interest income
 − Interest expense
 = Earnings before taxes (EBT)
 − Taxes
 = Net income
 − Dividends
 = Net to retained earnings

These are the basic elements of the income statement, and we will use these and the format shown with the EBITDA line for our modeling template.

THE BALANCE SHEET

The balance sheet is a snapshot of the company's numbers at one point in time: the end of the reporting period. Compare this with the idea behind the income statement, which contains numbers that have been accumulated over the entire 12 months. The two statements have different time frames, but they are presented as of the same day. (By the way, as far as the language of accounting is concerned, don't be surprised to come across the expression "at December 31," rather than the usual "on December 31.")

Current and Noncurrent

Current describes the span of time of the business period, typically a year. So a current asset is an asset with a life of less than a year. The same is true with a current liability. Basically, unless there is a continuous addition to the account, a current item on the balance sheet today would not be there in next year's balance sheet. For example, the particular accounts receivable on the books in one year's balance sheet would be gone by next year's balance sheet, given a typical collection period of no more than several months. The accounts receivable shown in the next year's balance sheet are new receivables not yet collected at that reporting date.

All shareholders' equity is assumed to be noncurrent.

Items on a Balance Sheet

Following is a look at the "typical" balance sheet:

Assets
Cash
Marketable securities
Accounts receivable
Inventory
Current assets
Total current assets

Fixed assets
Accumulated depreciation
Net fixed assets
Investment in affiliates
Goodwill

Intangibles
Other long-term assets
Total assets

Liabilities
Notes payable (short-term debt)
Accounts payable
Other current liabilities
Current portion of long-term debt
Total current liabilities
Senior debt
Subordinated debt
Other long-term liabilities
Total liabilities

Shareholders' equity
Common stock
Preferred stock
Treasury stock
Retained earnings
Other equity account
Total shareholders' equity
Total liabilities and shareholders' equity

If you are still new to accounting, there is no need to be anxious about understanding these accounts. Remember the general description: assets are what you "have," liabilities are what you "owe," and shareholders' equity is what you "own." Let's look at the accounts one by one.

Assets

Cash   Cash is cash.

Marketable Securities   These are short-term securities held as investments. They are convertible to cash at a moment's notice. A company may have them when it has excess cash and wishes to produce a higher interest income from the holdings.

Accounts Receivable   Moneys owed by a company's customers for services billed but not paid for. It is important that a company collect on these as quickly as possible. *Accounts receivable* are a "loan" that the company makes to its buyers. Note that the accounts payable section in the current liabilities section is the reverse: it is a "loan" that a company gets from its suppliers.

Inventory   Raw materials and other supplies needed for production, or goods waiting to be sold.

Other Current Assets   Anything else that is an asset and is not a long-term asset.

Fixed Assets   Generally any long-term asset used for production. This is often called gross plant, property, and equipment (Gross PPE).

Accumulated Depreciation   This is the total amount of cost that has been used up or depreciated over the life of the fixed assets.

Net Fixed Assets   Fixed assets less accumulated depreciation. As you work with different models for different analytical needs, you may find that you need to show only this line and not (gross) fixed assets and accumulated depreciation on the balance sheet. This line is often called Net PPE.

Investment in Affiliates   This shows the investments held by the company under the equity method. When a company holds between a 20 and 50 percent interest in another company and has significant influence (but not a controlling interest) over that company, that investment is held in this category.

Goodwill   When a company buys another company using the purchase accounting method and pays a price that is higher than the net assets (the value of the assets less the value of the liabilities), the difference is held in this account. There is no identifiable asset to this account—it's just a place to note that the purchase price was more than the value purchased. Such goodwill used to be required to be amortized over a set period of years, up to 40 years, depressing the earnings figure. (From a cash flow point of view, there is no effect, as the amortization is a noncash expense.) However, this rule was changed in 2001, and goodwill can remain unamortized, subject only to a periodic test for impairment.

Intangibles   Though similar to goodwill in that its amortization is a noncash expense, *intangibles* represent identifiable assets such as patents and trademarks and proprietary technology.

Other Long-Term Assets   These are other assets that are non-current. Depending on your modeling needs, you can include more than one long-term assets account.

Liabilities

Short-Term Debt   Debt payable within one year. There is another account in the current liabilities that is also debt, and that is "Current portion of long-term debt." This is the portion of long-term debt that is known to be payable within the year because of a company debts' amortization schedules. You can list this as a separate account, or you can show this as part of the short-term debt account.

In general modeling, you may not need to show the current portion of long-term debt in the current liabilities section. This is because it is usually more useful to see all of the long-term debt as a total in the long-term liabilities section. In this way, you will not make the mistake of overlooking the amount in the current section. Doing it this way understates the current liabil-ities section, of course. The only ratios that are subsequently affected will be the *current ratio*, which looks at the ratio of cur-rent assets to current liabilities, and the *quick ratio*, which looks at (current assets less inventory) to current liabilities. If these two ratios play critical measures for the type of analysis you do, then by all means you should have current liabilities include the current portion of long-term debt.

Accounts Payable   This represents the amounts owed to suppli-ers for products or services that the company has purchased. An important point to make here is that accounts payable are like an interest-free short-term loan from a company's suppliers. The longer a company can delay in paying off the suppliers, the longer it holds on to "free money."

Accrued Expenses   These are expenses that the company has incurred, but has not paid off yet.

Other Current Liabilities   These represent any accounts that the company has to pay off within one year, such as taxes payable or dividends payable.

Debt   These can include bank debt, bonds, and subordinated debt, to name a few examples.

Long-Term Liabilities   Any other obligations that are noncurrent.

Common Stock   This lists the amount of common stock issued at par. Common stock pays dividends.

Additional Paid-In Capital (APIC)   This lists the difference between the proceeds of the common stock issued and the par value of the common stock. In our modeling, we can simplify this by showing the two accounts together as *Common stock and APIC*.

Preferred Stock   This is another kind of stock that has priority in dividends and has priority claims on assets if a company is in liquidation. Preferred stock pays preferred dividends.

Treasury Stock   This is stock that has been issued but has been later reacquired by the company. There are several reasons that a company may do so: (1) To help keep the stock price high, (2) to acquire shares for distribution to employees under bonus plans, (3) to avoid takeovers by an outside party that is buying up shares in the open market.

Retained Earnings   This is capital that increases through earnings. This is the connection point between the income statement and the balance sheet: the net income after dividends flows into this account.

Other Equity Account   It is useful to have an extra account. This is for listing such item as *Translation gains or losses,* or, if your model is using non-U.S. settings, for certain equity reserves.

CHAPTER 9

Putting Everything Together

In Chapter 7, we went over how to make the balance sheet balance, and in Chapter 8, the types of accounts in the income statement and the balance sheet.

In this chapter, we will put everything together in order to build a working financial model. This will be a model that is more advanced than the one we created in Chapter 7. But in the scheme of things, it is still a simple model: a basic income statement, balance sheet, and cash flow statement, with just the "typical" accounts that you would see in a financial report. We will lay out the framework to get a projection model "up and running."

STRUCTURE OF OUR MODEL

The model structure that we will be using will consist of:

- An "Input" sheet
- An "Income Statement" output sheet
- A "Balance sheet" output sheet
- A "Cash flow" output sheet

We will be entering our historical data and forecast assumptions in the "Input" sheet only, and having the other three sheets show the results.

As noted before, this structure is just one of the virtually limit-less number of modeling approaches that you can have for creating a financial projection model. Generally, there are two main app-roaches to building a model if we want to organize the inputs and outputs: (1) to put both the input and the output on one sheet and (2) to separate the input and the output onto separate sheets. However, I propose a third way in which the input sheet of the model contains both rows for inputs and rows to show the results. There still will be the output sheets, but these will read the results already calculated in the input sheet.

Put Inputs and Outputs on One Sheet

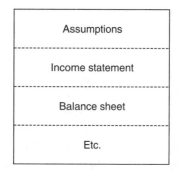

Doing it this way can lead to a very long sheet, with the input assumptions block at the top, and the income statement, balance sheet, and other sections arrayed below. This is best for a small model, where a quick Page Down or Page Up will get you to where you want to go. It gets a little more tedious when there are many hundreds of rows.

Put Inputs and Outputs on Separate Sheets

Assumptions	Income statement	Balance sheet	Cash flow, etc.

Here, the input assumptions are on one sheet, typically on the first of many sheets, and the output sheets follow after that. With this approach, we can lay out the different statements and other outputs such as the ratios on different sheets, with each sheet tab identified accordingly. This approach makes more sense with bigger models.

Put Inputs/Outputs First, Followed by Pure Output Sheets

Input sheet for assumptions and output results	Income statement (reads Input sheet's output results for the income statement)	Balance sheet (reads Input sheet's output results for the balance sheet)	Cash flow, etc.

The first two approaches lack something from a usability point of view. It would be nice to enter the input and then, instead of tapping away from that particular block to see the output, to be able to see the output nearby, one or two rows away. This way, the feedback of your inputs is immediate and near, and it gives you a sense of whether it is correct or not.

This third approach is possible if we interleaved the inputs and outputs of the individual accounts first, as follows:

Row 1: Inputs for revenues
Row 2: Output for revenues
Row 3: Input for COGS
Row 4: Output for COGS
Etc.

Once we have this block of inputs/outputs done, then organizing the outputs is a simple matter of referencing only the finished output lines. In fact, we still have a choice of organizing the final numbers for either an "all on one sheet" or "separate sheets for separate statements" presentation. One major advantage of the interleaved approach is that you can write and check your formulas very easily since the inputs and outputs are next to each other. Moreover, as you write the formulas, there is no need to tap PageUp/PageDown or Ctrl+PageUp/Ctrl+PageDown across sheets.

This third approach is the one that will be used here, because we want to be able to:

- Easily check the results of our inputs
- Show historical interrelationships in a meaningful way
- Format the input for maximum clarity and ease of use, and format the output for maximum visual polish in the final presentation

Some other features we want to have:

- To input the historical data in columns, and once that is done, to continue in the same rows with entering forecast numbers or assumptions.
- To be able to specify forecast numbers in two general forms: in hard-coded numbers or as other inputs such as percent growth or percent of sales, among other metrics. We would need the former because we may need to use the model to replicate another model's forecasts exactly, number for number. In the latter case, the model should do the calculation to produce the final number.

The number of historical and forecast periods can also be flexible. We can have 5 years of historical data, followed by 10 years of projections; or the reverse; or whatever combination, even all historical and all projected (although the latter should have at least one year of historical data to start with). We can make the model as flexible as possible on this account, but for our model-building purposes at this stage, let's set the model to have three historical periods, followed by three forecast periods. If you want to increase the forecast horizon, copy out the last columns on each sheet.

WHAT WE WANT TO GET TO

Here are several screens that show the model that we want to end up with. These have been laid out so that you can recreate them on your own. In fact, for the best learning experience, I encourage you to create for yourself the model being illustrated here. Not only will you get a hands-on experience of developing a model, but you will also have a fully functioning model by the end of the exercise.

In the section that follows, we will go over the model, row by row.

We are laying out the rows on the sheet that is called "Input." So open a new workbook in Excel, pick a new sheet, and then rename that sheet "Input" by double-clicking on the sheet tab. When the sheet tab becomes highlighted, simply type the name onto it. Press "Enter" when you are done.

Let's start.

The shaded cells (shown in gray) are the input cells. A good choice of color would be pale yellow, the palest in Excel's palette. If that is still too strong, remember you can change the shading for that (or any other color choice in the palette) through the Tools>Options>Color>Modify setting. Please refer to Chapter 3, "Starting Out."

The Income Statement Input

	A	B	C	D	E	F	G
1	First Corporation						
2							
3					Proj	Proj	Proj
4	INCOME STATEMENT	2000	2001	2002	2003	2004	2005
5							
6	Revenues	825.0	900.0	1,000.0			
7	Percent growth %	na	9.1%	11.1%	10.0%	10.0%	10.0%
8	Revenues	825.0	900.0	1,000.0	1,100.0	1,210.0	1,331.0
9							
10	COGS	450.0	490.0	55~			
11	As % rev				55.0%	55.0%	55.0%
12	COGS				605.0	665.5	732.1
13	Gross pro...	~~~.~	410.0	450.0	495.0	544.5	599.0
14	Gross margin	45.5%	45.6%	45.0%	45.0%	45.0%	45.0%
15							
16	SGA	125.0	135.0	150.0			
17	As % revenues	15.2%	15.0%	15.0%	15.0%	15.0%	15.0%
18	SGA	125.0	135.0	150.0	165.0	181.5	199.7
19							
20	Operating expenses	25.0	28.0	30.0			
21	As % revenues	3.0%	3.1%	3.0%	3.0%	3.0%	3.0%
22	Operating expenses	25.0	28.0	30.0	33.0	36.3	39.9
23	EBITDA	225.0	247.0	270.0	297.0	326.7	359.4
24	EBITDA margin	27.3%	27.4%	27.0%	27.0%	27.0%	27.0%
25							
26	Depreciation	60.0	75.0	80.0			
27	As % prior Net PPE	na	8.6%	8.4%	8.5%	8.5%	8.5%
28	As % revenues	7.3%	8.3%	8.0%			
29	Depreciation	60.0	75.0	80.0	85.0	91.8	102.5
30							
31	Amort of intangibles	4.0	4.0	4.0	4.0	4.0	4.0
32	Amort of intangibles	4.0	4.0	4.0	4.0	4.0	4.0
33	EBIT	161.0	168.0	186.0	208.0	230.9	252.9
34	EBIT margin	19.5%	18.7%	18.6%	18.6%	19.1%	19.0%
35							
36	Non-oper expenses	10.0	10.0	8.0	10.0	11.0	12.0
37	As % revenues	1.2%	1.1%	0.8%			
38	Non-oper expenses	10.0	10.0	8.0	10.0	11.0	12.0
39							
	Input						

The Income Statement Input (Part 2)

	A	B	C	D	E	F	G
40	Interest income	3.0	5.0	6.0			
41	Surplus funds				2.3	3.6	1.3
42	Cash				4.0	4.0	4.0
43	ST investments				1.7	1.7	1.8
44	Interest income	3.0	5.0	6.0	7.9	9.3	7.1
45							
46	Interest expense	50.0	50.0	50.0			
47	Necessary to finance				0.0	0.0	1.0
48	ST notes				1.4	1.4	1.4
49	Debt 1				15.0	15.0	15.0
50	Debt 2				22.5	22.5	22.5
51	Debt 3				8.8	8.8	8.8
52	Interest expense	50.0	50.0	50.0	47.7	47.7	48.7
53	EBT	104.0	113.0	134.0	158.2	181.5	199.3
54	EBT margin	12.6%	12.6%	13.4%	14.4%	15.0%	15.0%
55							
56	Provision for taxes	360	40.0	47.0			
57	Tax rate %	34.6%	35.4%	35.1%	35.0%	35.0%	35.0%
58	Provision for taxes	36.0	40.0	47.0	55.4	63.5	69.7
59	Net income	68.0	73.0	87.0	102.7	118.0	129.5
60	Net margin	8.2%	8.1%	8.7%	9.3%	9.7%	9.7%
61							
62	Dividends	10.0	12.0	11.0			
63	Payout ratio %	14.7%	16.4%	12.6%	10.0%	10.0%	10.0%
64	Dividends	10.0	12.0	11.0	10.3	11.8	13.0
65	Net to ret'd earnings	58.0	61.0	76.0	92.6	106.2	116.6
66							
67							
	Input						

The Balance Sheet, Current Assets Input

	A	B	C	D	E	F	G
68							
69					Proj	Proj	Proj
70	BALANCE SHEET	2000	2001	2002	2003	2004	2005
71	ASSETS						
72	Surplus funds	0.0	0.0	0.0	90.0	52.7	0.0
73	Interest rate %				5.000%	5.000%	5.000%
74	Interest income				2.3	3.6	1.3
75							
76	Cash	60.0	75.0	80.0	80.0	80.0	80.0
77	% of revenues	7.3%	8.3%	8.0%			
78	Cash	60.0	75.0	80.0	80.0	80.0	80.0
79	Interest rate				5.000%	5.000%	5.000%
80	Interest income				4.0	4.0	4.0
81							
82	ST investments	30.0	32.0	33.0	34.0	35.0	36.1
83	% growth	3.6%	3.6%	3.3%			
84	St investments	30.0	32.0	33.0	34.0	35.0	36.1
85	Interest rate				5.000%	5.000%	5.000%
86	Interest income				1.7	1.7	1.8
87							
88	Accounts receivable	60.0	75.0	90.0			
89	% of revenues	7.3%	8.3%	9.0%			
90	Days of revenues	26.5	30.4	32.9	30.0	30.0	30.0
91	Accounts receivable	60.0	75.0	90.0	90.4	99.5	109.4
92							
93	Inventory	120.0	135.0	150.0			
94	% of revenues	14.5%	15.0%	15.0%			
95	Days of COGS	97.3	100.6	99.5	98.0	95.0	95.0
96	Inventory	120.0	135.0	150.0	162.4	173.2	190.5
97							
98	Other current assets	10.0	10.0	12.0			
99	% of revenues	1.2%	1.1%	1.2%	1.0%	1.0%	1.0%
100	Other current assets	10.0	10.0	12.0	11.0	12.1	13.3
101	Current assets	280.0	327.0	365.0	467.9	452.5	429.3
102							
	Input						

The Balance Sheet, Long-Term Assets Input

	A	B	C	D	E	F	G
103	Net PPE	870.0	950.0	1,000.0			
104	Capex	130.0	155.0	130.0			
105	% of revenues	15.8%	17.2%	13.0%	15.0%	18.0%	20.0%
106	Capex	130.0	155.0	130.0	165.0	217.8	266.2
107	Depreciation	60.0	75.0	80.0	85.0	91.8	102.5
108	Net PPE	870.0	950.0	1,000.0	1,080.0	1,206.0	1,369.7
109							
110	Intangibles	58.0	54.0	50.0			
111	Amortization				4.0	4.0	4.0
112	Intangibles	50.0	50.0	50.0	46.0	42.0	38.0
113							
114	Long-term assets	92.0	116.0	150.0			
115	% of revenues	11.2%	12.9%	15.0%	14.0%	14.0%	14.0%
116	% growth	na	26.1%	25.0%			
117	Long-term assets	100.0	120.0	150.0	154.0	169.4	186.3
118	Total assets	1,300.0	1,447.0	1,565.0	1,747.9	1,869.9	2,023.3
119							
	Input						

The Balance Sheet, Liabilities Input

	A	B	C	D	E	F	G
120	**LIABILITIES**						
121	Short-term notes	10.0	12.0	14.0	14.0	14.0	14.0
122	Short-term notes	10.0	12.0	14.0	14.0	14.0	14.0
123	*Interest rate*				10.000%	10.000%	10.000%
124	Interest expense				1.4	1.4	1.4
125							
126	Accounts payable	60.0	70.0	80.0			
127	% of revenues	7.3%	7.8%	8.0%			
128	Days of COGS	48.7	52.1	53.1	55.0	55.0	55.0
129	Accounts payable	60.0	70.0	80.0	91.2	100.3	110.3
130							
131	Other current liabilities	10.0	20.0	20.0			
132	% of revenues	1.2%	2.2%	2.0%	2.0%	2.0%	2.0%
133	Other current liabilities	10.0	20.0	20.0	22.0	24.2	26.6
134	**Current liabilities**	**80.0**	**102.0**	**114.0**	**127.2**	**138.5**	**150.9**
135							
136	Necessary to finance				0.0	0.0	19.4
137	*Interest rate*				10.000%	10.000%	10.000%
138	Interest expense				0.0	0.0	1.0
139							
140	Debt 1	200.0	225.0	150.0			
141	Debt 1	200.0	225.0	150.0	150.0	150.0	150.0
142	*Interest rate*				10.000%	10.000%	10.000%
143	Interest expense				15.0	15.0	15.0
144							
145	Debt 2	200.0	200.0	225.0			
146	Debt 2	200.0	200.0	225.0	225.0	225.0	225.0
147	*Interest rate*				10.000%	10.000%	10.000%
148	Interest expense				22.5	22.5	22.5
149							
150	Debt 3	110.0	110.0	110.0			
151	Debt 3	110.0	110.0	110.0	110.0	110.0	110.0
152	*Interest rate*				8.000%	8.000%	8.000%
153	Interest expense				8.8	8.8	8.8
154							
155	Long-term liabilities	40.0	38.0	37.0			
156	% of revenues	4.8%	4.2%	3.7%	4.0%	4.0%	4.0%
157	% growth	na	(5.0%)	(2.6%)			
158	Long-term liabilities	40.0	38.0	37.0	44.0	48.4	53.2
159	**Total liabilities**	**630.0**	**675.0**	**636.0**	**656.2**	**671.9**	**708.6**
160							
	Input						

The Balance Sheet, Shareholders' Equity Input and Balancing Rows

	A	B	C	D	E	F	G
161	SHAREHOLDERS' EQUITY						
162	Common stock	460.0	500.0	580.0	650.0	650.0	650.0
163	Common stock	460.0	500.0	580.0	650.0	650.0	650.0
164							
165	Retained earnings	200	261.0	337.0			
166	Net to retained earnings				92.6	106.2	116.6
167	Retained earnings	200.0	261.0	337.0	429.6	535.7	652.3
168							
169	Other equity acct	10.0	11.0	12.0			
170	% of revenues	1.2%	1.2%	1.2%	1.1%	1.0%	0.9%
171	Other equity account	10.0	11.0	12.0	12.1	12.3	12.4
172	Total SH equity	670.0	772.0	929.0	1,091.7	1,198.0	1,314.8
173	Total liabs & SH equity	1,300.0	1,447.0	1,565.0	1,747.9	1,869.9	2,023.3
174							
175							
	Input						

You may be wondering what the final printout will be. Remember that this is the input sheet. So what we need to do is to create several other sheets whose job is basically nothing more than to read the results of the input sheet (not the yellow input lines themselves). These sheets can be named, for example, "Income Statement," "Balance Sheet," and "Cash Flow." You will see how they look at the end of the chapter.

First, let's look at the elements of the "Input" sheet, and I will explain them as we go along.

HOW TO READ THE ILLUSTRATIONS

In order to illustrate the formula-writing as fully as possible, I have included small sections of our model showing the formulas that need to be written into the various rows. The notation ">>>" means "copy this across the columns to the right." For space reasons, the illustrations only go to column F. As you set up your own model, you can copy the columns out beyond this, to as many columns as you want.

Formulas in the Titles

For all the titles, there should be a way of allowing the labels to be changed and having those changes read by the output. A good way to do this, rather than having to retype the labels, is simply to have the "output" row read the label for that block. For example, for revenues, the formula in A8 should read as shown:

$$A8 = A6$$

You should feel free to add in these formulas yourself in the model shown below. Use Excel's Copy and Paste commands to enter the same data in the cells.

Dates and Revenues

	A	B	C	D	E	F
1	First Corporation					
2						
3					Proj	Proj
4	INCOME STATEMENT	2000	=B4+1	>>>	>>>	>>>
5						
6	Revenues	825.0	900.0	1,000.0		
7	Percent growth %	na	=IF(B6,C6/B6−1,"na)	>>>	10.0%	10.0%
8	=A6	=B6	>>>	>>>	=IF(E6,E6, IF(ISNUMBER(E7), D8*(1+E7),0))	>>>

Title
A1   "First Corporation"
Date
B4   2000
C4   =B4+1. Copy this cell across to column G. Each looks to the previous cell and adds the value 1 to that number. You can use the DATE function if you want to use a more sophisticated dating system that uses months and years as described in Chapter 5 in the Section "Functions for Dates."

Revenues
B7   This is "na" because there is no prior year for measuring growth.
C7   =IF(B6,C6/B6 − 1, "na")

TCG.org   username - 052910013
            password - 052910013

Chad TCG username - cstewart p'word - ~~chazza~~ chazza

Long Dist Code - ~~##~~ 191

Tax ID - 86-0211777

Bank One Accounts
        User -
                bklaztheatre

        P'word - acctg1$1057

Bank One CC's

        User - aztheabreccV
        p'word - acctg Ø;la3

ArizonaTheatreCompany

THE STATE THEATRE

David Ira Goldstein
Artistic Director

Jessica L. Andrews
Managing Director

Gate key
works for
other
buildings

Building Alarm Code - 2431
- just punch the numbers to arm/disarm
- one minute grace period

My extension is 8120 (this is also voicemail password)

To dial out use 9 then the number

To dial out to phoenix area dial 4 then number

Computer login - chazza01

Login password - trebbie02

Ticketing System password - callie03

G/L - login - chad
p'word - trebbie02

Blackbaud RE login - Chad
p'word - money38

David Ira Goldstein
Artistic Director

Jessica L. Andrews
Managing Director

Sue IT
8130

Alarm Code—
for My   2431
Building   one minute

New Alarm Code For
New Building
5233
JADE

Lock Deadbolt

x 8120 — my extension
also voice mail code

Dial 9 to get out
Dial 4 to get out to Phenix

login — chazza01

password 1 - trebbie$02

password 2 - callie0$3

D7   The same formula as C7 with the column
                references shifted. Both these formulas simply
                calculate the growth rates for the historical
                inputs. In this way, you can see the growth
                trends in the historical periods to help you as
                you make your forecast assumptions.
B8   = B6. Copy this cell across to column D.
                These cells are a direct read of row 6, which
                may seem to make them redundant. However,
                having the full time series of the historical and
                forecast revenues numbers in this one row
                makes it easy to send these numbers to the
                output sheets.
E8   = IF(E6,E6,IF(ISNUMBER(E7),D8*(1+E7),0)).
                Copy this cell across to column G.
                This formula looks at the hard-coded entry
                row first. If that is a zero, it looks to the Percent
                growth entry row and checks that it is a number
                by using the ISNUMBER function. This means
                that if this second row is blank, the formula will
                return a zero. If it had not used the ISNUMBER
                check, the formula will return the prior year's
                sales number.

COGS and Gross Profit

	A	B	C	D	E	F
10	COGS	450.0	490.0	550.0		
11	As % revenues	=IF(B$8,B10/B$8,0)	>>>	>>>	55.0%	55.0%
12	=A10	=B10	>>>	>>>	IF(E10,E10, E11*E$8)	>>>
13	Gross profit	=B8-B12	>>>	>>>	>>>	>>>
14	Gross margin	=IF(B$8,B13/B$8,0)	>>>	>>>	>>>	>>>

COGS
B11   =IF(B$8,B10/B$8,0). Copy this cell across to
                column D.
                Create these so that you have an indication
                of the historical margins as you make your
                forecast assumptions.

Note the use of the absolute reference ($) for the row number only. This allows the formula to be copied into other rows below without losing the reference to the revenues row. Note also that the reference is to the final result of revenues (row 8), not to the hard-coded input row (row 6), which may be empty in the forecast years if you are defining revenues by the growth rate.

B12   = B10. Copy this cell across to column D.

E12   = IF(E10,E10,E11*E$8). Copy this cell across to column G.

The use of the absolute reference ($) for the row number only means you can copy this formula into other rows that use the same pattern. Again, the formula looks to the final results row for revenues.

B13   = B8−B12. Copy this cell across to column G.

B14   = IF(B$8,B13/B$8,0). Copy this cell across to column G.

The use of the IF statement here prevents the #DIV/0! error messages from showing up when the model is empty. You can write the formulas without the IF test if you do not mind seeing the error messages.

SGA and Operating Expenses

	A	B	C	D	E	F
16	SGA	125.0	135.0	150.0		
17	As % revenues	=IF(B$8,B16/B$8,0)	>>>	>>>	15.0%	15.0%
18	=A16	=B16	>>>	>>>	IF(E16,E16, E17*B$8)	>>>
19						
20	Operating expenses	25.0	28.0	30.0		
21	As % revenues	=IF(B$8,B20/B$8,0)	>>>	>>>	3.0%	3.0%
22	=A20	=B20	>>>	>>>	IF(E20,E20, E21*B$8)	>>>
23	EBITDA	=B13-B18-B22	>>>	>>>	>>>	>>>
24	EBITDA margin	=IF(B$8,B23/B$8,0)	>>>	>>>	>>>	>>>

SGA

B17 = IF(B$8,B16/B$8,0). Copy this formula across to column D. Alternately, copy the formulas from the COGS section (B11–D11) here to create these rows quickly.

B18–G18 Likewise, you can copy the formulas from the COGS section (B18–G18) here to create these rows.

Operating expenses

Rows 20–22 These rows in the model are, except for the title of the account, the same as the block in rows 16–18 (for SGA). So a quick way to create this in the model is to copy those rows and paste them here. You can use this same approach in adding other sections in the income statement.

B23 =B13–B18–B22. Copy this cell across to column G.

B24–G24 Copy the cells from the gross margin row (row 14) to the EBITDA margin row.

Depreciation, Amortization of Intangibles, EBIT, Non-operating Expenses

	A	B	C	D	E	F
26	Depreciation	60.0	75.0	80.0		
27	As % prior Net PPE				8.5%	8.5%
28	As % revenues	=IF(B$8,B26/B$8,0)	>>>	>>>		
29	=A26	=B26	>>>	>>>		
30						
31	Amort of intangibles	4.0	4.0	4.0	4.0	4.0
32	=A31	=B31	>>>	>>>	>>>	>>>
33	EBIT	=B23-B29-B32	>>>	>>>	>>>	>>>
34	EBIT margin	=IF(B$8,B33/B$8,0)	>>>	>>>	>>>	>>>
35						
36	Non-oper expenses	10.0	10.0	8.0	10.0	11.0
37	As % revenues	=IF(B$8,B36/B$8,0)	>>>	>>>		
38	=A36	=B36	>>>	>>>	=IF(E36,E36, E37*B$8)	>>>
39						

Depreciation

B27	"na"
C27	= IF(B108,C29/B108,0). Copy this to D27.

This formula looks to the prior year's Net PPE (that's why B27 is just an "na"), but as we begin to create this sheet (and the balance sheet is not yet created at this time), there is no reference for row 108 for Net PPE. In this case, leave this formula blank and return to it only after the balance sheet is complete.

B28	Copy the formulas from any of the lines that use the "As % revenues" input here, such as row 17 for SGA. But adjust the reference to read B33/B$8.
B29	= B26. Copy this across to column D.
E29–G29	As we are still in the process of building this model and we don't have a reference for the Net PPE (row 108) in the model yet, leave this formula blank and return to it when the balance sheet is complete.

Amortization of intangibles

B32	= B31. Copy this across to column G.

This input section with only one input line, followed by a row that directly reads the input line, may seem to be an exercise in redundancy. This is true. However, a consistent approach is always helpful in building models, and here we are being consistent in having an input row where we can manipulate our entries, and a resulting "output" row that is being read for the model's calculations.

EBIT

B33	= B23−B29−B32
B34	= IF(B$8,B33/B$8,0). Copy this across to column G. You can create this row quickly by simply copying the formulas from row 24 for the EBITDA margin.

Non-operating expenses
Rows 36–38   This block is similar to rows 20–22. Copy
             those rows here and change the titles to show
             "non-oper expenses."

Interest Income, Interest Expense, and EBT

	A	B	C	D	E	F
40	Interest income	3.0	5.0	6.0		
41	Surplus funds				2.3	3.6
42	Cash				4.0	4.0
43	ST investments				1.7	1.7
44	=A40	=B40	>>>	>>>	=IF(E40,E40, SUM(E41:E43))	>>>
45						
46	Interest expense	50.0	50.0	50.0		
47	Necessary to finance				0.0	0.0
48	ST notes				1.4	1.4
49	Debt 1				15.0	15.0
50	Debt 2				22.5	22.5
51	Debt 3				8.8	8.8
52	=A46	=B46	>>>	>>>	=IF(E46,E46, SUM(D47:51)	>>>
53	EBT	=B33-B38+B44-B52	>>>	>>>	>>>	>>>
54	*EBT margin*	*=IF(B$8,B53/B$8,0)*	>>>	>>>	>>>	>>>

Interest income
B41–D43   This block of three rows for the historical
             rows are blank because, in these three
             periods, we expect that the interest income
             number will be provided from the
             historical reports. We do not need to
             calculate them.
E41–G43   The cells in this block will have the interest
             income of the related balance sheet assets. Since
             we do not have the balance sheet built yet and
             therefore don't know the rows to reference at
             the moment, leave these cells blank for the
             moment.

B44   =B40. Copy this to column D.
                   This is to enable the straight read from the input of
                   the historical interest income.
E44   =IF(E40,E40,SUM(E41:E43)).
                   This formula will show the number in row 40 if
                   there is a value other than 0 there (and, if so, it
                   will disregard other values in rows 41–43).
                   Otherwise, it will read the sum of the rows 41
                   to 43.
Interest expense
B46–G52   This block for interest expense is similar to
                   the block for interest income, and you should
                   build it the same way. For the moment, leave
                   the formulas in cells E47–G51 blank since there
                   are no balance sheet references to link to.
EBT
B53   =B33−B38+B44−B52. Copy this across the
                   row to column G.
B54   =IF(B$8,B53/B$8,0). Copy this across the row
                   to column G. You can create this row quickly by
                   simply copying the formulas from row 23 for
                   the EBITDA margin, or row 34 for the EBIT
                   margin.

Provision for Taxes, Net Income, Dividends, and Net to Retained Earnings

	A	B	C	D	E	F
56	Provision for taxes	360	40.0	47.0		
57	Tax rate %	=IF(B53,B56/B53,0)	>>>	>>>	35.0%	35.0%
58	=A56	=B56	>>>	>>>	=IF(E56,E56, E53*E57)	>>>
59	Net income	=B53-B58	>>>	>>>	>>>	>>>
60	Net margin	=IF(B$8,B59/B$8,0)	>>>	>>>	>>>	>>>
61						
62	Dividends	10.0	12.0	11.0		
63	Payout ratio %	=IF(B59,B62/B59,0)	>>>	>>>	10.0%	10.0%
64	=A62	=B62	>>>	>>>	=IF(E62,E62, E59*E63)	>>>
65	Net to ret'd earnings	=B59-B64	>>>	>>>	>>>	>>>

Provision for taxes

A reminder here: As we are building the model at the moment, the numbers that you see in your model will not be the same as the ones shown in the illustration. Those represent the final numbers of the working model, so don't be concerned if your model-in-progress has different numbers.

B57	= IF(B53,B56/B53,0). Copy this across the row to column D.
B58	= B56. Copy this across to column D.
E58	= IF(E56,E56,E53*E57). Copy this across to the end, column G.

Net income

B59	= B53−B58. Copy this across to the end, column G.
B60	= IF(B$8,B59/B$8,0). Copy this across to the end, column G.

Dividends

B63	= IF(B59,B62/B59,0). Copy this across the row to column D.
B64	= B62. Copy this across to column D.
E64	= IF(E62,E62,E59*E63). Copy this across to the end, column G.

Net to retained earnings

B65	= B59−B64. Copy this across the row to the end, column G.

Surplus Fund, Cash, and ST Investments

	A	B	C	D	E	F
68						
69					Proj	Proj
70	BALANCE SHEET	=B4	>>>	>>>	>>>	>>>
71	ASSETS					
72	Surplus funds					
73	*Interest rate %*				*5.000%*	*5.000%*
74	Interest income				=E73*SUM(D72:E72)/2	>>>
75						
76	Cash		60.0	75.0	80.0	80.0	80.0
77	*% of revenues*	*IF(B$8,B76/B$8,0)*	>>>	>>>		
78	=A76	=B76	>>>	>>>	=IF(E76,E76, E77*E$8)	>>>
79	*Interest rate*				*5.000%*	*5.000%*
80	Interest income				=E79*AVERAGE(D78:E78)	>>>
81						
82	ST investments		30.0	32.0	33.0	34.0	35.0
83	*% of revenues*	*3.6%*	*3.6%*	*3.3%*		
84	=A82	30.0	32.0	33.0	34.0	35.0
85	*Interest rate*				*5.000%*	*5.000%*
86	Interest income				=E79*AVERAGE(D78:E78)	>>>
87						

We are now beginning the balance sheet section. Some cells are left blank (cells E72–G72, and others in later illustrations) to indicate that you should leave them blank until everything else is in place. The numbers that are already there in the illustration are the numbers that will eventually appear at completion.

Dates
B70   =B4. Copy this across to column G.

Surplus funds
B72–D72   Blank. These are the cells that otherwise would be for the asset plug calculations. For historical numbers, there should be no need for plugs since the numbers will come from reported source data.

Note: You may want to put in the "Surplus funds" (and the "Necessary to finance") formulas for the historical periods, which can be a useful way of checking if the source (i.e., hard-coded) data are out of balance. Just look at the "Surplus funds" and the "Necessary to finance" lines in the historical periods. There should be 0 numbers on these two lines.

E72–G72   Since we are in the process of building the balance sheet and do not yet have a row for the plug calculations, leave these blank for the moment.

E74–G74   = E73*SUM(D72:E72)/2. Copy across to column G. We will need to calculate the interest income from any surplus funds. Note the use of SUM/2, rather than AVERAGE. This is because we expect D72 to be blank, so a formula such as =E73*AVERAGE(D72:E72) would be considered by Excel to be the same as =E73*E72. Excel's AVERAGE function does not consider a blank cell as a cell to be counted. Since we want the interest income to be on the basis of the average of the starting and ending numbers, we need to use the SUM/2 approach. In columns F and G, we can use AVERAGE. Likewise, to use AVERAGE in column E, another way would be to put the 0 digit in cell D72.

Cash

B77   IF(B$8,B76/B$8,0). Copy across to column D.

B78   = B76. Copy across to column D.

E78   = IF(E76,E76,E77*E$8). Copy across to column G.

B80–D80   Leave these cells blank, as we will not be calculating the interest income for cash for the historical years. Typically, historical interest income is shown as one number combining the earnings of all the different assets; there is no need to calculate the interest income from the different assets separately.

E80   = E79*AVERAGE(D78:E78). Copy across to
              column G.

              We can use the AVERAGE function here because
              the formula is looking to cell that will always
              have a number (even if it is zero). In this way,
              the AVERAGE function will calculate properly.
              Compare this with the case of the "Surplus
              funds" above, where we have to use the SUM/2
              approach.

ST investments

This is similar in all respects to the "Cash" block above. Copy
the "Cash" block here. The use of the absolute reference ($)
in some of the formulas will ensure that the references are
correct.

Accounts Receivable, Inventory, and Other Current Assets

	A	B	C	D	E	F
88	Accounts receivable	60.0	75.0	90.0		
89	% of revenues	=IF(B$8,B88/B$8,0)	>>>	>>>		
90	*Days of revenues*	=IF(B$8, B88/B$8*365,0)	>>>	>>>	30.0	30.0
91	=A88	=B88	>>>	>>>	=IF(E88,E88, IF(E89,E89*E$8, E90/365*E$8))	>>>
92						
93	Inventory	120.0	135.0	150.0		
94	% of revenues	=IF(B$8,B93/B$8,0)	>>>	>>>		
95	*Days of COGS*	=IF(B$12, B93/B$12*365,0)	>>>	>>>	98.0	95.0
96	=A93	=B93	>>>	>>>	=IF(E93,E93, IF(E94,E94*E$8, E95/365*E$12))	>>>
97						
98	Other current assets	10.0	10.0	12.0		
99	% of revenues	=IF(B$8,B98/B$8,0)	>>>	>>>	1.0%	1.0%
100	=A98	=B98	>>>	>>>	=IF(E98,E98, E99*E$8)	>>>
101	Current assets	=B72+B78+B84 +B91+B96+B100	>>>	>>>	>>>	>>>
102						

Accounts receivable

B89	= IF(B$8,B88/B$8,0). Copy across to column D.
B90	= IF(B$8,B88/B$8*365,0). Copy across to column D.

This is a formula to derive the "Days of revenues" of receivables turnover, or a measure of how many days elapse on average before the company collects cash on its receivables. We will use 365 as the number of days in the year, even for leap years. This formula can be made more elaborate by making it take into account the extra day in leap years. Some analysts also use 360 days as the year basis.

B91	= B88. Copy across to column D.
E91	= IF(E88,E88,IF(E89,E89*E$8,E90/365*E$8)). Copy across to column G.

This is an example of a nested IF statement and will calculate the accounts receivable based on any of the three inputs.

Inventory

In general terms, this block is similar to the "Accounts receivable," but if you create it by copying the block above, you should take care to make the appropriate changes in the formulas, especially the reference to COGS, rather than revenues, for rows 95 and 96.

B94	= IF(B$8,B93/B$8,0). Copy across to column D.
B95	= IF(B$12,B93/B$12*365,0). Copy across to column D.

This is a formula to derive the "Days of COGS" of inventory turnover, or a measure of how many days on average that a piece of inventory remains in the warehouse before it is used in the production line. We will use 365 as the number of days in the year, even for leap years. This formula can be made more elaborate by making it take into account the extra day in leap years. Some analysts also use 360 days as the year basis.

B96	= B93. Copy across to column D.
E96	= IF(E93,E93,IF(E94,E94*E$8,E95/365*E$12)).

Copy across to column G.

This is an example of a nested IF statement, and it will calculate the inventory based on any of the three inputs.

Other current assets

B99	= IF(B$8,B98/B$8,0). Copy across to column D.
B100	= B98. Copy across to column D.
E100	= IF(E98,E98,E99*E$8). Copy across to column G.

Current assets

E101	= B72+B78+B84+B91+B96+B100. Copy across to column G.

Net PPE, Intangibles, Long-Term Assets

	A	B	C	D	E	F
103	Net PPE	870.0	950.0	1,000.0		
104	Capex	130.0	155.0	130.0		
105	% of revenues	=IF(B$8,B104/B$8,0)	>>>	>>>	15.0%	18.0%
106	Capex	=B104	>>>	>>>	=IF(E104,E104, E105*E$8)	>>>
107	Depreciation	=B29	>>>	>>>	>>>	>>>
108	=A103	=B103	>>>	>>>	=IF(E103,E103, D108+E106-E107)	
109						
110	Intangibles	58.0	54.0	50.0		
111	Amortization				=E32	>>>
112	=A110	=B110	>>>	>>>	=IF(ISNUMBER(E110), E110,D112-E111)	>>>
113						
114	Long-term assets	92.0	116.0	150.0		
115	% of revenues	=IF(B$8,B114/B$8,0)	>>>	>>>	14.0%	14.0%
116	% growth	na	=IF(B117, C114/ B117-1,0)	>>>		
117	=A114	=B114	>>>	>>>	=IF(E114,E114, IF(E115,E115*E$8, D117*(1+E116)))	>>>
118	Total assets	=B101+B108 +B112+B117	>>>	>>>	>>>	>>>
119						

Net PPE

Net PPE is a little bit more complicated because there are a few more flows that affect the final numbers. For historical periods, only the entries on row 103 will matter. The entries in row 104 for capital expenditures ("Capex") are there for informational purposes only, mainly so that we have a measure of Capex as a percentage of revenues to use as a forecasting yardstick. The line for "Depreciation" in the historical years is also not strictly needed. The depreciation in the forecast columns is used, however, for calculating the Net PPE number when there is no hard-coded input for this account.

B105	= IF(B$8,B104/B$8,0). Copy across to column D.
B106	= B104. Copy across to column D.
E106	= IF(E104,E104,E105*E$8). Copy across to column G. This formula shows the Capex, either as the hard-coded input or as a percentage of revenues.
B107	= B29. Copy across to column G.
B108	= B103. Copy across to column D.
E108	= IF(E103,E103,D108+E106−E107). Copy across to column G. This formula shows the Net PPE, either as a hard-coded input, or as a calculation based on the prior Net PPE + the Capex number previously calculated − Depreciation. We could have referenced the formula directly back to the income statement, but there is something to be said for having first brought the depreciation values down (to row 107), clearly labeling that, and then using that in this formula.

Intangibles

Whether we have the amortization numbers for the historical years is not important, as the model will read the hard-coded inputs for these years.

B111–D111	These can be left blank, or you can write =B32 and copy to column D.

E111   = E32. Copy across to column G.
B112   = B110. Copy across to column D.
E112   = IF(ISNUMBER(E110),E110,D112−E111).
                Copy across to column G.
                The ISNUMBER function is important here. With
                this in use, you can bring the account down to
                zero by entering a 0 in the input. Without the
                ISNUMBER, entering a 0 will give a FALSE
                result for the IF statement, and the result is the
                prior year's number less the amortization for
                the year.

Long-term assets

There are two subentry lines for long-term assets, one for "% of
revenues" and the other for "% growth." This gives flexibility for
defining this account: The first input defines the account as a
function of revenues and thus operations, and the second defines
the account by growth, as an investment account.

B115   = IF(B$8,B114/B$8,0). Copy across to
                column D.
B116   "na"
C116   = IF(B117,C114/B117−1,0). Copy to column D.
B117   = B114. Copy across to column D.
E117   = IF(E114,E114,IF(E115,E115*E$8,
                D117*(1+ E116))). Copy across to column G.
                This is a nested IF with three levels for calculating
                the long-term assets. The formula reads row 114
                first. If that is 0, then it reads the next row, and
                so on.

Total assets

B118   = B101+B108+B112+B117. Copy this across to
                column G.

ST Notes, Accounts Payable, and Other Current Liabilities

	A	B	C	D	E	F
120	LIABILITIES					
121	Short-term notes	10.0	12.0	14.0	14.0	14.0
122	=A121	=B121	>>>	>>>	>>>	>>>
123	Interest rate				10.000%	10.000%
124	Interest expense				=E123*AVERAGE (D122:E122)	>>>
125						
126	Accounts payable	60.0	70.0	80.0		
127	% of revenues	=IF(B$8,B126/B$8,0)	>>>	>>>		
128	Days of COGS	=IF(B$12,B126/ B$12*365.0)	>>>	>>>	55.0	55.0
129	=A126	=B126	>>>	>>>	=IF(E126,E126, IF(E127,E127*E$8, E128/365*E$12))	>>>
130						
131	Other current liabilities	10.0	20.0	20.0		
132	% of revenues	=IF(B$8,B131/B$8,0)	>>>	>>>	2.0%	2.0%
133	=A131	=B131	>>>	>>>	=IF(E131,E131, E132*E$8)	>>>
134	Current liabilities	=B121+B129+B133	>>>	>>>	>>>	>>>
135						

Short-term notes

B122   = B121. Copy across to column G.

B124–D124   This is left bank as these are for the historical years. In these years, we would expect to have the interest expense for the company to be shown as one number for all debt accounts, so there is no need to show it separately for the different types of debt.

E124   = E123*AVERAGE(D122:E122). Copy across to column G.

Accounts payable

This block is similar to the inventory section, including the use of COGS rather than revenues, for the secondary inputs.

B127   = IF(B$8,B126/B$8,0). Copy across to column D.

B128   = IF(B$12,B126/B$12*365,0). Copy across the
              column D.
              This is a formula to derive the "Days of COGS"
              of accounts payable turnover, or a measure of
              how many days on average the company holds
              its payables before actually paying them off. The
              longer it is, the more of a "free loan" from its
              suppliers the company enjoys. We will use 365
              as the number of days in the year, even for leap
              years. This formula can be made more elaborate
              by making it take into account the extra day in
              leap years. Some analysts also use 360 days as
              the year basis.
B129   = B126. Copy across to column D.
E129   = IF(E126,E126,IF(E127,E127*E$8,
              E128/365*E$12)). Copy across to column G.
              This is an example of a nested IF statement and
              will calculate the accounts payable based on a
              hierarchy of the three inputs.
Other current liabilities
B132   = IF(B$8,B131/B$8,0). Copy across to column D.
B133   = B131. Copy across to column D.
E133   = IF(E131,E131,E132*E$8). Copy across to
              column G.
Current liabilities
B134   = B122+B129+B133. Copy across to column G.

Necessary to Finance, Debts 1 to 3, and Long-Term Liabilities

	A	B	C	D	E	F
136	Necessary to finance					
137	*Interest rate*				10.000%	10.000%
138	Interest expense				=E137*SUM(D136:E136)/2	>>>
139						
140	Debt 1	200.0	225.0	150.0		
141	=A140	=B140	>>>	>>>	>>>	>>>
142	*Interest rate*				10.000%	10.000%
143	Interest expense				=E142*AVERAGE(D141:E141)	>>>
144						
145	Debt 2	200.0	200.0	225.0		
146	=A145	=B145	>>>	>>>	>>>	>>>
147	*Interest rate*				10.000%	10.000%
148	Interest expense				=E147*AVERAGE(D146:E146)	>>>
149						
150	Debt 3	110.0	110.0	110.0		
151	=A150	=B150	>>>	>>>	>>>	>>>
152	*Interest rate*				8.000%	8.000%
153	Interest expense				=E152*AVERAGE(D151:E151)	>>>
154						
155	Long-term liabilities	40.0	38.0	37.0		
156	*% of revenues*	IF(B$8,B158/B$8,0)	>>>	>>>	4.0%	4.0%
157	*% growth*	na	=IF(B158,C155/B158-1,0)	>>>		
158	=A155	=B155	>>>	>>>	=IF(E155,E155,IF(E156,E156*E$8,D158*(1+E157)))	>>>
159	Total liabilities	=B134+B136+B141+B146+B151+B158	>>>	>>>	>>>	>>>
160						

Necessary to finance (NTF)

This is the plug for the liabilities side, and it is assumed to be debt.

B136–D136   These cells should always be blank, since there should be no plugs for the historical years.

See the comment under "Surplus funds,"
regarding using formulas for the historical
periods.

E136–G136   For the moment, leave this blank because we
have not created the calculation lines at the
bottom of the balance sheet. We will get back to
this as we complete the model.

E138–G138   = E137*SUM(D136:E136)/2. Copy across to
column G.

We will need to calculate the interest expense from
any NTF. Note the use of SUM/2, rather than
AVERAGE. This is because we expect D136 to
be blank, so a formula such as
=E137*AVERAGE (D136:E136) would be
considered by Excel to be the same as
=E137*E136. Excel's AVERAGE function does
not consider a blank cell as a cell to be counted.
Since we want the interest expense to be on the
basis of the average of the starting and ending
numbers, we need to use the SUM/2 approach.
In columns F and G, we can use AVERAGE.
Likewise, to use AVERAGE in column E, another
way would be to put the 0 digit in cell D136.

Debt 1

The description for Debt 1 will apply as well to Debt 2 and Debt
3, so I will describe only how to build Debt 1. Once this block is
built, simply copy it to create the other two debt blocks.

B141   = B140. Copy across to column G.

B143–D143   This will remain blank as we will not need to
calculate the interest income separately for debt
in the historical years. Typically, historical
interest expense is given as one number
representing the interest expense of all interest-
bearing liabilities.

E143   = E142*AVERAGE(D141:E141). Copy across
to column G.

The interest expense is calculated on the basis
of the average of the beginning and ending

outstandings. We can use the AVERAGE function here because the formula is looking to cells that will always have a number (even if it is zero). In this way, the AVERAGE function will calculate properly. Compare this with the case of the NTF (and Surplus funds) above, where we have to use the SUM/2 approach.

Debt 2
Copy the Debt 1 block to create this second block. Remember to change the title.

Debt 3
Copy the Debt 1 block again to create this third block. Remember to change the title.

Long-term liabilities
Like long-term assets, this may or may not be related to operations. For this reason and to be flexible, we will have two subentry lines.

B156	=IF(B$8,B158/B$8,0). Copy across to column D.
B157	"na"
C157	=IF(B158,C155/B158−1,0). Copy to column D.
B158	=B155. Copy across to column D.
E158	=IF(E155,E155,IF(E156,E156*E$8, D158*(1+E157))). Copy across to column G. This is a nested IF with three levels for calculating the long-term liabilities.

Total liabilities
B159	=B134+B136+B141+B146+B151+B158

Common Stock, Retained Earnings, and Other Equity Account

	A	B	C	D	E	F
161	EQUITY					
162	Common stock	460.0	560.0	580.0	650.0	650.0
163	=A162	=B162	>>>	>>>	>>>	>>>
164						
165	Retained earnings	200	261.0	337.0		
166	Net to retained earnings				=E65	>>>
167	=A165	=B165	>>>	>>>	IF(E165,E165, D167+E166)	>>>
168						
169	Other equity acct	· 10.0	11.0	12.0		
170	% of revenues	=IF(B$8,B169/B$8,0)	>>>	>>>	1.1%	1.02%
171	=A169	=B169	>>>	>>>	=IF(E169,E169, E170*E$8)	>>>
172	Total SH equity	=B163+B167+B171	>>>	>>>	>>>	>>>
173	Total liabs & SH equity	=B159+B172	>>>	>>>	>>>	>>>
174						

Common stock

B163   = B162. Copy across to column G.

B166–D166   Leave this blank because, for the historical years, retained earnings will be defined by the numbers from the data source, which will be entered in the input cells in row 165.

E166   = E65. Copy across to column G.

                This is the reference to the "Net to retained earnings" row in the income statement.

B167   = B165. Copy across to column D.

E167   = IF(E165,E165,D167+E166).

                For the forecast periods, we are most probably going to rely on retained earnings being calculated as the prior period's number plus the current period's net to retained earnings. So the formula need only be =D167+E166 in cell E167. Nevertheless, on the off chance that you would want to use a specific input, we will use the IF formula shown to give you the ability to specify retained earnings by specific hard-coded inputs.

Other equity account
B170   = IF(B$8,B169/B$8,0). Copy across to
              column D.
B171   = B169. Copy across to column D.
E171   = IF(E169,E169,E170*E$8). Copy across
              to column G.
Shareholders' equity
B172   = B163+B167+B171. Copy across to
              column G.
Total liabilities and shareholders' equity
B173   = B159+B172. Copy across to column G.

BALANCING THE BALANCE SHEET

Now that we have completed the first sweep through the income statement and the balance sheet, let's put in the balancing formulas. After that, we will go back and fill in those rows that we have left blank. When these rows are completed, we will have a fully functioning model. *Reminder*: Excel's Iteration setting must be on.

Remember: There are two ways to balance the model. I will include both here, but you should choose **only one**. For the model at this point, there is no benefit or disadvantage to using either one. However, at a later point, if you want to include the automatic repayment of debt through surplus funds, that feature can be added only if you use the first method.

Balancing Method No. 1

	A	B	C	D	E	F
175						
176	Assets without SF	=IF(ISERROR(B78+B84+B91+B96+B100+B108+B112+B117), 0, B78+B84+B91+B96+B100+B108+B112+B117)				
177	Liabs, Eq w/out NTF	=IF(ISERROR(B134+B141+B146+B151+B158+B172), 0, B134+B141+B146+B151+B158+B172)				
178						
179						
180	Surplus funds	=MAX(B177-B176,0)	>>>	>>>	>>>	>>>
181	Necessary to finance	=-MIN(B177-B176,0)	>>>	>>>	>>>	>>>
182						

This method first takes the totals of the left-hand side and the right-hand side of the balance sheet, excluding the rows for the plugs. We take the difference between the two and put the difference either as "Surplus funds" (the asset plug) or "Necessary to finance" (the liabilities plug).

B176   = IF(ISERROR(B78+B84+B91+B96+B100+
                 B108+B112+B117),0,B78+B84+B91+B96+
                 B100+B108+B112+B117).
                 The use of the ISERROR is very important
                 here. Since this formula is part of the
                 circular reference that we are deliberately
                 establishing in the model, the use of this func-
                 tion will ensure that if there are any error mes-
                 sages, the formula will flip to 0, essentially
                 breaking the loop of the circular reference and
                 preventing any error messages from being
                 "trapped" in the loop. With this error trap, once
                 the error is removed, the formula runs as it
                 should and the iterative loop is re-established
                 automatically.
B177   = IF(ISERROR(B134+B141+B146+B151+
                 B158+B172),0, B134+B141+B146+B151+
                 B158+B172)
                 This is the formula for the right-hand side of
                 the balance sheet. This also must have the
                 ISERROR function.
B180   = MAX(B177-B176,0).
                 The use of the MAX function means that this row will
                 show a number only when liabilities + equity
                 exceeds assets—precisely the calculation for the
                 asset plug that we want. This is the row that the
                 "Surplus funds" line in the balance sheet will read.
B181   = −MIN(B177−B176,0).
                 The use of the MIN function *with the negative
                 sign* means that this row will show a number
                 when assets exceed liabilities + equity. This
                 will give the "Necessary to finance" plug that
                 we want. You can reverse the calculation and

use a MAX but without a negative sign
(i.e., =MAX(B176–B177.0) for the same effect.

Balancing Method No. 2

	A	B	C	D	E	F
175						
176	Assets WITH SF	=B118	>>>	>>>	>>>	>>>
177	Liabs, Eq WITH NTF	=B173	>>>	>>>	>>>	>>>
178	Difference	=B177-B176	>>>	>>>	>>>	>>>
179	Accumulated difference	IF(ISERROR (B178+B179),0, B178+B179)	>>>	>>>	>>>	>>>
180	Surplus funds	=MAX(B179,0)	>>>	>>>	>>>	>>>
181	Necessary to finance	=-MIN(B179,0)	>>>	>>>	>>>	>>>
182						

This method uses the total assets, *including the Surplus funds*, and
the total liabilities and equity, *including the NTF*. The lines shown
here are for ease of illustration: row 178, which takes the difference between the two sides of the balance sheet, could just as
easily look at the totals directly from the balance sheet rows, in
which case we can omit row 176 and row 177.

B176	=B118. Copy across all columns to column G.
B177	=B173. Copy across all columns to column G.
B178	=B177–B176. Copy across all columns to column G.

The order of using liabilities and equity less assets
is helpful in that if the difference is positive, it
indicates an asset plug; if negative, it indicates a
liabilities plug.

B179   =IF(ISERROR(B178+B179),0,B178+B179).
Copy across all columns to column G.

This is the supremely elegant formula that makes
this second method work. The ISERROR function is included here and is the error-trapping
mechanism in case there is an error message
produced in the model. This is the line that
calculates the plug that the model needs.

B180   =MAX(B179,0). Copy across all columns to
column G.

B181

This formula looks to the previous row and shows the result for an asset plug if the row is positive. = −MIN(B179,0). Copy across all columns to column G.

This formula looks to the previous row and shows the result for a liabilities plug if the row is negative, *but shows the result as a positive.*

CONNECTING THE BALANCING LINES

In the model shown in the illustrations, the row references for this section are the same whether for Balancing Method No. 1 or Balancing Method No. 2.

Surplus Funds

	A	B	C	D	E	F
68						
69					Proj	Proj
70	BALANCE SHEET	2000	2001	2002	2003	2004
71	ASSETS					
72	Surplus funds				=E180	>>>
73	*Interest rate %*				*5.000%*	*5.000%*
74	Interest income				2.3	3.6
75						

E72

= E180. Copy across all columns to column G. This connects the row to the Surplus funds balancing calculation.

Necessary to Finance

	A	B	C	D	E	F
136	Necessary to finance				=E181	>>>
137	*Interest rate*				*10.000%*	*10.000%*
138	Interest expense				0.0	0.0
139						

E136

= E181. Copy across all columns to column G. This connects the row to the Necessary to finance balancing calculation.

CONNECTING OTHER ROWS
TO COMPLETE THE MODEL

When we were building the model, we left some lines blank because we did not have the rows fully laid out. Now that the model is set in place in row positions, let's go back and make sure all the connections are now in place.

Interest Income

	A	B	C	D	E	F
40	Interest income		3.0	5.0	6.0	
41	Surplus funds				=E74	>>>
42	Cash				=E80	>>>
43	ST investments				=E86	>>>
44	Interest income		3.0	5.0	6.0	7.9	9.3
45						

E41   = E74. Copy across all columns to G.
E42   = E80. Copy across all columns to G.
E43   = E86. Copy across all columns to G.

Interest Expense

	A	B	C	D	E	F
46	Interest expense		50.0	50.0	50.0	
47	Necessary to finance				=E138	>>>
48	ST notes				=E124	>>>
49	Debt 1				=E143	>>>
50	Debt 2				=E148	>>>
51	Debt 3				=E153	>>>
52	Interest expense		50.0	50.0	50.0	47.7	47.7

E47   = E138. Copy across all columns to G.
E48   = E124. Copy across all columns to G.
E49   = E143. Copy across all columns to G.
E50   = E148. Copy across all columns to G.
E51   = E153. Copy across all columns to G.

Depreciation

	A	B	C	D	E	F
26	Depreciation	60.0	75.0	80.0		
27	As % prior Net PPE	na	=IF(B108, C29/B108,0)	>>>	8.5%	8.5%
28	As % revenues	7.3%	8.3%	8.0%		
29	Depreciation	60.0	75.0	80.0	=IF(E26,E26,IF(E27, E27*D108,E28*E8))	>>>
30						

C27   = IF(B108,C29/B108,0). Copy to column D.

E29   = IF(E26,E26,IF(E27,E27*D108,E28*E8)).
             Copy across columns to column G.

CONGRATULATIONS

If you have followed the steps in this chapter and have used the numbers shown in the illustrations, you should have a model that is fully functioning and dynamically balancing with the same output numbers shown on pages 160–165. Now begin experimenting with changing various inputs and see how the balance sheet always balances, no matter what input changes you make.

In the next chapter, we will look at how to extract the output lines from this Input sheet and create other sheets, including the cash flow statement. In this way, we can organize the presentation of the lines more easily to get the format of the output we want.

CHAPTER 10

The IS and BS
Output Sheets

If we have followed the steps in Chapter 9 properly, we will have a fully working model. But it is still in a "raw" state. This chapter shows how to create the first output sheets to show the results with greater visual polish.

CREATING NEW OUTPUT SHEETS

Although the name of the sheet is *Input sheet*, in actuality there is a fully working model on the sheet. However, it looks quite ugly. It has the mish-mash of the input and the calculation lines and lots of extra lines at the bottom for the balancing formulas. This is not the kind of printouts that you want to put in front of your audience. Let's create output sheets that are neater, presentation-ready, and, yes, more impressive.

At this point, we can create just another sheet that we can call, say, "Output," that will show not only the two financial statements (in a neater format), but also the cash flow statement and perhaps other sections that you want to add such as ratios. But this may make the sheet too long and cumbersome to navigate.

Let's add, instead, several more sheets, with each sheet containing only one specific section. This chapter will show you how. Of course, if you wish to have your output as just one sheet, by all means create the output that way.

ADD FOUR MORE SHEETS

Using Excel's own commands, add four more sheets and label them:

* IS
* BS
* CF
* Ratios

I could have spelled them out as "Income Statement," "Balance Sheet," and "Cash Flow," or only partially shortened them to "IncStatement," and so on. This is not important. However, if you have many sheets in a file, the shorter the tab names, the more tabs you can see across the bottom of the screen.

If you did decide to spell out the names, you should avoid having spaces in them. If you have spaces in them, Excel automatically adds single quotes outside sheet tab names with spaces, so a reference to a sheet with a space in its name ("Income Statement") will appear as ='Income Statement'!A1. If you are typing in this formula as you build cross-sheet references, you must remember to put these single quotes in. So you will have created the minor, but repeated, inconvenience of having to put in these quotes.

The IS and BS sheets will have references to the Input sheet, reading directly off the calculated lines from that sheet. The CF and Ratios sheets (and other sheets that you may want to add later on) will read the numbers from the IS and BS. So the Input sheet feeds only the starting two sheets, and everything else reads these two sheets. It's a good way to streamline the flow of numbers through a model.

THE IS SHEET

The following illustration is what the IS sheet will look like. The first year's column (column B) is shown with the formulas in them. Copy these formulas across all the columns to column G. To have the titles on this sheet reflect the titles on the Input sheet, copy the formulas to column A, also.

Since all the numbers have been calculated in the Input sheet, it is an easy task to simply bring them to this IS output sheet. As a matter of preference, you can also directly read the Input numbers for the subtotal lines, such as "Gross profit" or "EBITDA." In the illustration, these subtotals are calculated again; this is a good double-check on the accuracy of the original calculations in the Input sheet.

IS Sheet

	A	B	C	D	E	F	G
1	=Input!A1						
2							
3					Proj	Proj	Proj
4	INCOME STATEMENT	=Input!B4	2001	2002	2003	2004	2005
5							
6	Revenues	=Input!B8	900.0	1,000.0	1,100.0	1,210.0	1,331.0
7	COGS	=Input!B12	490.0	550.0	605.0	665.5	732.1
8	Gross profit	=B6-B7	410.0	450.0	495.0	544.5	599.0
9	Gross margin	=IF(B$6,B8/B$6,0)	45.6%	45.0%	45.0%	45.0%	45.0%
10							
11	SGA	=Input!B18	135.0	150.0	165.0	181.5	199.7
12	Operating expenses	=Input!B22	28.0	30.0	33.0	36.3	39.9
13	EBITDA	=B8-B11-B12	247.0	270.0	297.0	326.7	359.4
14	EBITDA margin	=IF(B$6,B13/B$6,0)	27.4%	27.0%	27.0%	27.0%	27.0%
15							
16	Depreciation	=Input!B29	75.0	80.0	85.0	91.8	102.5
17	Amort of intangibles	=Input!B32	4.0	4.0	4.0	4.0	4.0
18	EBIT	=B13-B16-B17	168.0	186.0	208.0	230.9	252.9
19	EBIT margin	=IF(B$6,B18/B$6,0)	18.7%	18.6%	18.6%	19.1%	19.0%
20							
21	Non-oper expenses	=Input!B38	10.0	8.0	10.0	11.0	12.0
22	Interest income	=Input!B44	5.0	6.0	7.9	9.3	7.1
23	Interest expense	=Input!B52	50.0	50.0	47.7	47.7	48.7
24	EBT	=B18-B21+B22-B23	113.0	134.0	158.2	181.5	199.3
25	EBT margin	=IF(B$6,B24/B$6,0)	12.6%	13.4%	14.4%	15.0%	15.0%
26							
27	Provision for taxes	=Input!B58	40.0	47.0	55.4	63.5	69.7
28	Net income	=B24-B27	73.0	87.0	102.7	118.0	129.5
29	Net margin	=IF(B$6,B28/B$6,0)	8.1%	8.7%	9.3%	9.7%	9.7%
30							
31	Dividends	=Input!B64	12.0	11.0	10.3	11.8	13.0
32	Net to retid earnings	=B28-B31	61.0	76.0	92.6	106.2	116.6
33							
	IS						

THE BS SHEET

The BS sheet follows the same approach. With most of the work already done in the Input sheet, laying out this sheet is also a fairly simple task.

BS Sheet

	A	B	C	D	E	F	G
1	=Input!A1						
2					Proj	Proj	Proj
3	BALANCE SHEET	=Input!B4	2001	2002	2003	2004	2005
4	ASSETS						
5	Surplus funds	=Input!B72	0.0	0.0	90.0	52.7	0.0
6	Cash	=Input!B78	75.0	80.0	80.0	80.0	80.0
7	St investments	=Input!B84	32.0	33.0	34.0	35.0	36.1
8	Accounts receivable	=Input!B91	75.0	90.0	90.4	99.5	109.4
9	Inventory	=Input!B96	135.0	150.0	162.4	173.2	190.5
10	Other current assets	=Input!B100	10.0	12.0	11.0	12.1	13.3
11	Current assets	=SUM(B5:B10)	327.0	355.0	467.9	452.5	429.3
12							
13	Net PPE	=Input!B108	950.0	1,000.0	1,080.0	1,206.0	1,369.7
14	Intangibles	=Input!B112	50.0	50.0	46.0	42.0	38.0
15	Long-term assets	=Input!B117	120.0	150.0	154.0	169.4	186.3
16	Total assets	=B11+SUM(B13:B15)	1,447.0	1,565.0	1,747.9	1,869.9	2,023.3
17							
18	LIABILITIES						
19	Short-term notes	=Input!B122	12.0	14.0	14.0	14.0	14.0
20	Accounts payable	=Input!B129	70.0	80.0	91.2	100.3	110.3
21	Other current liabilities	=Input!B133	20.0	20.0	22.0	24.2	26.6
22	Current liabilities	=SUM(B19:B21)	102.0	114.0	127.2	138.5	150.9
23							
24	Necessary to finance	=Input!B136	0.0	0.0	0.0	0.0	19.4
25	Debt 1	=Input!B141	225.0	150.0	150.0	150.0	150.0
26	Debt 2	=Input!B146	200.0	225.0	225.0	225.0	225.0
27	Debt 3	=Input!B151	110.0	110.0	110.0	110.0	110.0
28	Long-term liabilities	=Input!B158	38.0	37.0	44.0	48.4	53.2
29	Total liabilities	=B22+SUM(B24:B28)	675.0	636.0	656.2	671.9	708.6
30							
31	SHAREHOLDERS' EQUITY						
32	Common stock	=Input!B163	560.0	580.0	650.0	650.0	650.0
33	Retained earnings	=Input!B167	261.0	337.0	429.6	535.7	652.3
34	Other equity account	=Input!B171	11.0	12.0	12.1	12.3	12.4
35	Total SH equity	=SUM(B32:B34)	772.0	929.0	1,091.7	1,198.0	1,314.8
36	Total liabs & SH equity	=B29+B35	1,447.0	1,565.0	1,747.9	1,869.9	2,023.3
37							
	BS						

Copy the formulas shown in column B across to column G. To copy the titles from the Input sheet, copy column B back to column A (notice that A1 already has a formula so that the name of the company also appears on this sheet). However, copying back to column A does not work for the "totals" rows with the summing formulas.

So, in very short order, we have created presentation-ready sheets for the income statement and the balance sheet. Let's go to the next chapter for the CF sheet.

CHAPTER 11

The CF Sheet

In Chapter 10 we moved the model into a working state and a set of output sheets that looked pretty nice. This chapter goes over the creation of the third important output: the cash flow statement.

A NEW SHEET: THE CASH FLOW STATEMENT

The *cash flow statement* (CF) is a new sheet that we have to work on. Unlike the IS and the BS, whose formats follow the Input sheet, we have to create a new sheet altogether.

Because the numbers from the Input sheet have already been brought into the IS and the BS sheets, the CF sheet will just read from these two statements. The exception, as you will see, is the capital expenditures (capex) number, which is not represented in the balance sheet. This number will be read from the Input sheet.

The cash flow statement is a way of showing how much cash is coming into a company and how it is being used. Cash is critical for operations: a business that is running out of cash is one that is in trouble, no matter how "profitable" it may seem from its net income number and how large its asset base is. The cash flow statement is key in showing exactly where a company's cash "sources" are and where the cash "uses" are.

FLOWS IN THE CASH FLOW STATEMENT

The cash flow statement's flows fall into three categories:

- Cash flow from operations
- Cash flow from investments
- Cash flow from financing

Each category shows the sources and uses of cash, so that at the end we have a total of the cash remaining from the year's earnings. This CF total should match, or "foot," with the *change* (which can be an increase or decrease) of cash on the balance sheet. The BS cash total is not the same as the CF cash, because BS cash includes the accumulated cash from previous year's earnings.

Sources

A source of cash is:

- Any decrease in the assets components
- Any increase in the liabilities and shareholders' equity components
- An accounting "credit" in the T-account (see p. 116)

Uses

Conversely, a use of cash is:

- Any increase in the assets components
- Any decrease in the liabilities and shareholders' equity components
- An accounting "debit" in the T-account (see p. 116)

From this listing of sources and uses, we can also make a connection to the discussion of debits and credits in Chapter 5. A source of cash is an *accounting credit*, and a use of cash is an *accounting debit*. So, finally, the system of debits and credits, which has been confusing and hard to remember, makes sense. Selling an asset (a credit) adds that much cash into a business (a source of cash). By the same token, buying inventory (a debit) or having capital expenditures (another debit) uses cash (a use of cash). We will use these rules as we build our cash flow statement.

Cash Flow from Operations

This includes:

+ Any flows from the income statement
+ Any changes in balance sheet accounts that are related to operations. Usually, these are all or most of the current assets, *excluding* cash and cash equivalents, and all or most of current liabilities, *excluding* any debt items such as short-term notes or current portion of long-term debt. These will appear in the "Cash from financing" section.

Cash Flow from Investments

This includes:

+ Capital expenditures
+ Any changes in the balance sheet accounts that are related to investments

Cash Flow from Financing

This includes:

+ Any changes in the balance sheet accounts that are related to debt or equity financing
+ Dividends

Usually, it is easy to identify flows that are related to operations or to financing. If you are not sure if it is an investment-related flow, simply ask yourself if it is an operating or financing flow. If the answer is no, then it *must* be a flow from investments.

Positive for Source, Negative for Use

The titles to these sections say "Cash from..." so, in the cash flow statement, it is a good idea to follow the system that a *source of cash* is shown as a *positive number*, but a *use of cash* is shown as a *negative number*.

RECONCILIATIONS

Even in the simple model that we are building, there are a few places where we can run into trouble if a "flow" number (such as depreciation or capex) does not match with the change in the corresponding balance sheet account. You may wonder how this could be so, since the numbers should foot with each other. Certain balance sheet accounts can be defined either by (1) hard-coded inputs or (2) automatic running additions of the prior year's numbers plus the flows from the current year's income statement. In some cases, where there has been an error in the input, or where the source data (e.g., another model you are trying to replicate) have a mismatch error, the model will have such discrepancies. We can avoid the resulting incorrect flows in the cash flow statement through the use of reconciliation tables.

Let's use the net PPE (Plant Property and Equipment) account, as an example. In fact, this account has two flows going into it. From one year to the next, it increases by the amount of capex and decreases by the amount of deprecation. In the cash flow statement, the capex and depreciation numbers will be shown, and they *should* account fully for the change in the net PPE in the balance sheet. And if they do not, we have to make sure that the discrepancy is included in the cash flow statement. If we ignore it, the cash flow will not foot.

A reconciliation table for net PPE would look like the following exhibit. I've used some quick "dummy" numbers to illustrate. The beginning net PPE on the balance sheet, equivalent to the prior year's net PPE, is 100, and the ending number is 125. However, the flows suggest the ending number should be different.

Beginning net PPE on balance sheet	100
+ Capex	50
− Depreciation	30
= Expected Ending net PPE	120
Ending net PPE on balance sheet	125
Other (increase) decrease	(5)

Here, the table keeps track of the flows and comes up with what it "expects" to be the final number. But the balance sheet number is different, so the final Other (increase) decrease line shows a number. The discrepancy is shown as a negative number, and here you have to recall what a source is and what a use is. In this case, because the ending net PPE on the balance sheet is more than what is expected, there has been an unexplained increase in this asset, which is therefore a use of cash. And in the cash flow statement, a use is shown as a negative number.

It is important to do these reconciliation tables for *all the accounts in the balance sheet that are affected by "flow" numbers* and include them in the cash flow statement itself. You do not need these reconciliation tables for accounts that exist only on the balance sheet. In the model we are building, there are three such accounts, shown with their flow numbers as follows.

Balance Sheet Account	Flow Numbers
Net PPE	Depreciation and capex
Intangibles	Amortization of intangibles
Retained earnings	Net to retained earnings

The reconciliation tables are built just under the cash flow statement itself, and their lines are read into the lines of the statement.

The following exhibit is what the CF will look like. The first full column of numbers is shown as formulas. This column reads the second year's column in the IS and BS. There is no first year in the CF because this sheet has to look at the changes in the balance sheet accounts from year to year, and the first year has no "prior" year.

The exception is the line for cash, which must begin with a starting number, in this case, the amount of cash and cash equivalents (surplus funds, which should be 0 of course, since this is a historical year, and marketable securities) at the beginning of the second year. This point in time is the same as the end of the first year.

The reconciliation tables are shown separately, but with the row numbers still in sequence with this first part of the cash flow statement.

To fully flesh out the cash flow statement, once you have written in these formulas, copy the column C across to all the columns up to column G.

	A	B	C
1	First Corporation		
2			
3			Proj
4	CASH FLOW	=IS!B4	=B4+1
5			
6	Net income		=IS!C28
7			
8	Add back:		
9	Depreciation		=IS!C16
10	Amort of intangilbles		=IS!C17
11	Operating cash flow		=C6+SUM(C9:C10)
12			
13	(Inc) in Accts receivable		=BS!B8-BS!C8
14	(Inc) in Inventory		=BS!B9-BS!C9
15	(Inc) in Other current assets		=BS!B10-BS!C10
16	Inc in Accts Payable		=BS!C20-BS!B20
17	Inc in Other current liabs		=BS!C21-BS!B21
18	(Inc) in Oper working capital		=SUM(C13:C17)
19	Cash from operations		=C11+C18
20			
21	Capex		=-Input!C106
22	Other (inc) dec in net PPE		=C54
23	Other (inc) dec in intangibles		=C61
24	(Inc) dec in long-term assets		=BS!B15-BS!C15
25	Cash from investments		=SUM(C21:C24)
26			
27	Inc (dec) in ST notes		=BS!C19-BS!B19
28	Inc (dec) in nec to finance		=BS!C24-BS!B24
29	Inc (dec) in debt 1		=BS!C25-BS!B25
30	Inc (dec) in debt 2		=BS!C26-BS!B26
31	Inc (dec) in debt 3		=BS!C27-BS!B27
32	Dividends		=-IS!C31
33	Inc (dec) in long-term liabs		=BS!C28-BS!B28
34	Inc (dec) common stock		=BS!C32-BS!B32
35	Other inc (dec) ret'd earnings		=C68
36	Inc (dec) in other equity acct		=BS!C34-BS!B34
37	Cash from financing		=SUM(C27:C36)
38			
39	Change in cash and equiv		=C19+C25+c37
40	Cash and equivalents	=SUM(BS!C5:C7)	=B40+C39
41			
42	Cash and equiv in B/S		=SUM(BS!C5:C7)
43	Parity check		=C40-C42
44			

	A	B	C
45			Proj
46	RECONCILIATION	=B4	=C4
47			
48	Net PPE		
49	Beginning amount		=BS!B13
50	Capex		=-C21
51	Depreciation		=C9
52	Expected ending amount		=C49+C50-C51
53	B/S amount		=BS!C13
54	Other (inc) dec Net PPE		=C52-C53
55			
56	Intangibles		
57	Beginning amount		=BS!B14
58	Amortization		=C10
59	Expected ending amount		=C57-C58
60	B/S amount		=BS!C14
61	Other (inc) dec Intangibles		=C59-C60
62			
63	Retained earnings		
64	Beginning amount		=BS!B33
65	Net to retained earnings		=IS!C32
66	Expected ending amount		=C64+C65
67	B/S amount		=BS!C33
68	Other inc (dec) ret'd earnings		=C67-C66
69			
70			

CF

And this is what the final set of numbers should look like:

	A	B	C	D	E	F	G
1	First Corporation						
2							
3					Proj	Proj	Proj
4	CASH FLOW	2000	2001	2002	2003	2004	2005
5							
6	Net income		73.0	87.0	102.8	118.0	129.5
7							
8	Add back:						
9	Depreciation		75.0	80.0	85.0	91.8	102.5
10	Amortization of intangibles		4.0	4.0	4.0	4.0	4.0
11	Operating cash flow		152.0	171.0	191.8	213.8	236.0
12							
13	(Inc) in Acct receivable		(15.0)	(15.0)	(0.4)	(9.0)	(9.9)
14	(inc) in Inventory		(15.0)	(15.0)	(12.4)	(10.8)	(17.3)
15	(inc) in Other current assets		0.0	(2.0)	1.0	(1.1)	(1.2)
16	Inc in Accts payables		10.0	10.0	11.2	9.1	10.0
17	Inc in Other current liabs		10.0	0.0	2.0	2.2	2.4
18	(Inc) in Operating working capital		(10.0)	(22.0)	1.3	(9.6)	(16.0)
19	Cash from operations		142.0	149.0	193.2	204.2	220.0
20							
21	Capex		(155.0)	(130.0)	(165.0)	(217.8)	(266.2)
22	Other (inc) dec net PPE		0.0	0.0	0.0	0.0	0.0
23	Other (inc) dec in Intangibles		0.0	0.0	0.0	0.0	0.0
24	Other (inc) dec in Long-term assets		(24.0)	(34.0)	(4.0)	(15.4)	(16.9)
25	Cash from investments		(179.0)	(164.0)	(169.0)	(233.2)	(283.1)
26							
27	Inc (dec) in Short-term notes		2.0	2.0	0.0	0.0	0.0
28	Inc (dec) in Necessary to finance		0.0	0.0	0.0	0.0	19.4
29	Inc (dec) in Debt 1		25.0	(75.0)	0.0	0.0	0.0
30	Inc (dec) in Debt 2		0.0	25.0	0.0	0.0	0.0
31	Inc (dec) in Debt 3		0.0	0.0	0.0	0.0	0.0
32	Dividends		(12.0)	(11.0)	(10.3)	(11.8)	(13.0)
33	Inc (dec) in Other long-term liabs		(2.0)	(1.0)	7.0	4.4	4.8
34	Inc (dec) in Common stock		40.0	80.0	70.0	0.0	0.0
35	Other inc (dec) in Ret'd earnings		0.0	0.0	0.0	0.0	0.0
36	Inc (dec) in Other equity account		1.0	1.0	0.1	0.1	0.1
37	Cash from financing		54.0	21.0	66.9	(7.3)	11.4
38							
39	Change in cash and equiv		17.0	6.0	91.0	(36.3)	(51.7)
40	Cash and equivalents	90.0	107.0	113.0	204.0	167.7	116.1
41							
42	B/S cash and equiv	90.0	107.0	113.0	204.0	167.7	116.1
43	Parity check	0.0	0.0	0.0	0.0	0.0	0.0
44							

	A	B	C	D	E	F	G
45					Proj	Proj	Proj
46	RECONCILIATON	2000	2001	2002	2003	2004	2005
47							
48	**Net PPE**						
49	Beginning amount		870.0	950.0	1,000.0	1,080.0	1,206.0
50	Capex		155.0	130.0	165.0	217.8	266.2
51	Depreciation		75.0	80.0	85.0	91.8	102.5
52	Expected ending amount		950.0	1,000.0	1,080.0	1,206.0	1,369.7
53	B/S amount		950.0	1,000.0	1,080.0	1,206.0	1,369.7
54	Other (inc) dec Net PPE		0.0	0.0	0.0	0.0	0.0
55							
56	**Intangibles**						
57	Beginning amount		58.0	54.0	50.0	46.0	42.0
58	Amortization		4.0	4.0	4.0	4.0	4.0
59	Expected ending amount		54.0	50.0	46.0	42.0	38.0
60	B/S amount		54.0	50.0	46.0	42.0	38.0
61	Other (inc) dec Intangibles		0.0	0.0	0.0	0.0	0.0
62							
63	**Retained earnings**						
64	Beginning amount		200.0	261.0	337.0	429.6	535.7
65	Net to retained earnings		61.0	76.0	92.6	106.2	116.6
66	Expected ending amount		261.0	337.0	429.6	535.7	652.3
67	B/S amount		261.0	337.0	429.6	535.7	652.3
68	Other inc (dec) Retained earnings		0.0	0.0	0.0	0.0	0.0
69							
70							

CHAPTER 12

Ratios: Key Performance Indicators

At this stage, we have a model with a complete set of the three financial statements. In this chapter, we will go through the types of ratios for showing how well a company is performing and a type of presentation called "common-size" that will show the income statement and balance sheet as—in effect—nothing but ratios.

COMPARING NUMBERS AGAINST ONE ANOTHER

Once we have a complete model for a company, we can now use the numbers being produced to gain an understanding of the company. We can look at the historical numbers to have an insight into how well the company has been performing. From these, we can make forecast assumptions based on the historical trends and what we know of developments in the company's industry and see how well we think the company will perform based on these assumptions.

Numbers are most useful when we can compare them against other numbers to show ratios. For example, let's say there are two companies, each with a net income of $10 million. With just this information, the two may seem to be equals. But as the table shows, when we compare this against other

209

numbers—in this case each company's revenues—we see a different picture:

	Company A	Company B
Net income	$10 million	$10 million
Revenues	$100 million	$200 million
Net margin	10%	5%

Now the fact emerges that the second company is only half as profitable on a net margin basis as the first.

By the same token, we can have two companies, one with profits twice as high as the other. Twice as profitable? Not necessarily:

	Company C	Company D
Net income	$10 million	$20 million
Revenues	$100 million	$200 million
Net margin	10%	10%

With one company's revenues twice as high as the other, the two have the same net margin profitability, even though they are of different sizes. This illustrates another valuable aspect of ratios: They allow us to compare risk and return relationships among firms of different sizes, though with the caveat that firms with greatly differing sizes operate in different economic environments, and that such comparisons should be made with this in mind.

(In common-size statements, which we will cover a little later in this chapter, we can also look at the performance of one company across time, even if that company has gone through considerable growth.)

Different industries also have different ratio benchmarks, so it is important to limit ratio analysis to companies within an industry, but not across industries. And as you work with ratios, you should also keep in mind that companies often have some "window dressing" to make ratios look better. As a simple example, many department stores choose a fiscal year-end of January or February, when their inventory is at the lowest point after the end-of-the-year holiday sales. Companies can pay off their short-term working capital loans just before their reporting date, so that their debt ratios may be more favorable. They then draw down on their credit lines again after the reporting date passes.

NEGATIVE NUMBERS

From a modeling viewpoint, negative numbers present some problems. Here is a return on equity (net income/equity) calculation:

	Company E	Company F
Net income	$10 million	($10 million)
Equity	$100 million	($100 million)
Return on equity	10%	10%

It seems that both companies earn the same return on their equity, but obviously one is healthy while the other one is dire straits. In such a case, you may want to use an IF statement that will calculate the ratio only if the denominator is positive and, if not, return a text message of "n/a" (for "not applicable").

Here is another example, with a negative dividend payout ratio (dividend/net income):

	Company G	Company H
Dividend	$10,000	$10,000
Net income	$50,000	($50,000)
Payout ratio	20%	(20%)

A negative payout ratio does not mean that Company H has a lower payout ratio than Company G. If anything, Company H has an exorbitantly high payout ratio, as seen from the fact that it is paying out more than what it can afford, from the net income point of view.

CATEGORIES OF RATIOS

When we look at companies and their ratios, there are six broad categories of metrics. These six apply to all types of companies, but within each category, there will be measures that are more important for some industries and less so—even disregarded—for others:

- ◆ Size
- ◆ Liquidity
- ◆ Efficiency
- ◆ Profitability
- ◆ Leverage
- ◆ Coverage

Some Important Terms

EBIT, or earnings before interest and taxes, is an important number in the income statement because it represents the company's ability to generate operating earnings before interest expense (a cost related to financing decisions, not operating decisions) and taxes (a cost related to running a business in a regulated economy). This is also called *operating profit* or *operating income*.

EBITDA is earnings before interest, taxes, depreciation, and amortization of intangibles. EBITDA is useful for comparing companies within and across industries, because it does not include the effects of many of the factors that differentiate companies in different sectors, such as interest (from different financing profiles), depreciation (from different fixed asset bases), amortization (from different holdings of intangibles), and taxes (from different tax treatments). Because depreciation and amortization of intangibles are noncash expenses, EBITDA shows the amount of cash a company can generate from its operations. This is the source of cash for any interest payments, so this is a measure that a company's creditors would examine very closely.

Net debt is total debt minus cash and cash equivalents. Cash equivalents are accounts such as short-term investments or marketable securities, which can be easily turned into cash. Net debt represents the net debt load that a company has to bear after using its cash and cash equivalents. Companies with a large cash position relative to their total debt will have a negative net debt.

For Size

All things being equal, the larger the company as shown by the measures that follow, the sounder it is.

1. Revenues
2. Total assets
3. Total shareholders' equity

For Liquidity

These measures give an indication of how much of a company's cash is invested in its current assets. However, they also show how well current assets can cover current liabilities if the company had to liquidate them into cash.

1. Working capital
2. Operating working capital
3. The current ratio, or current assets/current liabilities
4. The quick ratio, or (current assets − inventory)/current liabilities

Working capital (sometimes also called *net working capital*) is current assets minus current liabilities. Working capital is a measure of the cushion that a company has for meeting obligations within the ordinary operating cycle of the business.

Operating working capital (OWC) is a nonstandard term that means current assets *without cash* minus current liabilities *without short-term debt (which includes any current portion of long-term debt).* This measure looks at how much of its cash a company uses in maintaining its day-to-day operations. The higher the operating working capital, the less liquid a company is, because its cash is tied up in accounts such as accounts receivables and inventory.

The *current ratio* is current assets divided by current liabilities. The ratio measures the multiple by which a company can use its current assets (if it could convert them all to cash) to cover all its current liabilities.

The *quick ratio* is similar to the current ratio but is a more severe ratio (the ratio will be a lower number than the current ratio) in that it takes inventory out of the numerator. Inventory is very illiquid and usually cannot be turned into cash at a moment's notice, at least without resorting to deep discounts and "fire sale" prices.

In regard to the last two ratios, both ratios are only indications since they do not include information about when the current liabilities are due. A company that can stretch its accounts payable over a longer period will have a better ability to pay its other bills than a second company with the same ratios but with a shorter payables payment period. These ratios are also more popular in credit analysis than in mergers and acquisitions (M&A) work.

For Efficiency

The ratios that follow indicate how well or efficiently a company makes use of its assets to generate sales. The first five look at the amount of balance sheet accounts that are tied up in the creation of earnings. The last two look at how well the company's assets are utilized for sales.

1. Accounts receivable/sales * 365
2. Inventory/cost of goods sold * 365
3. Accounts payable/cost of goods sold * 365
4. [(Current assets – cash) – (current liabilities – short-term debt)]/sales
   or
   Operating working capital/sales
5. Change in OWC and Change in OWC/sales
6. Sales/net fixed assets
7. Sales/total assets

Accounts Receivable/Sale * 365

Accounts receivable/sales * 365 shows how many days it takes a company to collect on its receivables. The higher the number of days, the worse its receivables management. If the company has made a sale but has not collected the money from it, it is literally extending an interest-free "loan" to that customer, tying up the cash that could be put to productive use elsewhere.

Without the * 365, the ratio shows the fraction of the year's sales that is still tied up in receivables. By multiplying the number of days in a year into the fraction, we get not a fraction, but the number of days that represents how long the average receivable remains uncollected. Thus, the result is usually called "receivable days." (You can use 360 as the number of days, but if you do so, you should use the same number whenever you are calculating portions of years elsewhere in the model.)

Receivable days that have been increasing reflect declining sales and/or a poorly managed collection system.

A similar ratio to this is sales/accounts receivable, reversing the numerator and the denominator. This is a turnover ratio, and it describes how many times receivables turn over in the year (i.e., how many cycles of receivables are fully collected in the year). The higher the ratio, the better, since it would reflect a faster receivables collection system.

Inventory/Cost of Goods Sold * 365

Inventory/cost of goods sold * 365 shows how many days it takes a company to make use of a piece of inventory. The higher the number of days, the worse it is. Like the receivable days ratio, an "inventory days" ratio shows how long a company's cash is tied up in its inventory before that inventory is put into a product and sold. A high inventory days number suggests slowing sales and/or an inefficient production system.

Sales is sometimes used as the denominator and can show the same trend. However, if there are changes in the gross margin (i.e., in the relationship between sales and cost of goods sold), then the trend shown by the ratio using sales will be different from that using cost of goods sold.

Cost of goods sold/inventory is a ratio using the same numbers but in reversed positions, and without the 365 multiplier. This is a turnover ratio; it shows the number of times that inventory is turned over during the year. Think of this as the number of times that the inventory in the warehouse is completely changed during the year.

Accounts Payable/Cost of Goods Sold * 365

Accounts payable/cost of goods sold * 365 shows how many days its takes a company to pay its suppliers. The higher the number of "payable days," the more favorable it is for the company. Not paying a supplier means that the company is able to get an interest-free "loan" from its supplier. (This is a receivables collection issue from the supplier's point of view.)

The denominator is cost of goods sold, and not sales, because the unpaid bills usually relate to purchases of inventory. In production, inventory is used up and that use is recognized as cost of goods sold.

A low payable days number means that the company has an efficient payment system, which is well and good in itself. A higher number can mean that the company has a strong enough buying power to delay its payments and still not have its suppliers abandon it. Beyond a certain limit, and this is a judgment call, a high number can mean the deterioration of its cash position, and therefore its ability to pay its bills.

Cost of goods sold/accounts payable is the payable turnover ratio. It shows how many times in the year that the company has completely repaid its suppliers.

[(Current Assets – Cash) – (Current Liabilities – Short-Term Debt)]/Sales

[(Current assets – cash) – (current liabilities – short-term debt)]/sales, or Operating working capital/sales, is an interesting ratio and bears some attention. The numerator is almost like working capital, but not quite. This is why I am using the term *operating working capital*, or OWC.

For highlighting the operating decisions of a company, working capital (or, current assets minus current liabilities) has a flaw. Because it includes cash and cash equivalents and also short-term debt—both of which are related to financing decisions—working capital gives an unclear measure of the purely operating current investments a company has to make in its balance sheet. This is understandable as the original intent of working capital is to show the *cushion* that it has for meeting its current obligations.

For this reason, it is useful to look at current assets *without* cash and cash equivalents minus current liabilities *without* any sort of short-term debt. This will show only the company's operational investments, separate from financing effects. So, operating working capital is:

Current assets − cash

− (Current liabilities − short-term debt)

= Operating working capital

Thus the ratio OWC/sales is a measure of how much each dollar of sales is tied up in the current accounts of a company's balance sheet. OWC management is critical to a company's success, especially during periods of high growth.

Companies often fail during this growth spurt because their OWC goes out of control. They run out of cash as new buildups of receivables and inventory from the increased sales—combined with additional capital expenditures for expansion—lead to a depletion of their cash holdings, even if they manage to delay their payments to suppliers.

Change in OWC from one accounting period to the next as a dollar number, and change in OWC/sales in percentage are important corollary measures of operating working capital. The dollar number is the ongoing amount that the company has to invest in its current accounts to sustain its operations. The higher the number, the more cash a company has to find and use. The ratio of the change over sales gives an indication of how well a company continues to manage these required investments as a percentage of its revenue stream. A trend of increasing percentages is a cautionary one as they reflect buildups of OWC that proportionately take up more cash than what sales bring in.

Sales/Net Fixed Assets

Sales/net fixed assets measures sales as a percentage of the net fixed assets (i.e., gross fixed assets less accumulated depreciation). The higher the ratio, the more productively a company is making use of its fixed assets. This ratio is called the *fixed asset turnover ratio*. Another name for it is the *asset intensity ratio*. In general, industrial companies have lower ratios than service companies.

Sales/Total Assets

Sales/total assets measures sales as a percentage of the total assets of the company. This is the asset turnover ratio. The higher the ratio, the more productive the company. Comparing this ratio across companies in different industries is not particularly useful, as different industries can have vastly different average levels.

For Profitability

1. Gross margin, or gross profit/revenues
2. EBIT margin, or EBIT/revenue
3. EBITDA margin, or EBITDA/revenue
4. Net margin, or net income/revenue
5. Sales/(accounts receivable + inventory + net fixed assets)
6. EBIT/total invested capital
7. Return on average common equity
8. Return on average assets

The first four items listed above are metrics within the income statement. They look at how well the company manages its expenses relative to the revenues from sales, or, alternatively, how well its pricing strategies are working. They define profitability in terms of earnings after expenses.

The final four items listed above look at earnings relative to the balance sheet for a more complete picture and show how the earnings are relative to the investments that have been made to support those earnings. They define profitability in terms of returns on investment and compare earnings to different groups of balance sheet accounts. If revenues are small compared to the amount of assets on the balance sheet, this would indicate the company is making an unproductive use of its assets.

Gross Margin

The *gross margin* shows how much as a percentage of sales the company can make after paying for the raw materials that go into sales. The raw materials expense is seen as a cost of goods sold.

EBIT Margin

The *EBIT margin* is the percentage of sales that the company can make after paying other operating expenses such as SG&A (sales, general, and administrative expenses). This is also called *operating margin*.

EBITDA Margin

The *EBITDA margin* is the percentage of sales that the company can make on the EBITDA basis, with the noncash depreciation and amortization expenses added to the EBIT measure.

Net Margin

The *net margin* is the percentage of sales that the company clears after payments of taxes.

Sales/(Accounts Receivables + Inventory + Net Fixed Assets)

This ratio shows the relationship between sales and the operating and investment assets. (Receivables, inventory, and net fixed assets are often called the *core assets*.) *Accounts receivable* is an operating investment, essentially the amount of cash "invested" in customers who have not paid for their purchases. Likewise, *inventory* represents the "investment" in the amount of goods already purchased and kept in storage ready for production. *Net fixed assets* are the capital equipment required to produce the company's products, net of depreciation.

Return on Average Common Equity

The *return on average common equity,* sometimes just called *return on equity* (ROE), is based on the *average* of the starting and ending common equity for the year. (The starting common equity is equivalent to the ending number for the prior year.) This is because the earnings accrue over the year, so the return should be calculated over the common equity level that holds over the same period. The average of the beginning and ending numbers is the best proxy for this.

Return on Average Assets

Likewise, the *return on average assets*, sometimes just called *return on assets* (ROA), uses the same approach of using an average for the denominator.

For Leverage

The following ratios measure leverage, or the amount of debt that the company has relative to investments or to its earnings flow. In either case, the higher the ratio, the higher the leverage and the higher the chances for default.

Cash is the measure of things for repaying debt, which is why EBITDA is the preferred number for leverage ratios.

1. Total debt/shareholders' equity
2. Net debt/shareholders' equity
3. Total debt/total invested capital
4. Bank debt/EBITDA
5. Senior debt/EBITDA
6. Total debt/EBITDA
7. Net debt/EBITDA

Total Debt/Shareholders' Equity

Total debt/shareholders' equity shows the ratio of debt to equity. A high ratio, within limits, is not necessarily bad. You would have to look at it in the context of the company's ability to generate cash flow to cover its debt service (interest payments and principal repayments).

Net Debt/Shareholders' Equity

Net debt/shareholders' equity is a ratio similar to total debt/ shareholders' equity. Net debt is total debt minus cash and cash equivalents. Cash equivalents are accounts such as short-term investments or marketable securities that can be turned easily into cash. Net debt shows the debt load of a company as if it has used its available cash to repay some of its debt. Companies with a large cash position relative to their total debt will have a negative net debt.

Total Debt/Total Invested Capital

The denominator is total invested capital—the combination of shareholders' equity, total debt, and minority interests.

Bank Debt/EBITDA; Senior Debt/EBITDA; Total Debt/EBITDA; Net Debt/EBITDA

These ratios with debt measures in the numerator and EBITDA in the denominator show the size of each debt measure relative to the cash operating earnings of the company. In an annual model, the EBITDA will be the annual earnings, so each ratio is a way of expressing that the debt is equivalent to so many years' earnings. If you start building models that have nonannual periods—for example, if each column contains quarterly data— these ratios will not be useful unless the quarterly EBITDA numbers are annualized. For quarterly EBITDA numbers, the easy way is simply to multiply them by 4.

For Coverage

Coverage refers to the ability of the company's cash flows to cover its interest expense or debt obligations.

1. Times interest earned: EBIT/interest expense
2. EBITDA/cash interest expense
3. (EBITDA – capital expenditures)/cash interest expense
4. Fixed charge coverage
5. Cash fixed charge coverage
6. Operating cash flow/total debt
7. Operating cash flow/net debt
8. Operating cash flow/average total liabilities

Times Interest Earned

Times interest earned (TIE) is a ratio that compares the company's EBIT to its interest expense. This ratio is important to the lending decisions made by banks. If a company has a TIE of 3.0×, this means that its EBIT is enough to pay its interest expense three times over. Put another way, EBIT has to shrink more than two-thirds before it defaults, or cannot pay its interest payments. Lending banks want to see a high ratio because it means there is less likelihood that a loan to the company will become a "non-performing" loan.

EBITDA/Cash Interest Expense

EBITDA/cash interest expense is TIE on a cash basis. EBITDA is the cash earnings that a company has. The denominator uses the interest expense that is cash, as there are forms of debt where the interest is not paid out in cash but instead added to the outstanding debt. This kind of debt is called *accreting debt*. It is also called *payment-in-kind* (or PIK, pronounced "Pick") debt. Thus, the denominator is total interest (which may have both cash and noncash interest) less noncash interest. This ratio gives an extra measure of insight for coverage analysis, because EBITDA is a more accurate measure of the cash earnings a company has for paying its interest costs.

(EBITDA − Capital Expenditures)/Cash Interest Expense

(EBITDA − capital expenditures)/cash interest expense is a coverage measure of the ability to repay cash interest based on cash earnings after what usually is a required expense: capital expenditures. Capital expenditures do not appear in the income statement by accounting convention. By subtracting these expenditures from EBITDA, the ratio shows the company's ability to pay its cash interest expense. It may be that a company can reduce or defer its capital expenditures in order to pay its interest. But if it does so, it is likely to suffer diminished productivity in the long run (as its fixed assets age and fall into increasing disrepair) and, thus, interest-paying ability.

Fixed Charge Coverage

(EBIT + rent expense)/(interest expense + preferred dividends + rent expense). This ratio is more important in analyzing retail companies.

Cash Fixed Charge Coverage

This is similar to the ratio above, but we use (EBITDA + rent expense)/(cash interest expense + preferred dividends + rent expense). The cash interest expense makes a distinction between interest payments that are cash and those that are noncash.

Operating Cash Flow Ratios

Operating cash flow is an item from the cash flow statement and is the sum of net income (the first item on the statement) plus all the addbacks of noncash expenses. Put another way, this is net income on a cash basis and represents the cash earnings after interest and taxes from operations.

COMMON-SIZE STATEMENTS

Common-size statements, which can be prepared for the income statement, balance sheet, or the cash flow statement, express a firm's performance over time as a percentage of a base number.

For the income statement, the typical base is each year's revenue number. All the other income and expense numbers shown for each year are a percentage of that year's revenue. Revenue is shown as 100 percent. In effect, the whole income statement becomes a "margin statement." By expressing all the accounts in this manner, we can see how well the company maintains its margins, even if the underlying dollar numbers have undergone sizable changes over time.

For the balance sheet, the usual base is total assets, which are shown as 100 percent. Every other account on the balance sheet, whether assets, liabilities, or equity, are then shown as percentages of this total.

In addition to providing a yardstick for comparisons across time within a company, common-size statements also provide useful information for looking at the economic characteristics of different companies in the same industry, as well as in different industries.

You can add this to the model we have developed by adding an extra sheet for each financial statement you want to show in common-size terms. An easy way to do this is to make a copy of the sheet through the Excel commands. (Double-click on the sheet tab you want to copy, right-click and select "Move or copy...," select a position among the sheets shown in the list box, check the "Create Copy" check box, then click on OK. You can then rename the duplicate sheet by clicking on the sheet tab, and typing in a new name for the sheet). Then write the formulas this way. Let's say you have just made a duplicate of the "IS" sheet, and you have renamed the duplicate sheet "ISCS" (for Income Statement Common Size.) On "ISCS," create a formula that looks to its counterpart in "IS," but with a divisor of the Revenues line for that column. For example, in ISCS cell B6 for the first year's revenues, write the formula that at its core is the calculation IS!B6/IS!B$6. Note the use of the absolute reference for the row in B$6. Because some of the rows in "IS" may be holding zeros, write the full formula as =IF(B$6,IS!B6/IS!B$6,0) so that you do not get a #DIV/0! Error when the formula encounters a zero.

In "ISCS," copy this formula down the column and across all the columns. As long as you have not made any changes to the "IS" and "ISCS" after you made the duplicate—i.e., each sheet has the same layout in rows and columns—this copying sequence can be done quickly, as you can be assured that the formula references from one sheet to the other are correct.

As you copy the formulas down, there may be some formatting that you want to keep, such as the underline before the subtotals. Make use of Excel's ability to copy only the contents of a cell (which means that the formatting of the cell you are pasting into is not affected). After the Edit>Copy command, use the Edit>Paste Special>Formulas. Then, format all the cells with the new formula in the Percent format.

As a final step, the original lines in "IS" had margin percentages. In "ISCS," you can delete these rows. The final "ISCS" sheet will be a few lines shorter than "IS."

Go through the same steps for creating a common-size balance sheet, but with the divisor for the formulas being the total assets for each column.

This is what the "ISCS" sheet will look like:

Common-Size Income Statement

	A	B	C	D	E	F	G
1	First Corporation						
2							
3					Proj	Proj	Proj
4	INCOME STATEMENT	2000	2001	2002	2003	2004	2005
5							
6	Revenues	100.0%	100.0%	100.0%	100.0%	100.0%	100.0%
7	COGS	54.5%	54.5%	55.0%	55.0%	55.0%	55.0%
8	Gross profit	45.5%	45.6%	45.0%	45.0%	45.0%	45.0%
9							
10	SGA	15.2%	15.0%	15.0%	15.0%	15.0%	15.0%
11	Operating expenses	3.0%	3.0%	3.0%	3.0%	3.0%	3.0%
12	EBITDA	27.3%	27.4%	27.0%	27.0%	27.0%	27.0%
13							
14	Depreciation	7.3%	8.3%	8.0%	7.7%	7.6%	7.7%
15	Amort of intangibles	0.5%	0.4%	0.4%	0.4%	0.3%	0.3%
16	EBIT	19.5%	18.7%	18.6%	18.9%	19.1%	19.0%
17							
18	Non-oper expenses	1.2%	1.1%	0.8%	0.9%	0.9%	0.9%
19							
20	Interest income	0.4%	0.6%	0.6%	0.7%	0.8%	0.5%
21	Interest expense	6.1%	5.6%	5.0%	4.3%	3.9%	3.7%
22	EBT	12.6%	12.6%	13.4%	14.4%	15.0%	15.0%
23							
24	Provision for taxes	4.4%	4.4%	4.7%	5.0%	5.2%	5.2%
25	Net income	8.2%	8.1%	8.7%	9.3%	9.7%	9.7%
26							
27	Dividends	1.2%	1.3%	1.1%	0.9%	1.0%	1.0%
28	Net to retíd earnings	7.0%	6.8%	7.6%	8.4%	8.8%	8.8%
29							
30							
	ISCS						

Here is the balance sheet common-size statements, based on total assets:

Common-Size Balance Sheet

	A	B	C	D	E	F	G
1	First Corporation						
2					Proj	Proj	Proj
3	BALANCE SHEET	2000	2001	2002	2003	2004	2005
4	ASSETS						
5	Surplus funds	0.0%	0.0%	0.0%	5.2%	2.8%	0.0%
6	Cash	4.6%	5.2%	5.1%	4.6%	4.3%	4.0%
7	St investments	2.3%	2.2%	2.1%	1.9%	1.9%	1.8%
8	Accounts receivable	4.6%	5.2%	5.8%	5.2%	5.3%	5.4%
9	Inventory	9.2%	9.3%	9.6%	9.3%	9.3%	9.4%
10	Other current assets	0.8%	0.7%	0.8%	0.6%	0.6%	0.7%
11	Current assets	21.5%	22.6%	23.3%	26.8%	24.2%	21.2%
12							
13	Net PPE	66.9%	65.7%	63.9%	61.8%	64.5%	67.7%
14	Intangibles	4.5%	3.7%	3.2%	2.6%	2.2%	1.9%
15	Long-term assets	7.1%	8.0%	9.6%	8.8%	9.1%	9.2%
16	Total assets	100.0%	100.0%	100.0%	100.0%	100.0%	100.0%
17							
18	LIABILITIES						
19	Short-term notes	0.8%	0.8%	0.9%	0.8%	0.7%	0.7%
20	Accounts payable	4.6%	4.8%	5.1%	5.2%	5.4%	5.5%
21	Other current liabilities	0.8%	1.4%	1.3%	1.3%	1.3%	1.3%
22	Current liabilities	6.2%	7.0%	7.3%	7.3%	7.4%	7.5%
23							
24	Necessary to finance	0.0%	0.0%	0.0%	0.0%	0.0%	1.0%
25	Debt 1	15.4%	15.5%	9.6%	8.6%	8.0%	7.4%
26	Debt 2	15.4%	13.8%	14.4%	12.9%	12.0%	11.1%
27	Debt 3	8.5%	7.6%	7.0%	6.3%	5.9%	5.4%
28	Long-term liabilities	3.1%	2.6%	2.4%	2.5%	2.6%	2.6%
29	Total liabilities	48.5%	46.6%	40.6%	37.5%	35.9%	35.0%
30							
31	SHAREHOLDERS' EQUITY						
32	Common stock	35.4%	34.6%	37.1%	37.2%	34.8%	32.1%
33	Retained earnings	15.4%	18.0%	21.5%	24.6%	28.7%	32.2%
34	Other equity account	0.8%	0.8%	0.8%	0.7%	0.7%	0.6%
35	Total SH equity	51.5%	53.4%	59.4%	62.5%	64.1%	65.0%
36	Total liabs & SH equity	100.0%	100.0%	100.0%	100.0%	100.0%	100.0%
37							
	BSCS						

CHAPTER 13

Forecasting Guidelines

This chapter goes over the principles of good forecasting—the kind that will ensure that your analysis remains in the realm of realistic estimates, rather than going off into pipe-dream silliness.

By the way, now that you have built a working model from scratch, don't forget to pat yourself on the back.

KEY PRINCIPLES

- Good forecasts must be consistent with historical performance and the current industry outlook.
- Look at historical numbers in relationship to others and use these ratios, particularly the operating ratios, to make your projections.
- All forecasts are estimates and approximations. Spend the time thinking and developing your ideas about the big picture, not the third decimal place.
- If the forecast looks too good to be true, it probably is. Re-examine your assumptions.

INCOME STATEMENT ACCOUNTS

Revenues

For industrial/manufacturing types of companies, revenues drive the other numbers in the model. Here are things to think about as you make your forecast:

- Revenues are the result of three main components: price, industry growth, and market share. Isolating the price growth from inflation will give you the measure for volume growth. Understand that in the context of the economic cycle, and then concentrate on what the drivers for future industry growth and market share might be. Add back the inflation component (typically very low at 1–2 percent in the United States) to get the full estimate of future revenues growth.

- Unless you are looking at new industries (new drugs, new telecommunications), most businesses are mature and should grow at around the growth of the economy. Gross domestic product (GDP) growth rates would be a good proxy. Your particular company's sales growth will also be affected at different points of the product cycle by new entrants and competing new technologies. Remember also that fast-growing businesses have very dramatic price and volume falls as the demand reaches a certain point. If your company does not have a position of advantage, it will lose market share, and your volume estimates must reflect that.

- If your company has product lines that have very different characteristics, it would be worthwhile to forecast the individual product lines. Where they are similar enough, it is better to think in broad aggregate terms and forecast only one revenue line. There is no need to get super precise price and volume numbers for the forecast years.

- Take into account the characteristics of the industry your company is in. Some industries have price controls or restrictions, which would limit your own forecasts.

Margin Assumptions

- Analyze the trends in the historical accounts, such as cost of goods sold as percentage of sales, SG&A (sales, general & administrative) as percentage of sales, etc. Your forecasts should be consistent with these trends, while taking into account what you know of any improvements or changes in the company's operating systems.
- If there have been striking changes in the margins, you should try to understand the reason.
- Look at the trends in the context of the economic and product cycles.

Depreciation

- Although it can be convenient to forecast depreciation as a percentage of sales, the relationship to sales is indirect. Depreciation is determined by net PPE (plant, property, and equipment), which, in turn, is affected by capital expenditures. Capex typically vary with sales.
- If some precision is required, the best way to model depreciation is to lay out the depreciation that is associated with each year's new capital investments. This will mean creating a "depreciation triangle" as shown in Table 13-1. The longer the forecast period, the "deeper" the triangle has to be. However, it is generally acceptable to use the recent relationship between depreciation and the net PPE of the prior year.
- Depreciation for tax purposes and for book purposes can be different. This will lead to the creation of deferred taxes.

Interest Income

- Look to the effective rates of interest income that the company has been paying in the historical years. You can get this information simply by looking at interest income divided by the average of the beginning and ending total interest-yielding assets. The average is used to capture the changes that have happened over the year. This may not

T A B L E 13-1

Assumptions: Ten-Year Life, with Straight-Line Depreciation

Year	0	1	2	3	4	5
Capital expenditures	80	70	100	90	110	120
Depreciation schedule of:						
Capex of year 0	0	8	8	8	8	8
Capex of year 1			7	7	7	7
Capex of year 2				10	10	10
Capex of year 3					9	9
Capex of year 4						11
Capex of year 5						
Total depreciation	0	8	15	25	34	45
Gross PPE	80	150	250	340	450	570
Accumulated depreciation	0	8	23	48	82	127
Net PPE	80	142	227	292	368	443
Dep'n % prior net PPE		10%	15.3%	19.2%	24.1%	28.2%

be the actual interest earnings rate. Many companies keep cash as an operational cushion, and it is not necessarily in the bank earning interest. However, this effective interest rate is usually good enough for projections.

♦ Interest on cash should be less than the interest on debt.

Interest Expense

♦ Companies usually pay close to market rates, so get estimates of the benchmark being used (LIBOR, Prime, etc.) and then apply a spread over that. Check with the relationship banker or the debt pricing desk about what this spread should be. Generally speaking, the bigger and, therefore, the more creditworthy the company, the smaller the spread. Spreads are usually quoted as *basis points*. One basis point is one one-hundredth of a percent. So 100 basis points is equivalent to 1 percent.

- Check also the historical effective interest rates that the company has been paying. (Remember to do so by dividing the interest expense by the average of the beginning and ending total debt.) If these rates seem very high, they may be due to seasonal borrowings. The company draws down on its line of credit during the year and, therefore, pays interest, but pays off the debt before the reporting date. The result is that there is a record of the interest expense in the income statement, but no record on the balance sheet of the debt that produced it. This is normal operating procedure, by the way, and there is nothing sneaky about it.

Taxes

- Taxes should be taxed at statutory rates, and they should also reflect local rules in effect for the company. If there are any deviations from these rates, you should try to find out the reasons why, and if they are sustainable.
- Deferred taxes occur when the provision for taxes in the book basis is different from the actual taxes paid on the tax basis. These occur usually because of different book-basis and tax-basis depreciation schedules that the company has adopted, or from net operating losses. Their complexity puts them beyond the scope of this chapter.

Extraordinary Items

- This is a tricky line since, by its very nature, items here are not easily forecast. If you have specific information about these items from the company, by all means include it. Otherwise, it may be best not to try to do any forecasts.

Dividends

The best way to forecast dividends is by multiplying the number of shares by a historic dividends per share number grown at a reasonable rate. You should watch out for the following, though:

- Use the correct number of shares, which is the *weighted average* shares outstanding. The plain shares outstanding refers to the number at the reporting date, but this does not take into account that there may have been changes in the shares outstanding over the year. It is also important to reflect the timing of the changes, which is why the weighted average number is used. Typically, this information is available in the annual reports. If you do not have this number, a proxy is to take the average of the shares outstanding at the beginning and the end of the reporting period.

- Compute the historic dividends per share numbers yourself. If they reconcile with the historic figures, then you have a good basis for using them as the basis for calculations of future dividends, plus a growth rate that roughly equals the growth of the economy and/or the industry. If they do not reconcile, it may be because of stock splits or rights issues. Companies' dividends usually grow at a steady rate, but the growth can stop if earnings go into a dip.

BALANCE SHEET

Cash

There are two kinds of cash account in the model. One is the cash that the company needs to have on hand to handle day-to-day expenses. We can think of this as "minimum cash." You can attach an interest rate to this, but more likely than not, this cash is not kept in the bank and so it is not earning interest. Because this cash also reflects operational needs, it makes sense to forecast this as a percentage of sales.

The other is the cash that is automatically produced by the model when liabilities and equity exceed assets—the Surplus funds row. You do not forecast this account directly. Rather, it is a result of the forecast assumptions you make for other parts of the balance sheet and indeed the income statement, too. (It may be that your assumptions will create a need for additional debt, in which case you would not see the Surplus funds line.) To the extent that you will have Surplus funds, make sure that you enter an interest rate.

Short-Term Investments

If your company has this account, you may want to forecast the same level going forward, without any growth. By holding it steady, you will be able to see more clearly the rate of buildup in Surplus funds or Necessary to finance.

Operating Assets and Liabilities

A large part of the balance sheet is there to support sales. As sales grow, these operating assets and operating liabilities must also grow by a more-or-less proportionate rate. As a result, you can forecast them based on a relationship to revenues in the income statement.

The operating assets are:

- Accounts receivable
- Inventory
- Other current assets
- Net PPE
- Other assets. You should check if these are related to operations or investments; if the latter, they should be forecast at some growth rate, not as a percentage of sales.

The operating liabilities are:

- Accounts payable
- Other current liabilities

You can project these items on the basis of the last historical year, but you should take into account any variations from trends that are booming or reversing. Any unusual or extreme change is a call for delving further into the information to find out what the reasons may be.

The net PPE number is a tricky one to forecast, and the forecast numbers are determined by two main flows: capital expenditures (which add to the gross PPE number) and depreciation (which flows into accumulated depreciation and reduces the gross PPE number). The production base to support sales is a function of many things, including the product being produced, the technology in place, and the scale of production. These—and other factors—represent a "habit" of the production systems in the company. The net result is a net PPE number that should have some discernible and steady relationship to sales. Thus, a good way to forecast net PPE is first to determine the net PPE to sales ratio and then to use that as the basis of forecasting net PPE. If we have a depreciation schedule, then, in fact, the capital expenditures number becomes the "plug" number in the calculation of net PPE.

Some pointers:

◆ If the latest net PPE to sales ratio is high, this probably reflects recent investments to modernize the plant. We can let this ratio trend down to the historical rates, and, as a result, future capex will also show a downward trend until the ratio meets the historical levels.

◆ If the ratio is low, this probably means that there will be a need for heavy investments soon.

◆ This measure of net assets to sales should be relatively steady over the forecast period. The logical test is to extend the projection period into perpetuity. If this ratio is trending upward, then we will have a company that will be extremely asset intensive. Likewise, if it is trending downward, we will have a company that will generate huge revenues on a sliver of a PPE base.

Other Assets

You should find out if these other assets are operating or investment assets, and then forecast them accordingly. If they are operating, you should forecast them in some relationship to sales; if they are investments, then they should grow at some rate.

Other Liabilities

These can be either operating or financing assets. You should project them accordingly. Sometimes, when you have no information, the best recourse would be to hold them steady at the last reported date levels.

Taxes Payable

You should forecast these as a percentage of current taxes. Taxes payable reflect the part of taxes not paid until the next year.

Dividends Payable

This should be forecast as a percentage of current dividends. Like taxes, a part of dividends is not paid out until the following year.

Debt

You should forecast the debt based on known amortization schedules. Where debt is being amortized, you may find that the assets side of the balance sheet is now "higher" than the liabilities and equity side. In this case, a plug debt line appears that is the Necessary to finance line in our model.

Common Stock and Other Equity Accounts

Unless you have specific information about these accounts, hold them at the level of the last historical year.

Retained Earnings

Retained earnings in the equity account should not be directly projected in the balance sheet. Instead, this should grow in the model as a result of the flows from net income, which in turn have been produced by the assumptions in use in the income statement.

CHAPTER 14

The Cash Sweep

This chapter expands on what we have done so far. At this point, you should have a working model that not only allows you to make forecasts of a company's performance, but also presents the results in a format that is GAAP consistent. Now we will add the cash sweep feature.

THE CASH SWEEP

The cash sweep allows the model to repay debt tranches automatically using the cash being generated by the earnings in your company. The cash sweep uses the Surplus funds line. It does not use the cash line in the model. As the debt is repaid, the interest expenses associated with that debt also are reduced. Having this feature means that the model will be iterating a few more cycles before it reaches convergence. However, the additional time is minimal and, given the high processor speeds available in computers now, it is not perceptible.

These are the important points to keep in mind:

1. The cash sweep works only where there is a Surplus funds amount, and the cash sweep is for projected numbers only. There are no Surplus funds in a historical year, and we would not want to have

the model start changing the historical debt outstanding numbers.

2. The cash sweep is for long-term debt only, and usually only for bank debt. Short-term debt is any debt that will be repaid within a year. So, to the extent that we define it year after year in our forecast, it means that we intend to have that debt continuously renewed. Thus, we do not need to have the cash sweep work for the short-term debt.

   The cash sweep is also used for bank debt because this is the kind of debt that can be prepaid (repaid early when funds are available) without incurring penalties. Bonds, on the other hand, have specific maturities, and there are usually penalties if they are repaid early.

3. The cash sweep feature works only if we keep to our concepts of "static" and "dynamic" numbers (see p. 130). Thus, the balancing formulas we have to use for the cash sweep must be the one where we first find the difference between the two sides of the balance sheet without the inclusion of the plug lines (Variation 1 in the balance sheet method of balancing, Chapter 7). The balancing formulas that look at the totals on the balance sheet that include the plug numbers (Variation 2) cannot work for the cash sweep.

4. Having a cash sweep does not mean that the balancing plug on the liabilities side—the Necessary to finance line—is put out of commission. The cash sweep is just an additional feature to the whole balancing mechanism that produces the Surplus funds line.

HOW THE CASH SWEEP WORKS

Let's look at a schematic of the balance sheet. On the left side, I have simplified the balance sheet to show only two distinct parts: the Surplus funds plug and all other assets. On the right-hand side, the liabilities are divided into two parts: long-term bank debt and other liabilities that are not LT bank debt. The shareholders' equity is the third part.

In a cash sweep, what we want to do is make the model take any Surplus funds and reduce the LT bank debt.

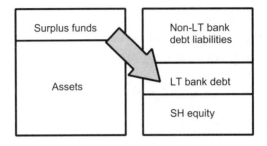

If the Surplus funds total exactly the LT bank debt, then the final result will look like this:

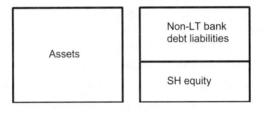

It is more likely, however, that there is not an exact match, in which case the end result will show a remaining amount of Surplus funds with no LT bank debt, or the reverse, with no Surplus funds, but with some LT bank debt remaining.

STRUCTURING A CASH SWEEP

Here are the steps for putting the cash sweep into your model. Let's assume the following facts to make the discussion a little clearer:

- Surplus funds will be 100
- LT bank debt 1 is 75
- LT bank debt 2 is 40
- LT bank debt 3 is 50

If you remember the definitions for the "static" and "dynamic" numbers (see p. 130), the following steps are directed at finding totals of the static numbers on the balance sheet for each period.

1. Find the static total for the assets side by summing:
   a. All current and long-term assets *without* the Surplus funds line.
2. Find the static total for the liabilities and equity side by summing:
   a. All current liabilities.
   b. All long-term liabilities *without* the Necessary to finance (NTF) plug and long-term bank debt.
   c. All long-term bank debt including known new additions and known amortizations over the forecast period *without* any of the automatic repayment that is the cash sweep for the current period. However, the long-term bank debt should include any cash sweep reductions from the previous period.
   d. The shareholders' equity total.
3. Find the difference by subtracting total (1) from total (2).
4. If the difference is negative, this means the model will show an NTF plug and there is no cash sweep possible for the period. The NTF plug will be the differences number, but is shown as a positive.
5. If the difference is positive, then that means that the model will show a Surplus funds plug, and this Surplus funds plug can be used to shave down the LT bank debt. In short, a cash sweep is possible for this period. In our assumptions for this illustration, we have a surplus funds amount of 100.
6. Take this starting surplus funds number and compare it with the LT bank debt 1, which is 75. Because Surplus funds are more than the debt, LT bank debt 1 is fully repaid. (We say the cash sweep is 75.)
7. Now we still have 25 of Surplus funds remaining. We apply all of this to pay down LT debt 2. LT bank debt 2 goes from 40 to 15.

8. LT bank debt 3 remains as 50. There are no more Surplus funds for the cash sweep.

9. At the end of this exercise, we connect the following numbers back up to the balance sheet:

   a. Any remaining Surplus funds number in our calculation block is referenced into the Surplus funds line on the balance sheet.

   b. Each cash sweep is referenced back to the corresponding bank debt. The bank debts shown in the balance sheet now show the reduced totals after the automatic repayments.

   c. Any NTF number is referred into the NTF line on the balance sheet.

You may be feeling quite confused now, so let's look at a simple model to see what everything would look like on the screen. The numbers are more fully fleshed out, so they are different from the simple numbers we used above. The full layout is shown below and is somewhat similar to the illustrations you have seen earlier regarding balancing the balance sheet. However, you will see that this has additional formulas for the cash sweep calculations. The inputs are also simplified as direct inputs. The intent of this illustration is to allow you to use test numbers to see the cash sweep calculations.

The gray areas shown in the model are the input cells. On the screen, these cells are marked in light yellow. But they come out as gray in a black-and-white printout.

	A	B	C	D	E
1	BALANCE SHEET	Year 1		Year 2	
2	Surplus funds plug	0	=B42	0	=D42
3	Current assets 1	200		220	
4	Current assets 2	600		500	
5	Long-term assets	800		1,000	
6	Total assets (TA)	1,600	=SUM(B2:B5)	1,720	=SUM(D2:D5)
7					
8	Necessary to finance plug	0	=B36	0	=D36
9	Current liabilities 1	80		100	
10	Current liabilities 2	80		90	
11	Debt 1	300	=B44	28	=D44
12	Debt 2	300	=B45	300	=D45
13	Debt 3	300	=B46	300	=D46
14	Total liabilities (TL)	1,060	=SUM(B8:B13)	818	=SUM(D8:D13)
15					
16	Common stock	500		800	
17	Retained earnings	40		102	
18	Shareholders' equity (SHE)	540	=SUM(B16:B17)	902	=SUM(D16:D17)
19	Total liabs & SH equity	1,600	=B14+B18	1,720	=D14+D18
20					
21	Debt 1 input	300			
22	Debt 1 before cash sweep	300	=B21	300	=IF(D21,D21,B44)
23					
24	Debt 2 input	300			
25	Debt 2 before cash sweep	300	=B24	300	=IF(D24,D24,B45)
26					
27	Debt 3 input	300			
28	Debt 3 before cash sweep	300	=B27	300	=IF(D27,D27,B46)
29					
30	Assets without SF	1,600	=SUM(B3:B5)	1,720	=SUM(D3:D5)
31	Total liabs (no NTF, before sweep)	1,060	=B9+B10+B22+B25+B28	1,090	=D9+D10+D22+D25+D28
32	Total SH equity	540	=B18	902	=D18
33	Total liabs + SHE (no NTF, bef sweep)	1,600	=B31+B32	1,992	=D31+D32
34	Difference (TL+SHE)-TA	0	=B33-B30	272	=D33-D30
35					
36	Necessary to finance	0	=-MIN(B34,0)	0	=-MIN(D34,0)
37					
38	Surplus funds before all cash sweeps	0	=MAX(B34,0)	272	=MAX(D34,0)
39	Cash sweep of debt 1	0	=MIN(B38,B22)	272	=MIN(D38,D22)
40	Cash sweep of debt 2	0	=MIN(B38-B39,B25)	0	=MIN(D38-D39,D25)
41	Cash sweep of debt 3	0	=MIN(B38-B39-B40,B28)	0	=MIN(D38-D39-D40,D28)
42	Surplus funds after all cash sweeps	0	=B38-SUM(B39:B41)	0	=D38-SUM(D39:D41)
43					
44	Debt 1 after cash sweep	300	=B22-B39	28	=D22-D39
45	Debt 2 after cash sweep	300	=B25-B40	300	=D25-D40
46	Debt 3 after cash sweep	300	=B28-B41	300	=D28-D41

Some general comments first.

The model shows two years of the balance sheet only. This is all that is needed for this first look. We will add the income statement later. For this approach, we do not need the cash flow statement.

Each year is stacked as a column, with assets at the top and liabilities and shareholders' equity at the bottom. There are only 10 items being input in each year: 3 for assets, 5 for liabilities, and 2 for equity.

I have assumed that the first year is a historical year and have made the numbers balance. There are no Surplus funds or Necessary to finance plugs. However, the balancing and cash sweep formulas that we are creating for this balance sheet will work for the first year. Once you have created this small example, you may want to change the inputs for the first year to see the cash sweep in the first year also.

The most unusual feature of the inputs is the separate inputs for the debt tranches 1, 2, and 3. Whereas all the other inputs are part of the balance sheet "block," these debt inputs are put separately below (rows 21, 24, and 27). The reason for this is that the inputs are where we specify the *starting pre-cash sweep* debt numbers. If there are any Surplus funds, then we want the cash sweep to automatically repay them to the extent possible. The debt numbers that appear as a part of the balance sheet (rows 11 to 14) are the debt outstanding *after* the cash sweep repayments.

We will connect the income statement later by (1) linking net income to the balance sheet's retained earnings and (2) linking the income statement's interest expense calculations to the final (post-cash sweep) debt numbers so that the model correctly reduces the interest as debt outstandings are reduced. The cash sweep mechanism will continue to work when you do this.

LOOKING AT THE MODEL ROW-BY-ROW

I will explain the model using the procedure laid out for building the balance sheet in Chapter 9.

Find the Static Total for the Assets Side

	A	B	C	D	E
1	BALANCE SHEET	Year 1		Year 2	
2	Surplus funds plug	0	=B42	0	=D42
3	Current assets 1	200		220	
4	Current assets 2	600		500	
5	Long-term assets	800		1,000	
6	Total assets (TA)	1,600	=SUM(B2:B5)	1,720	=SUM(D2:D5)
...					
...					
30	Assets without SF	1,600	=SUM(B3:B5)	1,720	=SUM(D3:D5)

Row 30

For each year, do a SUM function of the assets side. Make sure you do *not* include the line for the "Surplus funds" row (row 2). We want this total for the assets to be the static total—the total will not change during the balancing iterations.

Rows 21–28

These are the input rows for the starting (i.e., before the cash sweep) debt

Find the Static Total for the Liabilities

	A	B	C	D	E
7					
8	Necessary to finance plug	0	=B36	0	=D36
9	Current liabilities 1	80		100	
10	Current liabilities 2	80		90	
11	Debt 1	300	=B44	28	=D44
12	Debt 2	300	=B45	300	=D45
13	Debt 3	300	=B46	300	=D46
14	Total liabilities (TL)	1,060	=SUM(B8:B13)	818	=SUM(D8:D13)
...					
...					
21	Debt 1 input	300			
22	Debt 1 before cash sweep	300	=B21	300	=IF(D21,D21,B44)
23					
24	Debt 2 input	300			
25	Debt 2 before cash sweep	300	=B24	300	=IF(D24,D24,B45)
26					
27	Debt 3 input	300			
28	Debt 3 before cash sweep	300	=B27	300	=IF(D27,D27,B46)
...					
...					
31	Total liabs (no NTF, before sweep)	1,060	=B9+B10+B22+B25+B28	1,090	=D9+D10+D22+D25+D28

numbers. In the first year, you will notice that they are straightforward references to the input cells: row 22 simply reads the input cell on row 21 for debt 1, and so on. This ensures that the debt numbers are static and do not change with the iterations. For the second year, however, row 22 is a little more complicated. The formula in D22:

$$=IF(D21,D21,B44)$$

gives you the option of hard-coding a number for the second year. By leaving the input cell D25 blank, however, you let the model use the first year's *ending* (i.e., after the cash sweep) debt 1 number, which it takes from the cell B44. Cell B44 is not shown in this illustration.

Doesn't this mean that the formulas are now using dynamic numbers, and that we run the risk of flip-flopping as we run the calculations? No, because the key to thinking whether you are using static or dynamic numbers is whether they change during the iterations for the period they are in. For the second year, the formulas use post-cash sweep numbers from the *first* year. This means that so far as the *second* year is concerned, the formula is using static numbers.

Row 31   Add the "Current liabilities" rows (rows 9 and 10) and then add starting debt numbers (rows 22, 25, 28). Again, make sure that you do *not* include the line for "Necessary to finance" (row 8) because we want a static total. As you develop other models based on this template and you have more accounts in the liabilities, the important thing to

remember while you are creating the total
for the liabilities side is to *exclude* the NTF
line and to include only the starting debt
numbers that have been marked for the
cash sweep.

This is the total for the liabilities,
representing the static numbers (without
the NTF row) and the pre-cash sweep
debt numbers.

Find the Static Total for the Equity

	A	B	C	D	E
15					
16	Common stock	500		800	
17	Retained earnings	40		102	
18	Shareholders' equity (SHE)	540	=SUM(B16:B17)	902	=SUM(D16:D17)
...					
...					
32	Total SH equity	540	=B18	902	=D18

Row 18   This is a straightforward SUM formula
                    of the lines we have in "Shareholders'
                    equity."

Row 32   This is a direct reference to row 18, and
                    it is there for the visual proximity for
                    the next set of formulas.

Find the Difference Between (Total Liabilities + Equity) and Total Assets

	A	B	C	D	E
30	Assets without SF	1,600	=SUM(B3:B5)	1,720	=SUM(D3:D5)
31	Total liabs (no NTF, before sweep)	1,060	=B9+B10+B22+B25+B28	1,090	=D9+D10+D22+D25+D28
32	Total SH equity	540	=B18	902	=D18
33	Total liabs + SHE (no NTF, bef sweep)	1,600	=B31+B32	1,992	=D31+D32
34	Difference (TL+SHE)-TA	0	=B33-B30	272	=D33-D30
35					

Row 34   Subtract total assets (without surplus
                    funds) from the total liabilities (without
                    NTF) and shareholders' equity.

If a Negative Difference, This Is the Necessary to Finance Plug

	A	B	C	D	E
34	Difference (TL+SHE)-TA		0	=B33-B30	272 =D33-D30
35					
36	Necessary to finance		0	=-MIN(B34,0)	0 =-MIN(D34,0)
37					

Row 34   When this difference is negative, this indicates that the model is showing a funding deficit which will need to be met by the Necessary to Finance plug.

Row 36   Use the $-MIN(B34,0)$ formula (note the minus sign in front) to have the difference appear on row 36. The minus sign in the front will make this negative difference appear as a positive number. This will be referenced back into the balance sheet in the last steps in this procedure. If the calculations show an NTF plug, then there is no cash sweep to be done in the year, since the cash sweep is based on the availability of surplus funds.

If the Difference Is Positive, This Is the Surplus Funds Available for the Cash Sweep

	A	B	C	D	E
34	Difference (TL+SHE)-TA		0	=B33-B30	272 =D33-D30
35					
36	Necessary to finance		0	=-MIN(B34,0)	0 =-MIN(D34,0)
37					
38	Surplus funds before all cash sweeps		0	=MAX(B34,0)	272 =MAX(D34,0)
39	Cash sweep of debt 1		0	=MIN(B38,B22)	272 =MIN(D38,D22)
40	Cash sweep of debt 2		0	=MIN(B38-B39,B25)	0 =MIN(D38-D39,D25)
41	Cash sweep of debt 3		0	=MIN(B38-B39-B40,B28)	0 =MIN(D38-D39-D40,D28)
42	Surplus funds after all cash sweeps		0	=B38-SUM(B39:B41)	0 =D38-SUM(D39:D41)
43					

Row 38   If the difference is positive, then we can start the cash sweep process. Use the MAX(B34,0) formula to have the positive difference appear

on row 38. This is the row that shows the amount of surplus funds with which we can repay debt.

Use This Surplus Funds and Apply It for Payment of the Successive Debt Tranches

	A	B	C	D	E
38	Surplus funds before all cash sweeps	0	=MAX(B34,0)	272	=MAX(D34,0)
39	Cash sweep of debt 1	0	=MIN(B38,B22)	272	=MIN(D38,D22)
40	Cash sweep of debt 2	0	=MIN(B38-B39,B25)	0	=MIN(D38-D39,D25)
41	Cash sweep of debt 3	0	=MIN(B38-B39-B40,B28)	0	=MIN(D38-D39-D40,D28)
42	Surplus funds after all cash sweeps	0	=B38-SUM(B39:B41)	0	=D38-SUM(D39:D41)
43					

Row 39   This is the first debt on which we will be performing a cash sweep. The formula used is MIN(B38,B22), which is to say "the amount that is the lesser of (1) the surplus funds available for cash sweeps, and (2) the starting pre-cash sweep number for debt 1." We use the MIN function so that the formula does not overpay debt 1 by applying a repayment figure that is greater than the outstanding debt.

In the first year, since there are no Surplus funds, there is no cash sweep. In the second year, we see a cash sweep repayment of 272, thus reducing debt 1 to 28, from 300.

Row 40   This is the second debt for the cash sweep. In principle, we are using the same formula as the one used for debt 1, but with one difference: Because some of the surplus funds have been used to repay debt 1, the amount available for debt 1 must reflect that. Consequently, the formula is MIN(B38−B29,B25), which is to say "the amount that is the lesser of (1) the surplus funds available *less the cash sweep for debt 1*, and (2) the starting pre-cash sweep number for debt 2.

Since all the Surplus funds have been used up, there is no cash sweep for debt 2.

Row 41   This is the third debt. The formula takes into account the still reduced amount of Surplus funds available for debt 3, in this case 0. There is no cash sweep repayment possible for debt 3 in the second year.

If these lines are confusing for you, feel free to break them up into smaller "chunks" and insert more intermediate lines. This is always a good route to take when you are working with complex formulas doing many steps. For example, you can order the rows like this:

Surplus funds available for all cash sweeps

Cash sweep of debt 1

Surplus funds available for debt 2 and debt 3

Cash sweep of debt 2

Surplus funds available for debt 3

Cash sweep of debt 3

Surplus funds available after all cash sweeps

Connect the Remaining Surplus Funds, If Any, to the Balance Sheet; Do the Same for NTF

	A	B	C	D	E
1	BALANCE SHEET	Year 1		Year 2	
2	Surplus funds plug	0	=B42	0	=D42
...					
8	Necessary to finance plug	0	=B36	0	=D36
...					
36	Necessary to finance	0	=-MIN(B34,0)	0	=-MIN(D34,0)
...					
42	Surplus funds after all cash sweeps	0	=B38-SUM(B39:B41)	0	=D38-SUM(D39:D41)
43					

Row 2   In row 2 at the top of the model, write a formula that refers to the "Surplus funds" row *after* the cash sweeps.

Row 8   Likewise, in row 8, write a formula that refers to
                 the NTF row in row 36.

Calculate the Post-Sweep Debt Numbers and Connect Those to the Balance Sheet

	A	B	C	D	E
11	Debt 1	300	=B44	28	=D44
12	Debt 2	300	=B45	300	=D45
13	Debt 3	300	=B46	300	=D46
...					
44	Debt 1 after cash sweep	300	=B22-B39	28	=D22-D39
45	Debt 2 after cash sweep	300	=B25-B40	300	=D25-D40
46	Debt 3 after cash sweep	300	=B28-B41	300	=D28-D41

Rows 44–46   These three rows show the post-cash sweep debt
               numbers. They each take the pre-cash sweep
               inputs and subtract the calculated cash sweep
               numbers.

Rows 11–13   These are the rows in the balance sheet section.
               Write the references to rows 44–46 so that the
               final post-sweep numbers now appear in the
               balance sheet.

Now you can have a bit of fun changing the input numbers
so that you can test the cash sweep mechanism. The best way
to test is by increasing the liabilities and equity numbers. But
don't increase the debt numbers: remember that with the way
the balancing formulas are set up, increasing a debt number
increases the starting Surplus funds, which leads to a repayment
of the (increased) debt! Look what happens when you change
common stock in D16 to 1000.

CONNECTING THE INCOME STATEMENT

The illustration so far has excluded the income statement. You
can easily "attach" an income statement to this model. These are

the steps we will be taking:

1. Important! Turn on the Iteration setting in the calculation for the model by using the Tools>Options>Calculation tab and checking the Iteration check box, if this is not already done. You do not have to make any other changes to the default setting of Automatic calculation: a maximum number of iterations of 100, and a maximum change of 0.001.
2. Select a location in the model and create the income statement.
3. Specify interest income, interest expense, and tax rates, and set up the formulas in the income statement to make those calculations properly.
4. Link the income statement flows into the retained earnings formula in the balance sheet.
5. Introduce an error-trapping formula to ensure that error messages can clear themselves out of the model.

Turn on the Iteration Setting

It is now important that we turn the Iteration Setting on because the addition of the income statement creates interactive flows between it and the balance sheet that create circular references.

Create the Income Statement

I have added a simple income statement at the bottom of the balance sheet for ease of illustration and to keep the formula references we have been working with more or less the same. In any model you build, where you locate the income statement, balance sheet, and the cash flow statement (and other sheets) is up to you and should follow the principle of being the easiest to comprehend and interact with.

Here is the layout I have added at the bottom of the balance sheet.

	A	B	C	D	E
50					
51	INCOME STATEMENT	Year 1		Year 2	
52					
53	Revenues	250		300	
54	Expense	110		120	
55	Earnings before interest and tax	140	=B53-B54	100	=D53-D54
56					
57	Interest income surplus funds (5%)	0	=AVERAGE(0,B2)*5%	0	=AVERAGE(B2,D2)*5%
58	Interest expense NTF (10%)	0	=AVERAGE(0,B8)*10%	0	=AVERAGE(B8,D8)*10%
59	Interest expense debt 1 (10%)	30	=AVERAGE(B22,B11)*10%	16	=AVERAGE(D22,D11)*10%
60	Interest expense debt 2 (10%)	30	=AVERAGE(B25,B12)*10%	30	=AVERAGE(D25,D12)*10%
61	Interest expense debt 3 (10%)	30	=AVERAGE(B28,B13)*10%	30	=AVERAGE(D28,D13)*10%
62	Earnings before taxes	50	=B55+B57-SUM(B58:B61)	104	=D55+D57-SUM(D58:D61)
63					
64	Taxes (40%)	20	=B62*40%	41	=D62*40%
65	Net income	30	=B62-B64	62	=D62-D64
66					

Interest and Tax Rates

Rows 57–64   For interest income, the interest rate used is 5 percent, and for interest expense for debt (including the NTF debt), the interest rate used in 10 percent. The tax rate used is 40 percent.

You will notice also that I have inserted these rates directly into the formulas. I have done this as a "quick and dirty" way of creating the formulas, but for best practices, don't do it this way! Instead, we should keep these interest rates as separate inputs unto themselves in order to highlight what the inputs are, and to make quickly changing the assumptions possible by changing just that one cell.

Interest Calculations: Using the AVERAGE

Rows 57–61   For interest income and expense calculations, it is a good idea to use the AVERAGE formula to calculate the average values for the year based on the beginning and ending amounts. However, the first year is always tricky: What are the beginning amounts when there is no prior year? For Surplus funds and the Necessary to finance plugs, we can simply take the average of a starting 0 and the final number. Thus, the formula you see is written =AVERAGE(0,B2)*5% for the first year's interest income calculations for surplus funds. Admittedly, this is the long way of writing =B2/2*5% (half of the value in B2 multiplied by 5%), and it has been done this way to give a consistent form to the formula in the first and second years. The second year's formula uses the AVERAGE construction in a more expected way by taking the values from the first- and second-year columns.

The first column in a model is usually a historical year and there should not be any plugs, so the formulas we are considering here may be moot.

For the debt numbers, however, there is an additional consideration. Even in the first year, because there is a cash sweep, we do have a "prior" amount and an "ending" amount. The amount before the sweep can be assumed to be for the beginning of the year (equivalent to the ending number of a prior year). The amount after the sweep is then the amount for the end of the year. The formula for the debt lines, for example, debt 1, reflects this: =AVERAGE(B22, B11)*10%. Again, if the first year is historical, this may be a moot point. For historical years, you would have a combined interest expense number from the annual report, and you would not have to calculate it.

The Year 2 formula of =AVERAGE (D22,D11)*10% can also be written as =AVERAGE(B11,D11)*10%, as the two references of B11 and D22 refer to the same calculations.

Interest Calculations: Which Row Do We Refer To?

Row 59

For the first year, the formula =AVERAGE(B22,B11)*10% looks at cell B11 as the ending amount. If we look at cell B11, it is a reference to B44, which is the row where the post-sweep debt 1 is calculated. As a matter of good programming, we should write the formula =AVERAGE(B22,B44)*10% since B44 is where the number is first calculated. In this way, we do not ask Excel to calculate that number twice in B44 and B11 before we calculate it. But this delay is not at all important for a small model like the one we are working on, and I have written it and the other two similar debt lines this way because it helps in making the references clear.

For the second year, to keep things simple, we can also just write =AVERAGE(B11,D11)*10%.

Rows 60–61

The same applies for the other two interest expense rows for debt 2 and 3.

Link the Income Statement to the Retained Earnings

We now have to link the income statement to the balance sheet. We have already made some links in the interest calculations, but this is bringing the balance sheet data into the income statement. We have to do the same for bringing the income statement data into the balance sheet.

	A	B	C	D	E
15					
16	Common stock	500		800	
17	Retained earnings	40		102	=B17+D65
18	Shareholders' equity (SHE)	540	=SUM(B16:B17)	902	=SUM(D16:D17)
19	Total liabs & SH equity	1,600	=B14+B18	1,720	=D14+D18
20					

Row 17

The important change to make is the formula in the second year (cell D17). Rather than the input cell that we were previously working with, this is now a formula that reads the prior year's retained earnings (B17) and adds the net income line for the current year (D65) to it.

The first year remains as an input cell. In this case, we can assume that the number 40 is the sum of the net income for the first year, which is 30, plus the retained earnings of 10 from previous years. Remember, the first year in a model is usually a historical year, so it is within reason to specify the retained earnings as a hard-coded number for the year.

Add an Error-Trapping Formula

Row 34

Now to add the final touch. This is a minor change, but it is an important one, and it is something that you should always have when you are working with models with iterative calculations. This is an ISERROR error-trapping formula. I have put it in

row 38, which now looks like the
following:

For cell B34: $= \text{IF}(\text{ISERROR}(B33 - B30), 0, B33 - B30)$
For cell D34: $= \text{IF}(\text{ISERROR}(D33 - D30), 0, D33 - D30)$

Each column now has a circular reference, and the danger there is that any
error messages such as a #DIV/0! or
#VALUE! can get caught in the loop and
remain there even after the source of the
error has been removed or corrected.
When the formula encounters an error,
the ISERROR returns a 0, and this is then
read by the other formulas in the loop.
This has the effect of sweeping out the
error messages such that when the
calculation makes the full cycle and
comes to the ISERROR formula again, it
is no longer carrying the error message.
The ISERROR tests for the error, does not
find it, and so restores the formula
references again. The circular loop is
restored into working order.

CHAPTER 15

The Cash Flow Variation for Cash Sweep

When we covered the topic of balancing the balancing sheet in Chapter 7, we said there were two ways that it could be done: by looking at the balance sheet only (easier approach), or by looking at the cash flow statement (more difficult approach). A cash sweep is really a variation of a balancing exercise, but instead of creating a Surplus funds plug, we reduce debt amounts by the same amount. In Chapter 14, we looked at the cash sweep by expanding the balancing approach. In this chapter, in order to cover the subject more fully, we will look at expanding the second cash flow approach.

THE BASIC IDEA REMAINS THE SAME

For balancing the same set of company numbers, using the balance sheet method or the cash flow method will give us the same results. By the same token, the cash sweep in either approach will also give us the same results.

The basic idea remains the same: To find the available cash flow that can be used to repay debt. The available cash flow is similar to the Surplus funds plug on the balance sheet, but you need to keep in mind one difference. Because the available cash flow is derived from income statement flow and the changes in the balance sheet accounts for each year, it represents the changes for that one particular year. The Surplus funds number, on the other hand, is the cumulative total of all the changes in the balance sheet through the years.

Let's lay out another spreadsheet to show the cash sweep in this second way. The numbers we will be using will be identical to those used in the last chapter, and you will see that we will end up with the same numbers. But the layout will be quite different.

IT'S MORE COMPLICATED

Whereas we could experiment with creating a cash sweep using just the balance sheet as a start, we cannot do so in this case. In fact, we have to go the whole nine yards and include the balance sheet *and* the income statement *and* the cash flow statement. This is the same approach that would be required for merely balancing the flows. Having to work with all three statements at once to make the model run properly is the reason the cash flow approach is much more cumbersome. Nevertheless, let's plunge ahead and explore the complexity involved. It may be that you will be asked to review a model that uses this approach, and being familiar with this method will give you a head start in orienting yourself in that model.

STRUCTURING THE CASH SWEEP

The steps laid out are broadly similar to the steps laid out in the previous chapter. Again, the name of the game is to work with the static numbers as opposed to the dynamic numbers. The static numbers in this case would be the debt numbers before any cash sweep effects. As we start, make sure that you have turned on the Iteration for calculations through the Tools > Options > Calculation tab. The steps are:

1. Lay out the assets side.
2. Lay out the liabilities and equity.

3. Lay out the income statement and calculate the net income.

4. Find the available cash flow by subtracting all the changes in the balance sheet from the net income. Remember that a source of cash is from a decrease in an asset or an increase in a liability. A use of cash is from an increase in an asset or a decrease in a liability.

5. If the available cash flow is negative, then there is no cash sweep possible. The negative flow must be *added to the prior year's NTF* before it is connected to the Necessary to finance plug line in the balance sheet.

6. If the available cash flow is positive, then it is applied for repayment of the debt 1 amount. If there is any excess remaining, apply it for repayment of debt 2. Any excess after that is applied for debt 3. You must also apply the positive available cash flow for repayment of any Necessary to finance, and this may in fact be the first level of the cash sweep. More on this later.

7. Any remaining cash flow is *added to the prior year's Surplus funds amount* and then connected to the Surplus funds line.

LET'S BEGIN

Lay out the sheet in this way. The flow is:

- Assets
- Liabilities and equity
- Input for debt
- Income statement
- Cash flow

This is different from the layout we used in the last chapter, but as you work with it, I hope you will see the method in the madness. Because we will need more lines, I have split the screen into two pages.

	A	B	C	D	E
1	BALANCE SHEET	Year 1		Year 2	
2	Surplus funds plug		There is no plug here	0	=D68
3	Current assets 1	200		220	
4	Current assets 2	600		500	
5	Long-term assets	800		1,000	
6	Total assets (TA)	1,600	=SUM(B2:B5)	1,720	=SUM(D2:D5)
7					
8	Necessary to finance plug		There is no plug here	0	=D69
9	Current liabilities 1	80		100	
10	Current liabilities 2	80		90	
11	Debt 1	300	=B71	28	=D71
12	Debt 2	300	=B72	300	=D72
13	Debt 3	300	=B73	300	=D73
14	Total liabilities (TL)	1,060	=SUM(B8:B13)	818	=SUM(D8:D13)
15					
16	Common stock	500		800	
17	Retained earnings	40		102	=B17+D44
18	Shareholdersí equity (SHE)	540	=SUM(B16:B17)	902	=SUM(D16:D17)
19	Total liabs & SH equity	1,600	=B14+B18	1,720	=D14+D18
20					
21	Debt 1 input	300			
22	Debt 1 before cash sweep	300	=B21	300	=IF(D21,D21,B71)
23					
24	Debt 2 input	300			
25	Debt 2 before cash sweep	300	=B24	300	=IF(D24,D24,B72)
26					
27	Debt 3 input	300			
28	Debt 3 before cash sweep	300	=B27	300	=IF(D27,D27,B73)
29					
30	INCOME STATEMENT	Year 1		Year 2	
31					
32	Revenues	250		300	
33	Expense	110		120	
34	Earnings before interest and tax	140	=B32-B33	180	=D32-D33
35					
36	Interest income surplus funds (5%)	0	0	0	=AVERAGE(B2,D2)*5%
37	Interest expense NTF (10%)	0	0	0	=AVERAGE(B8,D8)*10%
38	Interest expense debt 1 (10%)	30	=AVERAGE(B22,B11)*10%	16	=AVERAGE(B11,D11)*10%
39	Interest expense debt 2 (10%)	30	=AVERAGE(B25,B12)*10%	30	=AVERAGE(B12,D12)*10%
40	Interest expense debt 3 (10%)	30	=AVERAGE(B28,B13)*10%	30	=AVERAGE(B13,D13)*10%
41	Earnings before taxes	50	=B34+B36-SUM(B37:B40)	104	=D34+D36-SUM(D37:D40)
42					
43	Taxes (40%)	20	=B41*40%	41	=D41*40%
44	Net income	30	=B41-B43	62	=IF(ISERROR(D41-D43),0,D41-D43)
45					

	A	B	C	D	E
46	CASH FLOW STATEMENT	Year 1		Year 2	
47					
48	Net income			62	=D44
49					
50	(Inc) dec in current assets 1			(20)	=B3-D3
51	(Inc) dec in current assets 2			100	=B4-D4
52	(Inc) dec in long -term assets			(200)	=B5-D5
53	Inc (dec) in current liabilities 1			20	=D9-B9
54	Inc (dec) in current liabilities 2			10	=D10-B10
55	Non-sweep inc (dec) in debt 1			0	=D22-B22
56	Non-sweep inc (dec) in debt 2			0	=D25-B25
57	Non-sweep inc (dec) in debt 3			0	=D28-B28
58	Inc (dec) in common stock			300	=D16-B16
59	Other inc (dec) in retained earnings			0	= D17-B17-D44
60	Available cash flow for cash sweep			272	=SUM(D48,D50:D59)
61					
62	Cash sweep of NTF			0	=-MIN(MAX(D60,0),B69)
63	Cash sweep of debt 1			(272)	=-MIN(MAX(D60,0)+D62, D22)
64	Cash sweep of debt 2			0	=-MIN(MAX(D60,0)+D62 +D63,D25)
65	Cash sweep of debt 3			0	=-MIN(MAX(D60,0)+D62 +D63+D64,0),D28)
66	Cash flow after cash sweep			0	=SUM(D60,D62:D65)
67					
68	Cumulative surplus funds			0	=MAX(D66,0)+B68
69	Cumulative necessary to finance	0	Enter 0 to start	0	=-MIN(D66,0)+B69
70					
71	Debt 1 after cash sweep	300	=B22	28	=D22+D63
72	Debt 2 after cash sweep	300	=B25	300	=D25+D64
73	Debt 3 after cash sweep	300	=B28	300	=D28+D65

General comments first:

The model shows two years, but the first year must be a historical year (i.e., one whose numbers are already balanced). This is because to find the balancing plug, we have to look at the changes in each account of the balance sheet from one year to the next. The first year's changes, without any prior years, cannot be calculated.

The model still retains the separate debt inputs shown in rows 21–28. This is constructed in the same way as the debt inputs in the previous chapter.

LOOKING AT THE MODEL ROW-BY-ROW

We will look at the model using the steps laid out.

Lay Out the Assets Side

	A	B	C	D	E
1	BALANCE SHEET	Year 1		Year 2	
2	Surplus funds plug		There is no plug here	0	=D68
3	Current assets 1	200		220	
4	Current assets 2	600		500	
5	Long-term assets	800		1,000	
6	Total assets (TA)	1,600	=SUM(B2:B5)	1,720	=SUM(D2:D5)
7					

Rows 2–6

This is a simple exercise. It is laying out the balance sheet items. For year 1, there is no plug for the Surplus funds, since we are assuming that it is a historical year. For the second year, the formula will ultimately read =D68. But at this point, since you have not set down row 68, you can leave it blank. You will complete this later. The "Total assets" is a sum of all the rows, including the Surplus funds line.

Lay Out the Liabilities and Equity

	A	B	C	D	E
8	Necessary to finance plug		There is no plug here	0	=D69
9	Current liabilities 1	80		100	
10	Current liabilities 2	80		90	
11	Debt 1	300	=B71	28	=D71
12	Debt 2	300	=B72	300	=D72
13	Debt 3	300	=B73	300	=D73
14	Total liabilities (TL)	1,060	=SUM(B8:B13)	818	=SUM(D8:D13)
15					
16	Common stock	500		800	
17	Retained earnings	40		102	=B17+D44
18	Shareholders' equity (SHE)	540	=SUM(B16:B17)	902	=SUM(D16:D17)
19	Total liabs & SH equity	1,600	=B14+B18	1,720	=D14+D18
20					
21	Debt 1 input	300			
22	Debt 1 before cash sweep	300	=B21	300	=IF(D21,D21,B71)
23					
24	Debt 2 input	300			
25	Debt 2 before cash sweep	300	=B24	300	=IF(D24,D24,B72)
26					
27	Debt 3 input	300			
28	Debt 3 before cash sweep	300	=B27	300	=IF(D27,D27,B73)
29					

Rows 8–19	This is also laying out the liabilities and equity. The only parts that need attention are rows 11–13, for the debt. Write these formulas now. Their values will appear when you complete rows 71–73.
Rows 21–28	Create this section as we did in the last chapter's model. This represents the inputs for the debt numbers *before* the cash sweep.

Lay Out the Income Statement and Calculate the Net Income

	A	B	C	D	E
30	INCOME STATEMENT	Year 1		Year 2	
31					
32	Revenues	250		300	
33	Expense	110		120	
34	Earnings before interest and tax	140	=B32-B33	180	=D32-D33
35					
36	Interest income surplus funds (5%)	0	0	0	=AVERAGE(B2,D2)*5%
37	Interest expense NTF (10%)	0	0	0	=AVERAGE(B8,D8)*10%
38	Interest expense debt 1 (10%)	30	=AVERAGE(B22,B11)*10%	16	=AVERAGE(B11,D11)*10%
39	Interest expense debt 2 (10%)	30	=AVERAGE(B25,B12)*10%	30	=AVERAGE(B12,D12)*10%
40	Interest expense debt 3 (10%)	30	=AVERAGE(B28,B13)*10%	30	=AVERAGE(B13,D13)*10%
41	Earnings before taxes	50	=B34+B36-SUM(B37:B40)	104	=D34+D36-SUM(D37:D40)
42					
43	Taxes (40%)	20	=B41*40%	41	=D41*40%
44	Net income	30	=B41-B43	62	=IF(ISERROR(D41-D43),0,D41-D43)
45					

Rows 30–44	This is similar to the layout we did in the last chapter.
Rows 36–37	These are the calculations for the interest income and expense linked to the plug lines. They are already in position in the balance sheet section, so go ahead and write these formulas. Because there are no plugs in the first year, you can simply hard-code the cells as 0 for the first year.
Rows 38–40	Just create these lines for the moment, even though they will not be calculating

correctly before everything is in place. This is one of the disadvantages of creating the balancing and cash sweep through the cash flow. Nothing will work properly until all the parts have been fitted properly together! Right now, since the debt numbers have not been reduced by cash sweeps, the interest expenses are still calculated at the maximum starting debt numbers.

Rows 41–44   Complete as shown.

Find the Available Cash Flow

	A	B	C	D	E
46	CASH FLOW STATEMENT	Year 1		Year 2	
47					
48	Net income			62	=D44
49					
50	(Inc) dec in current assets 1			(20)	=B3-D3
51	(Inc) dec in current assets 2			100	=B4-D4
52	(Inc) dec in long -term assets			(200)	=B5-D5
53	Inc (dec) in current liabilities 1			20	=D9-B9
54	Inc (dec) in current liabilities 2			10	=D10-B10
55	Non-sweep inc (dec) in debt 1			0	=D22-B22
56	Non-sweep inc (dec) in debt 2			0	=D25-B25
57	Non-sweep inc (dec) in debt 3			0	=D28-B28
58	Inc (dec) in common stock			300	=D16-B16
59	Other inc (dec) in retained earnings			0	= D17-B17-D44
60	Available cash flow for cash sweep			272	=SUM(D48,D50:D59)
61					

Rows 48–69   This is where the action happens for both the balancing and the cash sweep.

Rows 48–59   These 13 lines look at the individual accounts in the balance sheet, keep track of their changes, and show them as either a source of cash or a use of cash.

Rows 55–57   These are the changes in the debt *before* any changes that are the result of the cash sweep. This calculation is a way of identifying the static numbers that we need to work with.

Row 60   This is available cash for cash sweeps.

These 13 lines do the same job that was accomplished by five rows in the model seen in the last chapter (rows 30–34 in the illustration on page 246).

Apply the Available Cash Flow to the Cash Sweep

	A	B	C	D	E
60	Available cash flow for cash sweep			272	=SUM(D48,D50:D59)
61					
62	Cash sweep of NTF			0	=-MIN(MAX(D60,0),B69)
63	Cash sweep of debt 1			(272)	=-MIN(MAX(D60,0)+D62, D22)
64	Cash sweep of debt 2			0	=-MIN(MAX(D60,0)+D62 +D63,D25)
65	Cash sweep of debt 3			0	=-MIN(MAX(D60,0)+D62 +D63+D64,0),D28)
66	Cash flow after cash sweep			0	=SUM(D60,D62:D65)
67					

Row 60   If this row is positive, then a cash sweep is possible. If it is negative, then there is no cash sweep possible.

Row 62   This is an important line, so let's go slowly. One of the possibilities we have to consider is that there is an outstanding Necessary to finance from the previous period. As you expand this model to subsequent years, then this formula will be very important. Because the MIN function ignores blank cells, make sure you enter a 0 in cell B69 to make this formula work properly.

Essentially, the NTF becomes our fourth debt item that we need to apply the cash sweep to. We are putting NTF here so that it is the first line on which the cash sweep is applied. However, we could also place it as the fourth item, because we can rationalize that the NTF is the revolver facility that is being renewed from year to year. Consequently, under this thinking, the repayment of debts 1 to 3 would be considered more important. For this illustration, however, we will consider it as the first to be cash swept.

The formula first uses a MAX(D60,0) because we want to use the number from the available cash flow only if it is a positive number. We then use the MIN function to get the possible repayment for NTF. In the second year, the formula returns 0 because there is no NTF to be repaid.

The formula also uses a minus sign at the front, and this is true for all the repayments. Any repayment will show up as a negative number, consistent with the presentation in the cash flow statement that uses of cash are shown as negative numbers.

Row 63   This is the calculation for repaying debt 1. The formula adds the repayment amount of the previous line to the MAX(D60,0). This has the effect of reducing the available cash flow because the repayment is a negative number and adding a negative number is the same as subtracting it.

Rows 64–65   These continue the cash sweep calculations for debt 2 and debt 3.

Row 66   This is the end result of our calculations.

Calculate the Cumulative Surplus Funds

	A	B	C	D	E
66	Cash flow after cash sweep			0	=SUM(D60,D62:D65)
67					
68	Cumulative surplus funds	0		0	=MAX(D66,0)+B68
69	Cumulative necessary to finance	0		0	=-MIN(D66,0)+B69
70					
71	Debt 1 after cash sweep	300 =B22		28	=D22+D63
72	Debt 2 after cash sweep	300 =B25		300	=D25+D64
73	Debt 3 after cash sweep	300 =B28		300	=D28+D65

Row 68   We would see a 0 here if the starting total debt outstanding was more than the available cash flow, since all the available cash flow would have been used for repayment. If the starting debt was less, then there would be a remaining positive number here which would be equivalent to the increase in Surplus funds for the year.

The cash flow after cash sweep represents the *change* in available cash for the balance sheet, since it is derived by netting all the changes in the accounts in the balance sheet. Consequently, if we want to use this as a balance sheet number, we have to make it a *cumulative* number by adding the previous period's cash flow number to it. Hence the formula seen in D68 of =MAX(D66,0)+B68. The MAX function brings only the positive cash flow number into this calculation.

Calculate the Cumulative Necessary to Finance

Row 69   If the available cash flow were negative to begin with, we would see that same negative number here, since there would have been no cash sweeps to change that number. We will also have to convert this to a cumulative number by adding the prior period's negative flow.

As always when you are working with negative numbers, you have to be extra careful with the signs. This row uses only the negative number from row 66 by using the MIN(D66,0) function, but there is also a minus sign in front. This turns it back into a positive number, since this is the number that will appear

as the NTF on the balance sheet.
Consequently, when we add the previous
cumulative total (which is also a positive
number), we use a + sign.

Connect the Cumulative Plug Lines to Their Respective Rows on the Balance Sheet

	A	B	C	D	E
1	BALANCE SHEET	Year 1		Year 2	
2	Surplus funds plug		There is no plug here	0 =D68	
...					
...					
8	Necessary to finance plug		There is no plug here	0 =D69	
...					
...					
68	Cumulative surplus funds			0 =MAX(D66,0)+B68	
69	Cumulative necessary to finance			0 =-MIN(D66,0)+B69	

Rows 2 and 8   Write the reference to the lines in the cash
                        flow statement from the second year
                        onward.

Calculate the Debt Amounts After the Cash Sweep and Reference Them to the Balance Sheet

	A	B	C	D	E
11	Debt 1	300 =B71		28 =D71	
12	Debt 2	300 =B72		300 =D72	
13	Debt 3	300 =B73		300 =D73	
...					
71	Debt 1 after cash sweep	300 =B22		28 =D22+D63	
72	Debt 2 after cash sweep	300 =B25		300 =D25+D64	
73	Debt 3 after cash sweep	300 =B28		300 =D28+D65	

Rows 71–73   Write the formulas as shown. The first year
                       is not a cash sweep year, so you can
                       simply write the reference to the debt
                       inputs. For the second year and sub-
                       sequent years, the debt numbers after the
                       cash sweep are the starting numbers
                       (rows 22, 25, and 28) *less* the respective

Rows 11–13

cash sweep amounts. We use the + sign because the cash sweep amounts are already shown as negative numbers. Once you have rows 71–73, connect them back to rows 11–13 in the balance sheet.

Add an Error-Trapping Formula

As a last touch, we need to add an error-trapping formula. One good location is in the net income line, on row 44. There is no need for an error-trapping formula in the first year since there are no circular references there. For the second year, for cell D62, change it from:

$$=D41-D43$$

and just add the ISERROR function:

$$=IF(ISERROR(D41-D43),0,D41-43)$$

And we're done!

CHAPTER 16

Recording Macros

In this chapter, we begin to look at creating macros by recording our actions on the keyboard or via the mouse. Macros are automated sequences that you can launch whenever you want, so that you do not have to keep typing in the keystrokes yourself. Macros can be used to replicate any command sequences, and they use Excel's VBA programming language. At higher levels of programming, they can be made to operate other levels of Excel and interact with outside sources of data, for example. But don't worry, we will not go off that deep end in this chapter.

You can create a macro by writing the code for it, or you can have Excel automatically write the macro for you by setting it in a mode to record your keystrokes. We will get a little more deeply into macros in Chapter 19, but, even so, we will only be dipping our toes into the subject, as VBA is a subject that can fill volumes in its own right.

We will examine the steps for

- Recording a macro
- Running it again
- Looking at the macro itself

WHEN TO USE A RECORDED MACRO

A recorded macro gives a quick no-fuss way of getting some automation into your worksheet. You should use it when the model is fairly simple and is static: All the rows are fixed and you know the exact locations of the data points you want to work with, whether in copying and pasting, changing fonts or formats, or printing. If this is so, with the addition of on-screen controls (Chapter 17), you can get your basic model to look and function with more flourish.

RECORDING A MACRO

Let's start with a new file so that we can experiment to our hearts' content without jeopardizing anything that we have done.

Turn on the Recording Mode

Go to Sheet 1 first. Then do the sequence Tools > Macro > Record New Macro. You will see the dialog box shown as Figure 16-1 pop up in the middle of your screen.

You can leave everything as it is and just click on OK to begin recording your macro, but I want to point out something about the "Shortcut key" field.

F I G U R E   16-1

The "Shortcut key" entry is something that will enable you to launch this macro again just by pressing the Ctrl key and the key you specify here. The key that you specify can be lower case or upper case. You will see that if you enter in upper case letter, the sign will read Ctrl + Shift, and, in fact, you will have to press the additional Shift key to get to the upper case character.

Whenever you specify shortcut keys, be careful that you do not specify a letter that is already used by Excel. For example, the following keys are used by Excel in combination with the Ctrl key. (I have used the lowercase letter to indicate that you do not need to apply the Shift key.)

a	To select everything in the sheet; equivalent to clicking on the corner where the column letter A and the row number 1 meet
b	Apply bold type
c	Copy
f	Find
h	Find and replace
i	Apply italic type
n	Insert new worksheet
o	Open file
p	Print
s	Save
u	Apply underline format
v	Paste
x	Cut
y	Redo
z	Undo

If you do use one of these letters for a shortcut key, the native command in Excel will be overridden by your shortcut setting. A good approach you can use to avoid this kind of mix-up is to use the Ctrl + Shift combination, since none of the shortcuts in Excel uses this combination.

F I G U R E   16–2

Let's put the combination Ctrl + Shift + T in the dialog box shown as Figure 16-2. This will allow us to run this macro again just by pressing this combination. You can set (and reset) this shortcut key combination later on, by the way.

Enter These Steps

Click on OK. Now the recording mode is on. Let's do the following:

1. Go to cell C1 and enter 10.
2. Go to cell C2 and enter 20.
3. Go to cell C3 and enter 30.
4. Go to cell C5 and enter =SUM(C1:C3).
5. Copy the range C1:C5 to Sheet2, cell D1.
6. Go to Sheet2 and apply the Bold and Italic formats to cell D5.
7. Go to Cell A1.

Stop the Macro Recording

Stop the macro recording by going to Tools > Macro > Stop Recording.

Let's Check What We Did

Did we record the macro properly? Let's check by deleting all the entries in Sheet1 and Sheet2. Go back to Sheet1 and put the cursor anywhere. Now press the shortcut key combination Ctrl + Shift + T. Voilà! The two sets of numbers we recorded are run again, appearing once more.

RUNNING THE MACRO WITHOUT A SHORTCUT KEY

If we had not specified the shortcut key, running the macro again would require the following sequence: Tools > Macro > Macros. You will then see the dialog box in Figure 16-3.

Select the macro you want to run. In this case, there is only one and it is already highlighted. Then click on Run.

F I G U R E   16–3

Setting (and Resetting) the Shortcut Key

This dialog box will also give you the option of setting a new shortcut key or changing one that you have already assigned. Click on the Options button at the lower right-hand corner to see the dialog box in Figure 16-4. Type in the new shortcut key letter you want.

TURNING ON THE VB TOOLBAR

If you are going to do a lot of work with recording macros, or with the VBA code later on, it helps to have the Visual Basic toolbar visible in the toolbars at the top of the screen. Do the sequence View > Toolbars > Visual Basic and the Visual Basic toolbar will appear in the middle of the screen. It is shown in Figure 16-5.

You can drag this into the toolbar section and park it there. The important controls for what we need are the arrow key (▶), which is the icon to run a macro, and the circle (●), which is the record macro icon. When the recording mode is on, the circle will change to a square (■), which is the stop recording icon.

F I G U R E   16–4

F I G U R E 16–5

LOOKING AT WHAT WE RECORDED

Let's look at what we recorded. To do that, we have to go to the Visual Basic Editor (VBE). Every Excel file has two parts to it: the worksheet part, which is the worksheet part everyone sees when Excel first opens up on the computer screen, and the VBE, which can hold the VBA code.

Let's Go to the VBE

To go to the VBE, use either one of these steps:

- Tools > Macro >Visual Basic Editor

  or
- Alt + F11

Once you do this, you will see the screen that appears as Figure 16-6.

PARTS OF THE VBE

There are three main areas in the VBE:

1. Top left corner: This is the **Project Explorer** window, which shows you the items that the VB Editor has. If you do not see this window on your screen, or if you inadvertently closed it by clicking on the X box at its top right corner, you can make it reappear by going through this sequence *in the VB Editor* (and not in the worksheet part): View > Project Explorer.
2. Bottom left corner: This is the **Properties** window. It will show the properties of the item being highlighted in the Project Explorer window. To make this window appear if it is not there, use: View > Properties Window.
3. Right side of the screen: This is the **Code Editor** window. This is the window that will show the macros

F I G U R E   16–6

and where they can be edited. To make this window
appear if it is not there, use: View > Code.

Moving Between VBE and the Worksheets

Note that on the taskbar at the bottom of the screen, there are
now two buttons representing the active components of Excel:
the worksheet part and the VBE part.

You can now move between these two parts of the file by
simply clicking on a button. If you are in VBE, clicking on the
worksheet button will shift you there, and the VBE will remain
active—but in the background. When you want to go back to the
VBE again, click on the taskbar button for the VBE and you are
back there again.

If you are in the VBE and you press Alt + Q or you click on the X at the top right of the screen, you will close the VBE and then be back in the worksheet part. Of course, if you do it this way, if you want to get back to the VBE, you will have to restart it.

READING THE CODE WE RECORDED

Click on the Modules in the Project Explorer window, and then on Module 1 (see Figure 16-7). You will see the code appear in the Code Editor window on the right. Here is what it looks like:

```
Sub Macro1 ()
'Macro1 Macro
'
'Keyboard Shortcut: Ctrl + Shift + T
        '
  Range ("C1").Select
  ActiveCell.FormulaR1C1 = "10"
  Range ("C2").Select
  ActiveCell.FormulaR1C1 = "20"
  Range ("C3").Select
  ActiveCell.FormulaR1C1 = "30"
  Range ("C5").Select
  ActiveCell.FormulaR1C1 = "=SUM(R[−4]C:R[−2]C)"
  Range ("C1:C5").Select
  Selection.Copy
  Sheets ("Sheet2").Select
  Range ("D1").Select
  ActiveSheet.Paste
  Range ("D5").Select
  Selection.Font.Bold = True
  Selection.Font.Italic = True
  Range ("A1").Select

End Sub
```

F I G U R E 16–7

At first glance, this looks like gobbledygook. But just a little study will reveal how it works. VBA code is wonderful in one aspect: its code is reasonably close to normal English language. So let's try to decipher it line by line. Here is the translation in plain English of what each line means:

Range("C1").Select	Select cell C1.
ActiveCell.FormulaR1C1 = "10"	In the active cell (i.e., the one that we just selected, C1), enter the formula "10." Because there is no equal (=) sign within the double quotes, the code enters the number 10 in this cell.
Range("C2").Select ActiveCell.FormulaR1C1 = "20"	Select cell C2. In the active cell (C2), enter the number 20.
Range("C3").Select ActiveCell.FormulaR1C1 = "30"	Select cell C3. In the active cell (C3), enter the number 30.

Range("C5").Select	Select cell C5.
ActiveCell.FormulaR1C1 = "=SUM(R[-4]C:R[-2]C)"	This code writes the formula that begins with =SUM and then defines the rows from 4 rows above C5 to 2 rows above C5 and adds the closing parenthesis. If you remember, we were writing a formula for SUM(C1:C3).
Range("C1:C5").Select Selection.Copy	Select the range of 5 rows, and Copy.
Sheets("Sheet2").Select Range("D1").Select ActiveSheet.Paste	Select Sheet2, and then select D1 and Paste.
Range("D5").Select Selection.Font.Bold=True Selection.Font.Italic=True Range("A1").Select	Go to cell D5, apply Bold and Italic formatting, and then go to cell A1.

By the way, this macro has a shortcoming that you may or may not have noticed. Remember that the series of actions we were recording was about writing some simple formulas on Sheet1 and then copying them onto Sheet2. However, because we were already on Sheet1 when we started recording, the macro has no line that says

```
Sheets("Sheet1").Select
```

Consequently, if you were on another sheet and you launched the macro, the first block of formulas would be written on that active sheet, and not on Sheet1.

We can remedy this situation by adding our own code at the very top of this code. Just add the line at the very top of the macro so that it looks like what you see below. You can add a comment at the end of the line by first typing an apostrophe before entering your comments. The apostrophe tells VBA to disregard any text that follows it. You can write a whole line as a comment; just enter the apostrophe at the very beginning of the line. Once you have this line in, you can be anywhere in the file and the macro will write the formulas only on Sheets1 and Sheets2.

```
Sub Macro1 ()
'Macro1 Macro
'
'Keyboard Shortcut: Ctrl+Shift+T
'
    Sheets("Sheet1").Select 'This is the new line
      we are adding
    Range("C1").Select
    ActiveCell.FormulaR1C1 = "10"
    Range("C2").Select
    ActiveCell.FormulaR1C1 = "20"
    Range("C3").Select
```

EDITING THE CODE WE RECORDED

Once you have seen the recorded VBA code, you may notice that it gets to be repetitious. In fact, it is, and that is the result of the recording system that is transcribing in the most accurate way possible all the steps that you are specifying from the keyboard. When you do write your own code, you can directly write the code in a way that is more streamlined than what the VBE is producing.

Following are some beginning hints on streamlining the code.

Entering Values into a Cell

```
    Range("C1").Select
    ActiveCell.FormulaR1C1 = "10"
```

The two steps described here involve bringing the cursor to the cell, and then entering a value into it. In VBA, you can enter a value directly into a cell without selecting it, so this could be simplified into:

```
    Range("C1").FormulaR1C1 = "10"
```

An even simpler way to do this is to write:

```
Range("C1").Value = "10"
```

Anytime you wish to specify a value, Value will work as well as FormulaR1C1. You can even simplify it further and write Range("C1") = "10" but it is better as a programming style to specify what it is you want with that Range. In this case, let "the value of the Range be" x, so you should always specify Value. By the way, you should also use Value even if you are entering text. That's a "value," too, according to VBA.

Writing Formulas

The recorder constructs the code based on relative addresses. This is why you see

```
"=SUM(R[-4]C:R[-2]C)"
```

which describes the action of highlighting a range 4 rows to 2 rows above (notice the negative sign) the current active cell. If you know the range that you want to specify, then

```
Range("C5").Select
ActiveCell.FormulaR1C1 = "=SUM(R[-4]C:R[-2]C)"
```

could be rewritten as:

```
Range("C5").Value = "=SUM(C1:C3)"
```

Notice that we use Value even for writing formulas. To write a formula, start with an equals (=) sign and then write the formula within the double quotes. The code literally enters into the cell whatever it is told to, so in this case, with the beginning equal sign, it is writing the format that is required for entering formulas.

Copy and Paste

As already shown, we can shorten the Copy part from

```
Range ("C1:C5").Select
Selection.Copy
```

To something like this:

```
Range ("C1:C5").Copy
```

The next step specifies a different sheet. It's best to leave it as is for the moment:

```
Sheets ("Sheet2").Select
Range ("D1").Select
ActiveSheet.Paste
```

Other Tricks

When you see lines of code that look similar at the beginning and vary in the latter parts, you can use the With structure to make the code simpler and also faster to run. The best way to explain it is to show what it looks like before and after. Here it is before:

```
Range("D5").Select
Selection.Font.Bold=True
Selection.Font.Italic=True
```

Let's make the change that we already know how to make, to create a final form that is more apparent:

```
Range("D5").Font.Bold=True
Range("D5").Font.Italic=True
```

And here it is the final form:

```
With Range("D5").Font
    .Bold=True
    .Italic=True
End With
```

The With statement abbreviates all the identical references you have to specify for working with particular items in Excel and allows you to specify the actions on the different parts without specifying those references again. It's a great way to make the code simpler and easier to read, and also to make it run faster. The rule of thumb is that the fewer dots you see in the code (more specifically, they are called "dot operators"), the less time VBA needs to run through it.

Commenting

I mentioned that you can write descriptive comments in your code by entering an apostrophe and then writing the text after that. Comments are great for reminding you what the code is doing. You may think that you do not need comments as you will remember the purpose of the code, but it is easy to forget even your own genius in the code!

There is another use of the comment apostrophe, by the way: If you need to turn off code, simply put an apostrophe in front of it and it will be ignored by VBA.

CHAPTER 17

On-Screen Controls

A quick way to make your models more user-friendly is to put controls on the screen to allow the user to activate different settings or launch to macros to do various tasks. This chapter will show you how to use these on-screen controls.

THE CONTROL TOOLBOX

To place these controls—or more accurately—these control objects on the screen, use the Control Toolbox toolbar. This will appear in the middle of the screen when you select View > Toolbars and then select Control Toolbox. Under the View > Toolbars menu is actually another toolbar called the Forms toolbar, but you should not use this because it is the set of controls for versions of Excel earlier than Excel 97.

The Control Toolbox toolbar is shown in Figure 17-1.

You can reshape this so that it is a horizontal box. In any form, you can also just drag it up into the toolbar area and park it there.

The Control Toolbox gives you the controls that you can place on the screen, as well as other buttons for manipulating them.

How to Place a Control Object on a Sheet

Click on the control you want, then find a location on the worksheet. Click again and then drag to define the size of the control.

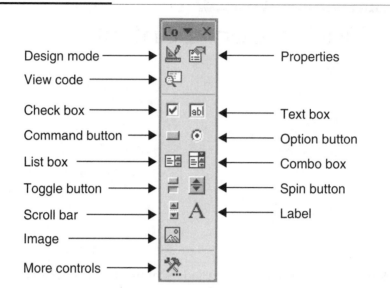

Release when you have the dimensions you want. Use the mouse again to readjust if necessary.

Design Mode

As you place a control on the sheet, the Design mode icon at the top left of the Control Toolbox toolbar will show that it has been activated: it has the appearance of being in a depressed position with borders around it. Once the control is in place and has been sized to what you want, turn off the Design mode by clicking on it again. This locks the control so it cannot be changed.

Later on, if you need to edit the control again, press the Design mode to put you in the edit mode.

Control Properties

Each of the controls has a set of properties associated with it. When you are designing the control, you can see its properties by clicking on the Properties icon on the Control Toolbox, or by right-clicking on the mouse when it is placed over the control.

Figure 17-2 shows what the Properties window looks like for the check box control.

CONTROLS TO KNOW

Check Box

A check box is used to show a choice, and typically it is either checked or unchecked. In the Design mode, show the Properties window. The properties you should work with are the following:

Caption: This is the text that will be shown as the check box description.

Value: This shows the state of the check box. It this is TRUE, it means that the check box is checked. If it is FALSE, it means it is unchecked.

LinkedCell: This is the location, either a cell address or a range name, that stores the value of the check box. When the check box state changes, so does the value of the linked cell, and this provides the direct link between this control and whatever IF formulas you have on the worksheet that will be driven by this. It also works the other way: if you change the value in the LinkedCell, then the check box will change also.

Text Box

This is a way to type text into a predefined area. You can set this text box control as part of a group of other controls that form a "control panel" in your model. Anything entered in the text box is automatically entered into a cell that you have identified as the LinkedCell. The properties you should work with are the following:

Text: This sets or shows the text in the control.

Multiline: If TRUE, the control will display text in multiple lines.

MaxLength: Enter 0 to allow any number of characters. Otherwise, enter an integer to set the maximum number of characters for the control.

LinkedCell: This is the cell that will store the Text property of the text box. Likewise, the text in this cell will determine what will appear in the text box.

Command Button

This is a button that typically is used to run a routine with a click of the mouse. The properties to work with are the following:

Caption: This determines what text is displayed in the button.

Picture: This allows you to display a graphic image on the button.

TakeFocusOnClick: When something in Excel is ready to receive input from a mouse or keyboard, that object has "focus." This property is best set to False for command buttons, so that other Excel objects can be accessed during a click of the command button.

Since there is usually a routine associated with the command button, once the button is set on the sheet and while it is still in the Design mode, click on the View Code icon in the Control Toolbox. This will show you the Visual Basic Editor, and it will show you where the code associated with the command button is located. Since no code has been written, at the start all you will see will be the lines:

```
Private Sub CommandButton1_Click()
[Empty. Macro goes here]
End Sub
```

CommandButton1 is the default name if this is the first command button control that you are setting up. The CommandButton1_Click means that with a click of the mouse on this button, the macro that appears here will run. If you have recorded a macro, you can copy that macro into the marked space.

Option Button

The option button also has the name "radio button." Like the check box, an option button gives either a selected or unselected state. However, unlike the check box, a group of option buttons can be linked together and work in a mutually exclusive way: if one option button is selected, then the others automatically unselect themselves.

By default, all the option buttons on a sheet will work together in this way. However, you can create different groups of option buttons so that they are mutually exclusive only within those groups that you have defined. There is no limit on the number of option buttons that can work together in a group. The properties to work with are the following:

Caption: This is the text that appears next to the option button.

GroupName: Enter a string to identify which mutually exclusive group the option button belongs in. By default, the group name is the name of the worksheet.

Value: TRUE means that it is selected; FALSE means that it is not.

LinkedCell: This can be a cell address or a range name and is the cell that holds the state of the option button. Each option button should have its own LinkedCell. You can then set your worksheet formulas to follow the setting established by the group of option buttons.

If you have three option buttons, what is the best way of translating the settings of the three LinkedCells into a value that can be used by, say, an IF formula? One way is to multiply the value of the first LinkedCell by 1, the second by 2, and the third by 3. Column D below shows the results of doing this. (Column E is used to illustrate the formulas used in column D.) Remember that TRUE has a value of 1 and FALSE has a value of 0 and they can be used in formulas. So in this set of TRUE/FALSE values from the selection of option button 1, we would have TRUE*1 = 1,FALSE*2 = 0, and FALSE*3 = 0. We sum these three calculations columns and get the value of 1. The selection of Option 2 and Option 3 would give 0 + 2 + 0 = 2 and 0 + 0 + 3 = 3, respectively. So in this way, we can use the SUM cell as the driver for any IF formulas that need to derive their condition from the LinkedCells. This approach would work for an unlimited number of LinkedCells.

	A	B	C	D	E
1	LinkedCell1	TRUE	1	1	=B1*C1
2	LinkedCell2	FALSE	2	0	=B2*C2
3	LinkedCell3	FALSE	3	0	=B3*C3
4				1	=SUM(D1:D3)

List Box

The list box control allows you to select an item from a list. The control can reference a large range of choices, and you can access the entire list through the arrow buttons that appear on the right side of the list box. The number of items that appear on the list is a function of the vertical size for the list box, which can be easily changed by manipulating the sizing handles. The properties to work with are the following:

ListFillRange: This is a range on the worksheet to which the list in the list box is referenced. This can be an address or range name.

LinkedCell: This is the cell that stores the selection from the list. The selection is also the Value property of the control.

MatchEntry: This determines how you can select from the list. In addition to using the scroll bar and then selecting from the list, you can also just type into the list box. The settings here will allow different ways of selecting the item you want. Suppose you have the names "New Jersey," "New Mexico," and "New York" in the list, and you want to select "New York." This is what you need to type to get to "New York" quickly:

```
FmMatchEntryFirstLetter   Type "N" three times.
FmMatchEntryComplete      Type "New Y."
```

Combo Box

The combo box is similar to the list box. However, it begins as only a one-line entry, but with a drop-down list box that is set by the ListRows property and not just sizing the control like the list box. Additionally, you can set the combo box to accept an entry that is not on the list of items linked to the combo box. In effect, this gives you a way to specify a new item on the fly. However, that new item remains excluded from the list of items. The properties to work with are the following:

ListFillRange: This is a range on the worksheet to which the list in the list box is referenced. This can be an address or range name.

ListRows: This is the number of items that will appear in the drop-down list.

LinkedCell: This is the cell that stores the selection from the list. The selection is also the Value property of the control.

MatchEntry: This property is the same as for the list box.
Style: Select FmStyleDropDownList and the combo box
will behave in the same way as a list box. Select
FmStyleDropDownCombo for the combo box to accept a
user entry into the control. This is assigned to the Value
property, but does not become part of the list.

Toggle Button

Although the toggle button looks like a command button, it is
most similar in function to the check box. The toggle can show
an on (TRUE) state and an off (FALSE) state. When it is on, the
button appears as if depressed. The properties to work with are
the following:

Caption: This is the text that is displayed on the toggle
button.
Value: Sets or returns the state of the control. TRUE
indicates depressed; FALSE indicates up.
LinkedCell: This is the cell that stores the Value. The
setting here also determines the state of the toggle button.

Here is a little bit of fun in macro writing that you can put
behind a toggle button. This assumes that ToggleButton1 is the
name of the control you are working with:

```
Private Sub ToggleButton1_Click()
    With ToggleButton1
        If .Value = True Then
            .Caption = "Turn OFF toggle"
        Else
            .Caption = "Turn ON toggle"
        End If
    End With
End Sub
```

We have not gone over any VBA code, so I will just ask you
to enter the above by clicking on the View Code icon while in the
Design mode for this control. When you get out of the Design

mode and start clicking on the toggle button, you will see the caption change, depending on the state.

Spin Button and Scroll Bar

The spin button and scroll bar are similar. They are controls to give you a quick way to vary values over a particular range. The spin button is less visually informative, because it is a set of buttons with up and down arrows. There is no indication of the range of values that you are working in if you are not already familiar with it. The scroll bar, however, is a bar with a slider, so that you can see the range. Moreover, the scroll bar allows you to adjust the value you want by either manipulating the slider bar, or by clicking on the end of the scroll bar that you want to move toward. For both of these, the properties to work with are the following:

Max: The maximum value. This must be a positive integer or zero.

Min: The minimum value. This must be a positive integer or zero. It must be less than the value set in Max.

Value: The current value of the scroll bar or the spinner.

LinkedCell: The cell that stores the Value property.

Label

Label is used for displaying static text, which is specified in the Caption property.

Image

Image is used to displaying images. You can have the image appear in this control by going to the Picture property in the Properties window. Click on that and a small button with three dots "..." appears. That is the "browse" button that will give you the Explorer to find the image you want to insert.

Frame

Frame is a control that is actually used only on user forms, which we are not covering. To draw a frame around controls just to visually group them together, use the group box control in the old Forms toolbar.

CHAPTER 18

Bells and Whistles

In this chapter, we will consider some more of the additional features—the "bells and whistles"—to make our financial model more functional.

A CAVEAT

When it comes to a model that you are sharing with others, you should consider carefully before you add more features to a core model that is already working well. Will the new features make the model run better and/or make it easier to operate? Sometimes, new features can mean new confusion for your users, who are used to doing things in a certain way. (And some of your users may prefer that they themselves add what they want to a bare-bones core model.) Even if the feature does make the model work better for the next user, adding more things also means there are more things that can go wrong.

If the model is for your own use, these concerns do not matter as much, since you will be your own judge of what makes sense and what doesn't.

In any case, as you make changes and add new features to a model that already works well, make sure you save the model under a different name after each successful modification. In this way, if you should decide to unwind a change that you have made, you can simply retrieve the last saved version from which to experiment again.

SCENARIOS

As you use the model for analysis, you will reach a time when you need to have different scenarios run through the model in order to test the possible outcomes given changes in your forecast assumptions. Usually, there are three types of scenarios that you would want to look at: the base case, the high case, and the low case.

It is not critical that we change every account in the model for the three scenarios. We need only to look at the main accounts that most affect the model's outcomes. In our model, there are only seven such accounts, called *drivers*:

- Sales
- COGS
- SGA
- Accounts receivable
- Inventory
- Capital expenditures
- Accounts payable

These seven drivers set a company's profitability and cash needs. The simplest arrangement is for all seven to move in tandem following one setting, called a *toggle*, and that is what the following illustration will show. If you want to have more possibilities, you can set seven toggles, one for each of the drivers, so that you can get permutations of combinations (base case on sales, but high case on COGS, low case on SGA, etc.). From an analysis point of view, however, this may be overdoing things. Remember, the numbers we are working with are assumptions, and there is very little to gain from putting in details that go beyond a broad-brush approach.

In the basic model, each one of the drivers has more than one input row, so as we develop scenarios, we should have the same number of rows. Here are the steps we must follow in order to have the scenario feature. We will be making these changes in the Input sheet, where each of the driver outputs will be calculated.

The resulting outputs will flow as before to the output sheets (IS, BS, etc.), so we won't need to make any changes on those sheets.

1. Set a cell that is the toggle.
2. Insert extra rows above each of the driver accounts.
3. Change the formula that reads the inputs so that it reads three scenario inputs based on the toggle setting.

Set a Cell That Is the Toggle

	A	B	C	D	E	F	G
1	First Corporation						
2	Scenario	1					
3					Proj	Proj	Proj
4	INCOME STATEMENT	2000	2001	2002	2003	2004	2005
5							
6	Revenues	825.0	900.0	1,000.0			
7	Percent growth %	Na	9.1%	11.1%	10.0%	10.0%	10.0%
8	Revenues	825.0	900.0	1,000.0	1,100.0	1,210.0	1,331.0
9							
10	COGS	450.0	490.0	550.0			
11	As % revenues	54.5%	54.4%	55.0%	55.0%	55.0%	55.0%
12	COGS	450.0	490.0	550.0	605.0	665.5	732.1
13	Gross profit	375.0	410.0	450.0	495.0	544.5	599.0
14	Gross margin	45.5%	45.6%	45.0%	45.0%	45.0%	45.0%
15							
	Input						

Here is the top section of the Input sheet. Let's select the cell B2 as the input cell and type the label next to it. We can also put a yellow shading to the cell (or whatever color you have been using to indicate an input cell).

Insert Extra Rows Above Each of the Driver Accounts

We will insert two more lines so that there are three growth percentage input rows, one for each of the scenario cases. The additional rows will be only for the forecast periods, since the historical periods do not need any alternative set of numbers. (Historical data are historical data.)

We could ponder here whether we need to "double up"—to have three couples of input rows, with each having a row for hard-coded inputs and a row for the percentage growths. This would be nice to have only if you were certain that you would be using this model to replicate another model's (precalculated) scenario numbers. For our model, however, we will keep to a simple design. Here is what the screen will look like, just for the revenues section:

	A	B	C	D	E	F	G
1	First Corporation						
2	Scenario	1					
3					Proj	Proj	Proj
4	INCOME STATEMENT	2000	2001	2002	2003	2004	2005
5							
6	Revenues	825.0	900.0	1,000.0			
7	Percent growth %	na	9.1%	11.1%	10.0%	10.0%	10.0%
8	Percent growth %				20.0%	20.0%	20.0%
9	Percent growth %				5.0%	5.0%	5.0%
10	Revenues	825.0	900.0	1,000.0	1,100.0	1,210.0	1,331.0
11							
	Input						

Change the Formula So That It Can Read the Three Scenario Inputs Based on the Toggle Setting

Now the magic begins for the scenario modeling. We need only to change the formulas for column E onward.

	A	B	C	D	E	F	G
1	First Corporation						
2	Scenario	2					
3					Proj	Proj	Proj
4	INCOME STATEMENT	2000	2001	2002	2003	2004	2005
5							
6	Revenues	825.0	900.0	1,000.0			
7	Percent growth %	na	9.1%	11.1%	10.0%	10.0%	10.0%
8	Percent growth %				20.0%	20.0%	20.0%
9	Percent growth %				5.0%	5.0%	5.0%
10	Revenues	825.0	900.0	1,000.0	1,200.0	1,440.0	1,728.0
11							
12	COGS	450.0	490.0	550.0			
13	As % revenues	54.5%	54.4%	55.0%	55.0%	55.0%	55.0%
14	As % revenues				54.0%	54.0%	54.0%
15	As % revenues				57.0%	57.0%	57.0%
16	COGS	450.0	490.0	55.0%	648.0	777.6	933.1
17	Gross profit	375.0	410.0	450.0	552.0	662.4	794.9
18	Gross margin	45.5%	45.6%	45.0%	46.0%	46.0%	46.0%
	Input						

E10   =IF(E6,E6,D$10*(1+CHOOSE($B$2,E7,E8,E9)))
                       Copy this cell across to column G.
                       The formula looks to the hard-coded revenue
                       entry first, and if that is a 0, it then looks to any
                       one of the three growth rate inputs. We use a
                       CHOOSE function using the cell B2 as the
                       toggle. The growth formula also has a reference
                       to the prior period's revenues, which will form
                       the basis for the growth rate. Note that the
                       reference is to the final (calculated) revenues
                       number (on row 10) and not the input line
                       (on row 6). The reason for this is apparent if we
                       look at the second forecast year: the formula
                       would have a base year of 0 if it looked to cell
                       E6, rather than cell E10.

E16   =IF(E12,E12,CHOOSE(B2,E13,E14,E15)*E$10)
                       Copy this cell across to column G.
                       We are using the CHOOSE function again, but
                       this is not a growth formula, rather it is a
                       formula that applies a percentage to the
                       Revenues line. The reference to the Revenues
                       line, E$10, has an absolute reference to the row
                       only because it is likely that we will copy this as
                       a way to quickly build other sections. The
                       absolute reference will ensure that the formula
                       continues to read row 10 as it is copied further
                       down. Note that the column reference *must not*
                       have an absolute reference as we want the
                       reference to move across as we copy the formula
                       across the model.

Scenario Formulas for More Than One Input Row

The examples used above show scenarios for only one of the
input rows (for growth of revenues, for example). When we
want to do two input rows, the formulas get complicated pretty
quickly. Here is an example for the accounts receivable section,

for which we have three input rows: hard-coded, as a percentage of revenues, and as days of sales. We will do scenarios for the latter two:

	A	B	C	D	E	F	G
93							
94	Accounts receivable	60.0	75.0	90.0			
95	As % revenues	7.3%	8.3%	9.0%			
96	As % revenues						
97	As % revenues						
98	Days of sales	26.5	30.4	32.9	30.0	30.0	30.0
99	Days of sales						
100	Days of sales						
101	Accounts receivable	60.0	75.0	90.0	90.4	99.5	109.4
	Input						

E101   =IF(E94, E94,IF(CHOOSE(B2,E95,E96,E97),
              CHOOSE(B2,E95,E96,E97)*E$10,
              CHOOSE(B2,E98,E99,E100)/365*E$10))

This is not an elegant formula. You can see that the middle nested IF statement has to test all three possibilities, and this makes for a very dense formula.

Often, the solution to this kind of modeling problem is to rethink the original situation. Do we really need two types of alternate inputs? If we keep the principle of KISS in mind, perhaps not.

DATA VALIDATION

With Data Validation, you can make your data entries more fool-proof by limiting the types of data that can be entered. The simplest limit may be the type of data (e.g., allow only date types, or integers), but you can also have it function with more sophistication, such as providing you with easy-to-build lists of the items that the worksheet can accept.

Additionally, because Data Validation also has pop-up boxes that alert you to the wrong type of data being input, you can use these pop-up boxes as a type of cell comment in their own right. Start Data Validation by the following steps:

1. Put your cursor on the cell for which you want to validate the data. Data Validation works on individual cells only, so if you have a range of cells where you want this feature, you can do it in the first cell and then copy the cell itself, or just its format, to the other cells.

2. Press the sequence Data > Validation, and you will see this user form:

3. Click on the Settings tab.

4. Specify the type of data that can be entered by clicking on the list box "Allow:" Let's say we choose "whole number." Specify under "Data:" the filter criterion. For example, you want to allow the data only to be "greater than or equal to." The drop-down list will show you the full list of criteria. Depending on what you chose in this step, the user form will show you additional edit boxes for specifying the value or values required.

At this step, one of the choices under "Allow:" is "list." This allows you to build a drop-down list very easily. After selecting this, enter the items that will appear in the list in the "Source:" edit box. Enter them each as a text string separated by commas. A check box option automatically appears on the user form marked "in-cell dropdown." If this is checked, then the items you selected will appear as a drop-down list when the cursor is on this cell. If not, no drop-down list appears.

The primary Data Validation settings have now been set. The next two steps are optional, but they add a nice level of control for what happens before and after you enter the data.

1. Select the "Input Message" tab. If the check box for "Show input message when cell is selected" is checked, then Data Validation can function as another form of cell comments. On this tab, you can enter the message or information that will appear when you put the cursor on this cell.

   You may want to have this function by itself, in lieu of cell comments, without the data filtering that we set on the "Settings" tab. In that case, simply leave the "Allow:" entry on that tab to read "Any value."

2. Select the "Error Alert" tab. If this is undefined, Excel will show a default error message after the invalid message is entered. But you can define the message yourself by entering it here. This tab also has the setting for what to do if invalid data are entered. Under the "Style:" list box, you can choose to have the sequence stopped, or only have a warning or information icon show up. The first one will not allow invalid data to be extended and is the default, but in some cases where you only need to remind the user that the data may not be right but you still want the model to accept them, then either of the latter two would be appropriate.

FORMATTING NUMBERS

Excel's features for formatting numbers are quite well developed. The menus under Format show the different ways that values can be formatted. In addition to this, you should know that Excel can make a distinction among positive, negative, and zero values and give different formats to each type of value. In addition, you can directly format a number to appear as if it were a text or a combination of number and text. So 0 can appear as "n/a" and so will not cause any formulas reading the value to go into error, which they would do if the cell actually did contain the text "n/a." Likewise, you can make a number, say 8, appear as "8 months" and still be read as a value.

Different Formats for Different Values

Excel's formats have three different sections. They are in the following order, separated by semicolons:

Format for positives; format for negatives; format for zero.

The format for positive numbers is required, but the other two are optional. If the other two are not specified, Excel will use the format for the positive as the default for all types of numbers.

You can set a different format, including a different color, for each of the three. To do this, you will have to define a custom format in Excel.

Let's look at a format. This one is to show numbers with one decimal place, with a comma for the thousand separators, and with parentheses as negative indicators:

```
#,##0.0_);(#,##0.0)
```

This format is only for the positive (left of the semicolon) and the negative (right of same). In this case, no format has been set for the zero value and a zero will follow the positive format. The negative is set so that parentheses show up; the positive formatting includes information in the "_)" that tells Excel to add a blank space at the end of the positive number equal to the space taken up by the ")" character. In this way, the last digit of the positive and negative numbers in a column will line up. Because of the syntax, we can make the format change to anything we want. Go to a cell in your

Excel screen, then do Format > Cells > Number tab. Select Custom from the list of formats, and then type this in the "Type:" box:

$$#,##0.0\_);(0.000);\text{"n/a"}$$

* Positive: one decimal place, thousand separators
* Negative: three decimal places, no thousand separators
* Zero: show as the text "n/a"

Or try this in the same "Custom" setting:

$$#,##0.0\_);(#,##0.0);\text{"--"}$$

* Positive: one decimal place, thousand separators
* Negative: one decimal place, thousand separators, parentheses
* Zero: show as a dash. This will give you a nice effect of showing those cells with zeroes only a dashes, making it easier for you to see the cells which do have numbers. You can enter just one hyphen, or two if you want to make it a dash. You should enter additional spaces after the hyphen(s) if you would like to see the dash farther away from the right border of the cell.

Don't forget to explore the other formatting categories. The Currency and Accounting formats share the same ability to include the currency symbol for virtually all possible currencies. The list of symbols also includes the standard three-letter abbreviations ("USD" for U.S. dollar, for example). The Accounting format has an added touch, however: it will set the currency symbol separate from the number, so that the symbol is flush-left in the cell, while the number is flush-right. A column of numbers set in the Accounting format will look very neat, with all the currency symbols hugging the left border of the column. The Accounting format also gives some choices for setting the currency symbols to appear after the number. The euro's €, for example, can be set to be a prefix or suffix to the number.

We can even add colors to each part. Try typing this as a custom format:

```
#,##0.0_);[Red](0.000);[Blue]"n/a"
```

If no color is specified, then Excel will use the default color. These other color settings are available, too:

- [Black]
- [Cyan]
- [Magenta]
- [White]
- [Blue]
- [Green]
- [Red]
- [Yellow]

In the zero format above, you can see that we do not have to put in a number format. Instead, we can directly enter a text string line "n/a." It is also possible to combine text strings and formats. Here, we continue our experimental formatting by saying that we want the positive number to appear as one decimal place and with the label " months" (note the space at the beginning of the label):

```
#,##0.0 " months"_);[Red](0.000);[Blue]"n/a"
```

With this formatting, this is what Excel will show for the following entries:

Enter this...	And it will appear as...	In this color
1234	1,234 months	Black
−1234	(1234.000)	Red
0	n/a	Blue

With custom formats, however, you are limited to changing only the numeric format of the cell and the color of the font. You cannot have the custom format change anything else. If you do want these additional controls, see the following section on conditional formatting.

I have combined the formats together in this way just to illustrate the variations possible. With these possibilities in mind, you can now set custom formats in your models that will highlight the information in the best way possible.

CONDITIONAL FORMATTING

Conditional formatting is a more advanced form of formatting. It allows you to change many more of the attributes of a cell and can be a useful alternative to using just Excel's custom formats you can change:

- ◆ The color/bold/italic of the font
- ◆ The border settings for the cell
- ◆ The background (pattern) color of the cell

Defining Conditional Formats

Start by putting your cursor on the cell you want to format. Then click on Format > Conditional Formatting to see the dialog box shown in Figure 18-1.

This is the setting for Condition 1. There are three conditional formats that you can apply in a cell, and you can set the other two by pressing on the Add >> button.

For any conditional format, you can choose to set it by one of two methods:

1. *By the "Cell Value Is" method.* In this setting, the conditional format will be driven by the current cell contents, which you can set using the condition operator

F I G U R E   18–1

(e.g., "between," "greater than," "less than or equal to," etc.) that is part of the dialog box. Depending on this choice, the dialog box will then show you inputs for one or two values.

2. *By the "Formula Is" method.* In this setting, the format will be determined by a formula that can refer to a cell or cells outside the current cell. (The formula can also refer to the current cell.) You will then have to define the condition that will trigger the conditional format in the formula. If the condition or set of conditions gets very complicated, you should make use of the other two settings available.

Be careful when you write the formula in the "Formula Is" method. You should define it the way you write a formula in a cell. In other words, make sure you begin the formula with the equal (=) sign. Otherwise, the formula will be regarded by Excel as a text string, much as any formula written without the beginning equal sign becomes a text string when entered in a cell. If you have written a conditional formula and it does not seem to be working, go back to this dialog box and make sure that it has not been entered as a text string.

Once you have defined the trigger for the conditional formats, click on the Format button to define the various attributes of the cell. If the starting cell has the plain, regular formatting, and you want it to change many of the attributes (e.g., to a cell with a bold, italic font, with borders and a different pattern background), it may be easier to "flip" how the conditional format works. In other words, make the starting cell carry the fancy attributes and have the conditional format be the "plain, regular" attributes. Of course, you have to make sure that the logic of the conditional format is working in the correct way.

To delete conditional formats, click on the Delete... button and you can delete any or all of the formats.

Finding Cells That Have Conditional Formats

Be careful about changing your worksheets after you define conditional formats. The formatted cells can stay in their original locations, even when new rows and/or columns have been inserted. A good way to check the location of cells that have conditional formats in them (which can remain apparently undifferentiated on the screen) is to use the F5 (Go to) key and then to click on the Special button on that dialog box. On the Special form, click on the Conditional Formats. This will cause any cells on the screen with conditional formats to be highlighted.

HIDING ROWS FOR PRINTING

The model we have been building is simple, but I hope that it will form the basis of more complex models that you will be building yourself. Once you have the basic model working, it will be easy to add more rows to capture more types of accounts. In fact, it is likely that you will want to develop a model that will include many types of accounts, not all of which will be used in any one modeling run. This will result in many printouts in which there will be some lines that contain nothing but zeroes. The model will continue to work in terms of its calculations, of course, but as a matter of visual polish, you may want to have those rows somehow hidden, whether for viewing on the screen or for printing.

Hiding Rows with the Group Command

There is a way of hiding rows easily, using the Data > Group and Outline > Group command, but this involves first highlighting the row or rows you want and then going through this sequence. A margin automatically appears on the left edge of the screen, which shows you the rows that you can hide. By clicking on the Minus button, you can hide the rows bracketed by the grouping line. The Minus button changes to a Plus button after you do this; clicking on this unhides the rows again. Alternately, you can click on the small numbers buttons at the top of the margin space. This hides and unhides according to the levels.

While this method gives a way of quickly hiding and unhiding rows, the disadvantage is that you will have to do this for each company that you are modeling in your model.

Different companies will be filling in different lines in the model, so you will have to go through the grouping sequence again and again for this to work properly.

Hiding Rows with Formulas

Here is another way of hiding rows with zeros, and we can make this work automatically for any set of numbers that you have in the model. This is the Autofilter command, which can be invoked through the Data > Filter > Autofilter sequence. The Autofilter feature is a way of filtering out (read: hiding) rows. It can be used for columns, too, but for our case, we need it only to hide rows.

The basic idea for the Autofilter feature is that it will show only those rows that contain the desired marker in a particular column. In our case, we will insert a new column at the extreme left (a new column A), which will contain the letter "y" (for yes) for the rows we want to print. By activating the Autofilter feature on this column, Excel will show only those rows with the letter "y", automatically hiding the other rows that do not have this marker.

But, of course, we want to avoid actually typing in the letter "y" for each row we want to print. This would be too tedious and violates the principle of letting Excel do most of the work for us. The solution is to write a formula in column A that tests that row for numbers other than zero and returns a "y" if the row meets this criterion. So these are the steps we have to do:

Insert a New Column A
Highlight the whole column of column A. Then use the Excel command to insert a new column: Insert > Column.

Adjust the Width of Column A
Adjust the column width to 3 by Format > Column > Width.

Write the Formula
This is going to be a long formula and, in essence, what we want is a way to identify the rows that the Autofilter command can act

on. The Autofilter command can be set to show only those rows that contain a certain content. For our formula we will simply set the Autofilter to do the following:

Show the row if column A shows the letter **y**.

Hide the row if column A shows the letter **n**.

Thus the task of the formula we want to write is that it should return a "y" if the row contains numbers other than zeros. Likewise, it should return an "n" if the row contains only zeros. (The Autofilter command will work on these letters whether they are in uppercase or lowercase.)

Let's assume that row 6 is the row that we want to test. The columns we want to test are C to H. So let's start by just writing the simplest possible formula. You will see that we will go through several versions of the basic formula, depending on how "smart" we want the test to be:

```
=IF(SUM(C6:H6),"y","n")
```

The SUM can work, but we run the risk of having a row that has positive numbers and negative numbers the sum of which net to exactly zero (a row for deferred tax buildups and reversals nets out to zero), in which case the formula will return an "n" when it should be a "y." Let's use the MAX function:

```
=IF(MAX(C6:H6)<>0,"y","n")
```

This is an interesting formula because it will work if the numbers on the line are positive or negative or both. However, it will not work if the line has negative numbers and zeros. It returns a zero in that case.

There may be some lines that will have only very small numbers. The plug lines in particular may show numbers that appear to be zeroes but contain a very small number like 0.00003. They are not zeros because in the balancing iterations Excel will stop once the maximum change number set in Tools > Options > Calculation is reached. If you do not want these near-zero lines to appear, then the formula becomes more complicated, because we would need to return a "y" only if the numbers on the line are outside the range of −0.001 to 0.001 (this range is set at your discretion):

```
=IF(OR(MAX(C6:H6)>0.001,
   MIN(C6:H6,0)<−0.001),"y","n")
```

Write this formula in the A column for each row that you want the Autofilter command to act on. The entries you should have in this column are as follows:

Enter This in Column A	To Have This Effect
y	For all rows that will always show when the Autofilter is on. This includes blank rows required for visual spacing, and title rows that need to appear.
n	For all rows that will always be hidden when the Autofilter is in effect. Examples would be rows used for internal calculations or for comments about the model.
The formula	For all rows that need to be shown only if they contain numbers other than zeros.

Activate the Autofilter

With the settings in place, select the column by clicking on the column letter A. Then select Data > Filter > Autofilter to turn the Autofilter on. You must already have the entries in column A in place to do this; otherwise, an error message that says "No list was found ..." will appear on the screen. A button with a downward arrow will appear in cell A1. Click on this and select "y" from the list of options. When you do this, only the "y" rows will appear on the screen; the "n" rows will be hidden from view.

You can print this page as it appears, and the "n" rows will remain hidden. Another thing you can do is to copy this filtered range to another sheet and the hidden rows will not be copied over. However, formulas in the original range become values in the target sheet. After printing, click on the button with the downward arrow and select "All" to show all the rows again.

CHAPTER 19

Writing a Macro in Visual Basic for Applications

In Chapter 16, we looked at macros and how to record them a little bit. In this chapter, we will see an overview of how to write a simple macro in VBA. I hope that this primer will get you started on your own road to mastery of this really easy-to-use and powerful language. The main purpose for using VBA in our model is to be able to manipulate elements in the model's cells and worksheets. VBA itself should not be used to do calculations on the worksheet. That's the work of the formulas and functions that we have created in the model.

The term *macro* is generally used to describe any code—also called a procedure—that can be run to manipulate and produce some effect on the balance sheet.

There is, however, another type of macro called the *function macro* for developing your own functions. This is covered briefly at the end of this chapter.

THE VISUAL BASIC EDITOR

Macros, whether they are recorded or ones that you create and write yourself, are kept in another part of the Excel file called the *Visual Basic Editor*, or *VBE*. This is the second part of the two parts that constitute a workbook file. The worksheets constitute the first part.

Let's Go to the VBE

To get from the worksheet part to the VBE, you have to go through one of two steps:
Use either:

- Tools > Macro > Visual Basic Editor

  or

- Alt + F11

If you do this, you will see the screen that appears as Figure 19-1.

F I G U R E   19–1

Note that on the taskbar at the bottom of the screen there are now two buttons representing the active components of Excel: the spreadsheet part and the VBE part.

There are three main areas in the VBE, as you can see.

- *Top left corner*: This is the **Project Explorer** window, and shows you the items that the VBE has. If you do not see this window on your screen, or if you inadvertently closed it by clicking on the X box, you can make it reappear by going through this sequence *in the VBE* (and not in the worksheet part): View > Project Explorer.

- *Bottom left corner*: This is the **Properties** window. It will show the properties of the item being highlighted in the Project Explorer window. To make this window appear if it is not there, use: View > Properties Window.

- *Right side of the screen*: This is the **Code Editor** window. This is the window that will show the macros and is where they can be edited. To make this window appear if it is not there, use: View > Code.

From the VBE Back to the Worksheet

There are several ways to move from the VBE to the worksheet:

- The easiest way is to click on the taskbar button for the Excel spreadsheet. This will shift the screen to the spreadsheet. The VBE is still running, but it is in the background. When you want to go back to the VBE again, click on the taskbar button for the VBE and you are back there again.

- Alt + Q. This will cause the VBE to close so that you are automatically put back in the worksheet part. To go back to the VBE, you will have to restart it again by going through the steps outlined above.

- Close the VBE window by clicking on the X at the top right of the screen. Like Alt + Q, you will need to restart VBE to get back to it.

INSERTING A VBA MODULE

We haven't yet seen any place specifically for writing code in the Project Explorer window. Let's insert a VBA module by Insert > Module while we are in VBE. (See Figure 19-2.)

You will then see an additional listing for Modules, and under that a module sheet with the name *Module1*. (See Figure 19-3.)

This is the default name; the next module sheet will be called *Module2*, etc. The cursor should now be in the Code Editor, the wide field on the right of the screen.

Module1 is just one of the many VBA modules that you can insert into the VBE. In fact, as you develop your macro writing skills and you write macros for data management, user

F I G U R E   19–2

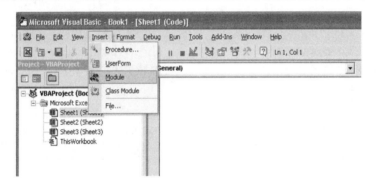

F I G U R E   19–3

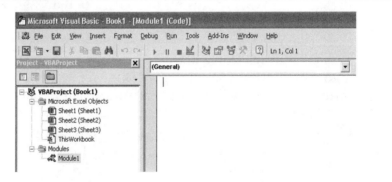

interfaces, printing, and so on, it is a good idea to write them on separate module sheets. You can rename the module sheets for greater clarity. So your collection of modules may be called, for example, modData, modValuation, modPrint, etc. You can rename a module by clicking on it and then putting the new name next to the item marked (Name) in the Properties window in the lower left-hand corner of the screen.

If you have experimented with recording macros, the VBE will already have created Module1 and perhaps other module sheets as a place where the recorded macros are kept.

Deleting a Module

If you want to delete a VBA module or a UserForm module, just click on the module name in the Project Explorer window and right-click on your mouse. On the short menu that appears, click on "Remove [your module name]..." You have a chance to remove it altogether or to save it as a separate file before you delete it.

OBJECTS

An object is anything in Excel that can be manipulated on the screen through manual input or by a macro. Objects are what VBA programming manipulates. An Excel object can be

- Excel itself
- The workbook (the .xls file)
- A worksheet or chart sheet in the workbook
- A column in the worksheet
- A row in the column
- A range

You will notice that this listing gives a range from large objects to small objects. This is the *object hierarchy* in Excel (and this hierarchy is called the *object model* in Excel, just to add to the arcania of your Excel knowledge). There are 128 objects in Excel. Don't worry. You need to know just a handful to start finding your way around VBA.

PROPERTY AND METHOD

Once you have defined the object you want to manipulate, then you have a choice of working with the *property* or the *method*. A good way to remember these terms is that a property describes what an object *is*, and a method describes what you *do* with it.

Property

Every object has a property, property in this case being the standard definition of an "essential or defining attribute." If the range that you are looking at contains the number *170853* in italics, then you can say that the range has the Value property of 170853 and the Format property of italics (or, more specifically, the Font Italic property is TRUE). A property always has a value, whether it is a string value, a numeric value, a Boolean value, or some other value.

Method

A *method* is an action that is performed with an object. Copying the range to another range is an example of the copy method. (Thus, this action has the effect of changing the property of the destination cell.)

If you are wondering how to tell a command for property and a command for method part, the property command has an equal (=) sign by itself. You may see an equal sign in a method command, but you will see this with a colon (":=") when the method has to show arguments that are part of the method command.

FOLLOW THE HIERARCHY

In a VBA macro, whether you want to apply a property or a method to an object, the way to do it is to start identifying it from within the hierarchy, from the largest object to the smallest. Most of the time, you do not have to specify the object that is

Excel itself (this is called the Application object), and you can start with the workbook. In the fullest approach, you would define it in this order:

- The workbook
- The worksheet
- The range

Each of these is separated from the next by a period. The period is called the "dot operator." Here is an example of the hierarchy structure if you want to put the number "123" in cell C10 in the sheet named "MySheet." The workbook is named "MyFile.xls." Write this as one line.

```
Workbooks("MyFile.xls").Sheets
("MySheet").Range("C10").Value = "123"
```

A shortened command will work, too:

```
Range("C10").Value = "123"
```

But note that in this case, as there is no definition of the workbook or the sheet, Excel will perform this command on whatever worksheet is currently active. So long as you are clear about where you are as you launch the subroutine, you can make the code short. However, when you are making the subroutine work across many worksheets or even many workbooks, it helps to write the longer code so you can specify exactly where the macro should work.

The .Value you see at the end of the code (note the dot operator) is another example of being specific. Writing

```
Range("C10") = "123"
```

works, too, but Excel has to evaluate what you mean by this. It is always better to be very specific so that Excel can work in the most immediate way to accomplish the task.

WRITING YOUR FIRST MACRO

Now that we know the lay of the land, let's try writing our first code. We will name the first macro FirstMacro. In the Code Editor window, enter the following line:

```
Sub FirstMacro
```

And then press Enter. Excel immediately adds to your entry so that it appears as:

```
Sub FirstMacro()
End Sub
```

The Sub is short for subroutine, and because Excel now recognizes this as the first line for the macro subroutine, it adds the "()" at the end. The parentheses can be used in more complex macros to hold information that the macro will work with. Most macros will just have these parentheses without anything between them. Excel also automatically adds a second line of "End Sub" at the end. The space between the two is where you write your macro, inserting additional lines as you go and, of course, deleting any extraneous lines. Another way of saying this is simply that the end of a macro must have the End Sub line.

Now let's add these lines

```
Sub FirstMacro()
    Sheets("Sheet1").Select
    Range("A1").Select
    ActiveCell.Value = 17
    Range("A2").Select
    Selection.Value=30
End Sub
```

The first line specifies the sheets that we want the macro to work on. This first step is equivalent to our selecting the Sheet1 sheet first to make that the active sheet. (Of course, for this macro to work every time also means that there should always be a sheet named "Sheet1." It does not have to be the first sheet, but it has to have this name.) Without this first line, the macro would work on whatever worksheet is the active sheet.

Once you have selected a cell, you have a choice of using either the ActiveCell keyword or the Selection keyword. Both point to the cell that the cursor is on, which is by definition the active cell, or the selection. In other cases where the macro is highlighting a multi-cell range, you cannot use the ActiveCell keyword, but you can use Selection.

Indents

Any line you write between the Sub and the End Sub lines should be indented. Just tap the Tab key once before you begin the line. This is really for ease in looking over the macro later on. In fact, you will see that as we add other programming sequences such as IF, it is helpful to indent those sections further to indicate the nested quality of those sequences within the main subroutine.

Automatic Capitalization for "Reserved Words"

Also, notice that if you enter the words *Select* and *Value* all in lowercase letters, VBA does an initial capitalization on them—it capitalizes the first letters of these words. This shows that these words are part of VBA's reserved words—words that are used within VBA to mean specific things or commands. You should not use them except for their specific meanings and effects in VBA.

RUNNING THE MACRO

Now that we have written this macro, let's run it. Go back to the worksheet of the file, to Sheet1. Once you are there, do Tools > Macro > Macros and, at the dialog box, select the macro name TestOne. Then click on Run. (See Figure 19-4.)

Once the macro is run, on your Sheet1, you will see the two cells A1 and A2 suddenly contain the numbers 17 and 30, respectively, written by this macro. At this point, you can also

F I G U R E   19–4

F I G U R E   19–5

define a shortcut key for this macro by clicking on the Options button. Figure 19-5 shows the dialog box that will appear.

Specify the letter in the Shortcut key definition box. Refer to Chapter 16 for a cautionary word on not using the shortcut key combinations already used by Excel.

FUNCTION MACROS

* ◆ A function macro creates your own custom function. It returns a value.
* ◆ All function macros begin with the Function keyword. They end with the End Function.
* ◆ They can be called from worksheet cells. This makes them work like any of the functions Excel already has (such as IF, SUM, etc.).

Here is a very simple function macro to get you started. It converts a temperature from the Fahrenheit scale to the Celsius scale. Let's call it ConvertFtoC:

```
Function ConvertFtoC(Arg1)
    ConvertFtoC=(Arg1-32)*5/9
End Function
```

Write this on a module sheet. For the moment, all you need to know is that the Arg1 is an argument. You can use any name of your own choosing instead of Arg1.

Now go to the worksheet part, select a cell anywhere, and write. Within the parentheses in the worksheet, enter the number you want to convert or the cell address holding the number to convert:

```
=ConvertFToC(68)
```
or
```
=ConvertFtoC(B1)
```

where the cell B1 holds the number 68.

When you do this, the cell returns the value of 20. Yes, 68 degrees Farenheit has just been converted to 20 degrees Celsius. You write the function in the worksheet in exactly the same way it is defined in the function macro. VBA makes the automatic connection between the value in the parentheses in the worksheet function and the function macro's argument Arg1 and makes the function work.

You can create a function macro that reads more inputs. Here is one that multiplies the three inputs:

```
Function Mult3 (Arg1,Arg2,Arg3)
    Mult3=Arg1*Agr2*Arg3
End Function
```

When you write the formula

```
=Mult3(B1,B2,B3)
```

it will return the results of multiplying the contents of the three cells on the worksheet.

OTHER IMPORTANT TOPICS TO COVER

Here is a brief road map of the subjects to cover as you begin your own exploration of VBA. I leave you with these:

- Variables
  - Declaring them using the Dim statement for the appropriate data type.
  - Declaring them at the local, module, or projectwide level
- Ways to control the execution of the code
  - If-Then, the VBA equivalent of the worksheet IF function.
  - Ways to repeat a block of instructions, e.g., the For-Next loop, and the Exit For statement to stop the loop when a condition is met.
  - Error trapping
- How to make procedures work with each other
- User forms: How to create your own dialog boxes for data input and display.
- Custom toolbars and custom menus: How to create your own toolbar for access to the features that you have in your model.

VBA AND BEYOND

I hope I have given you a useful tour of modeling and Excel's features in support of making user-friendly models. Knowing VBA adds to your ability to create even more powerful and functional models, and there are tremendous resources available now in bookstores and online for more advanced information about this programming language. This book covers only the beginning steps for learning VBA, and I invite you to turn to these other sources for continuing your learning.

INDEX

John S. Tjia (pronounced *"Chee*-ah") has 15 years of experience in developing financial models, including 7 years as head of the Models Group J.P. Morgan (now known as JPMorgan Chase) in New York. He was responsible for designing, developing, and providing the training for the firm's standard analysis and execution financial models for the Mergers & Acquisitions and Investment Banking divisions worldwide. Prior to that, he was an investment banker in the firm's Hong Kong office and had assignments in credit analysis and financial advisory in New York. Now a founding partner of the TMG & Associates, LLC modeling consulting company (*www.tmga.com*), he lives in Pleasantville, New York, with his wife and two children. He can be contacted at johntjia@buildingfinancialmodels.com.